SUPER SIGNS

TAKING YOUR BRAND TO THE ULTIMATE LEVEL

SAM HUA & NAN HUA

Published by
LID Publishing Limited
The Record Hall, Studio 204,
16-16a Baldwins Gardens,
London EC1N 7RJ, UK

524 Broadway, 11th Floor, Suite 08-120,
New York, NY 10012, US

info@lidpublishing.com
www.lidpublishing.com

A member of:

BPR
Business Publishers Roundtable

www.businesspublishersroundtable.com

© Sam Hua & Nan Hua, 2019
© LID Publishing Limited, 2019

Printed in P.R China by Beijing Congreat Printing Co., Ltd
ISBN: 978-1-912555-18-5

Cover and page design: Caroline Li

SUPER SIGNS

TAKING YOUR BRAND TO THE ULTIMATE LEVEL

SAM HUA & NAN HUA

LONDON   NEW YORK   SHANGHAI
MADRID   BARCELONA   BOGOTA
MEXICO CITY   MONTERREY   BUENOS AIRES

CONTENTS

FOREWORD

WHAT IS YOUR BRAND'S SUPER SIGN ?

When I received the manuscript of this book, I took a quick look at the table of contents and I was immediately impressed. I could not resist reading it, and once I started I could not stop. The end of the book left me wanting even more, and I was inspired to write a little about what I read, to share my thoughts and discuss them with readers and our colleagues in the business.

There has been no lack of bestselling books discussing marketing and branding, either in China or abroad. In recent years, marketing and brand management has become a hot topic. So many books claim to be the source of all the answers for readers and practitioners who are hungry for knowledge and insight. But behind the hype of these books, there always seems to be something missing – something that the reader can really put into practice. I've taught marketing for many years in a business school, and I see a real desire for a practical approach to brand marketing among my students.

This is the biggest difference between this book and other bestsellers and textbooks on marketing. First, its language and its ideas are simple and easy to understand. Its advice is direct and actionable. The authors have spent over a decade doing marketing consultancy, and their experience can be clearly seen.

The book contains a clear analysis of the consumer's multi-faceted role as both the starting point and ultimate objective of marketing. The analysis is both insightful and well-founded. I particularly like one passage: "Never count on your customers being loyal to you. *You* need to be loyal to your customers. Customers have no obligation to be loyal to you. Your entire responsibility is to be loyal to the customer." Just think about how Nokia once had a loyal base of customers who were always willing to buy their products, and yet now they are no longer part of the mobile phone market. This is a warning that we particularly need to remember.

In the chapter on brand strategies, the authors have described and reinforced Hua and Hua's real-world experiences from top-level design to practical implementation, taking the reader through numerous innovative case studies and the wisdom of their solution: when signs and language are taken to the ultimate level, they become super signs and super language.

As the Chinese economy has continued to develop and new and innovative methods for interactive marketing, such as social media, have emerged, companies and marketers now have even more tools at their disposal. If these tools are used well, then the company can even more effectively put their products and brands into the best position in customers' minds. But one thing we cannot forget is that the fundamental rules of marketing and appealing to the customer have never changed – how do you rapidly make customers aware of you, and persuade them to buy your product? Every company is looking to lower the cost of gaining customer awareness and persuading customers to action. Every company is looking for more effective and efficient ways to invest their resources into raising awareness. Hua and Hua's super sign approach is focused on using creativity to lower the cost of marketing and directly trigger customer behaviour.

This book is highly Chinese in its characteristics, with some classic cases of how to engage with the local market here. Yet at the same time, it has a clear international perspective and its methods are universal.

This book was clearly not written to win applause or admiration as a best seller; it was written to guide readers to think deeply about branding and marketing. It is a thought-provoking book, and the authors' unique perspectives on management deserve praise. If we can all be more open-minded in our values, we can create a 'platform ecosystem' that can truly drive industry growth and increase the general level of marketing knowledge in China.

After you read this book, try asking yourself: What is your brand's super sign?

Chiang Jeongwen, Ph.D.
Professor of Marketing
China Europe International Busines School

CHAPTER 1

YOUR BRAND IS A SIGN

WHAT IS A SUPER SIGN?

Is there a form of creativity so powerful that it takes only one look, one listen, for millions of consumers to remember it, know it, like it, be happy to buy it and even talk about it with other people?

Yes! That's what we call a super sign.

Super signs are the signs that people already remember, know and like. People are willing to follow super signs. Super signs are the Force embedded in human culture, hidden deep in the collective subconscious of our brains. Anyone who knows how to harness a super sign can release the power accumulated over thousands of years. Connect your brand to a super sign and you'll have super creativity, super products, super brands, super companies.

Over the past few decades, our company, Hua and Hua, has worked to help Chinese brands leverage the power of super signs. We've worked with brands in every industry, helping them achieve widespread recognition and goodwill – in other words, become leading brands in the China market. And we did this by using a system of ideas and practices we call the Hua and Hua way.

The Hua and Hua way is corporate semiotics: a method to harness super signs in your brand marketing, your corporate strategy and your product development.

Let's take a look at one example to show what super signs can do.

If you fly in China often, you've probably seen this advertisement many times in airlines' in-flight magazines – a location marketing campaign for the Gu'an Industrial Park in Hebei Province. To market a location, you have to find a *landmark*, a sign that can symbolize that location. For China, it might be the Great Wall; for Beijing, perhaps Tiananmen; for Shanghai, maybe the Bund; for Paris, it's the Eiffel Tower; for New York, Times Square.

Before 2003, Gu'an was just a small agricultural county in Hebei Province just south of Beijing. How do you market a location like this? How did we find a sign to make investors immediately know the place, like the place, and want to take a look? We didn't look for a landmark in Gu'an County. Instead, we employed the best-known landmark in all of China, a true super sign – Tiananmen Square. Then we connected it to the location – 50 kilometers south. '50 kilometers south of Tiananmen'. Anyone who saw it knew where Gu'an was, and the value of investing there became clear.

By connecting a widely recognized sign of Beijing to Gu'an, we infused Gu'an Industrial Park with the power of Beijing and Tiananmen.

Here you see the value of harnessing super signs. A place that was completely unknown becomes instantly familiar, even if it's someone's first time hearing of it. Isn't this what every new brand dreams of? You don't know Gu'an, but you know all about Tiananmen. When you know that Gu'an is 50 kilometers south of Tiananmen, it instantly becomes familiar, friendly and valuable – because this is a sign that people find familiar and friendly, and a sign that people see the value in. Using this sign allows us to tap into this treasure trove of shared memory. Your real estate investment will be 50 kilometers due south of Tiananmen – isn't that great?

But we weren't satisfied with the '50 kilometers south of Tiananmen' super sign. Our brand needed a pair of wings to take flight, and we only had one. So we found another super sign – the song 'I Love Beijing Tiananmen'. That gave us our full advertising slogan: 'I love Beijing Tiananmen, 50 kilometers south'.

'I Love Beijing Tiananmen' is a children's song that is practically China's second national anthem. This is the first song Chinese children learn in elementary school; it's a super sign that is familiar, resonant and friendly to every Chinese person. Connecting this song to Gu'an Industrial Park's brand was immensely powerful. The slogan 'I love Beijing Tiananmen, 50 kilometers south' became Gu'an Industrial Park's most important brand asset and the core of its brand experience.

The park also licensed the song 'I Love Beijing Tiananmen' and created an adaptation for the Gu'an campaign:

I love Beijing Tainanmen,
50 kilometers south.
We're a small city but we have big dreams –
We welcome you to Gu'an.

I love Beijing Tiananmen
50 kilometers south.
The people of Gu'an welcome you
The city of the future is here!

Advertisements are a way to encode signs. In this ad for the Gu'an Industrial Park, we also see a Caucasian man wearing a suit – a sign for an investor and entrepreneur – holding a sign that resembles the 'Long Live Solidarity for All the People in the World' sign in Tiananmen Square.

The harnessing of the super sign goes beyond the advertisement. In the planning center for Gu'an, where potential investors visit to learn more about the park, the song 'I Love Beijing Tiananmen' is played in various arrangements. The last activity for all visitors to the center is a photo op with the 'I love Beijing Tiananmen, 50 kilometers south' sign from the very same advertisement.

Tiananmen itself, and the song 'I Love Beijing Tiananmen', are the brand super signs for Gu'an Industrial Park.

'I love Beijing Tiananmen, 50 kilometers south' was a wonderfully creative – and immensely successful – idea that became a major asset for the Gu'an city brand and its cultural heritage. The people of Gu'an are proud of the concept, and have integrated the 'I love Beijing Tiananmen' theme into the city's sights, street furniture and festivals, in all sorts of ways.

Now, a decade later, 'I love Bejing Tiananmen, 50 kilometers south' has become a symbol of Gu'an. I am certain it will continue to be for a century, or even a millennium.

bms

TO ESTABLISH A BRAND
IS TO ESTABLISH A SIGN

If the word 'brand' had never been invented, we might have more accurately used the word 'sign' for the concept.

Saying 'we want to build a system of signs' would be more conducive to what we do than saying 'we want to build a brand'.

A super-brand is an exceptional system of signs. Brands are either derived from signs or become signs themselves – often both.

For example, the Gu'an Industrial Park brand was derived from the sign that is Tiananmen. Ten years later, 'I love Beijing Tiananmen, 50 kilometers south' has become a sign itself for Gu'an.

The Coca-Cola bottle design is based on a woman's curves – a sign that was appropriated by the Coca-Cola brand. As the Coca-Cola brand became successful, it became a cultural sign itself, widely recognized by all of humanity.

In theory, advertising and brand dissemination fall under the realm of propaganda. The *Encyclopedia Britannica* defines propaganda as follows: A systemic activity to manipulate the beliefs, attitudes or actions of others through the use of signs (such as words, gestures, flags, memorials, music, clothing, emblems, hairstyles, banknote designs and postage stamps).

From the above definition, we can see that propaganda is the use of a system of signs. For state propaganda, this includes elements straight out of the encyclopedia definition: words, gestures, flags, memorials, music, clothing, emblems, hairstyles, banknote designs and postage stamps.

A brand is also a system of signs. There is no essential difference between a brand and a state's system of signs. The only difference is that the goal of a state sign system is effective governance, while the goal of a brand is to drive sales.

States use signs to influence the beliefs, attitudes and actions of their people. Brands use signs to influence the opinions, ideas and behaviour of their consumers.

Some may disagree with the idea that advertising and brands are a form of propaganda. They think that the word propaganda itself is outmoded. But just as corporate management was based on military management techniques, the theories of brand dissemination were derived from political propaganda, which finds its highest form in war mobilization. The theories of propaganda were the root of advertising, and we must trace things back to their roots.

PRODUCTS ARE ALSO SIGNS

Products are signs. People define themselves through consuming signs. A woman who carries a Louis Vuitton bag is trying to convey something about her self-image through the meaning that this product signifies. Successful people build a system of signs around themselves, including what house and neighbourhood they live in, what car they drive and what clothes they wear. This system of signs defines and disseminates the identity and role of a successful person.

As a sign, a product defines its consumer. Meanwhile, the product is itself defined by signs. In other words: the sign defines the product, while the product, through what it signifies, defines a person.

Humans are sign-using animals. Signs contain meanings, whether implicit or explicit, that influence human actions on a deep level. We might say that signs control human behaviour; they are what drive us to consume.

Business magnate Li Ka-shing, the richest Chinese person in the world, made his fortune by using signs – more specifically, a sign representing flowers.

People like to decorate their homes with flowers in vases. It makes the home feel cozier and more comfortable. But fresh flowers are expensive, and they require constant watering and replacing.

In the 1960s, with the rise of the plastics industry, the artificial flower was invented – a sign *representing* flowers. You can buy an artificial flower, put it in a vase, and it will look good for years. Isn't that great? The invention was an overnight success.

After artificial flowers came on the market, companies began working to make them look even more like the real thing – how to make them look freshly cut, how to make them more beautiful, how to make it so they don't fade, how to make them so they keep their color even after washing, so that their beauty lasts forever. It didn't take long for all these technical problems to be solved. Artificial flowers always look beautiful and freshly cut. They grab your attention when you visit someone's living room: "These artificial flowers are beautiful!"

Well, it doesn't make people happy to hear this. They want you to think the flowers are real. So companies began adding fragrances to artificial flowers. The fragrance is a sign. When artificial flowers smell like real flowers, they become even more convincing to unsuspecting guests.

Eventually, artificial flowers became *too* real, *too* bright, *too* beautiful. They became a problem again. People began thinking that real flowers don't look like this. A real flower that's been picked from a real field will have a few withered petals, a few bug-bitten leaves. So a very smart person decided that the goal was no longer to look as perfect as possible – they added some bug bites to the fake flower.

Let's review: First, a sign was created to represent a real object. Then more and more elements were added – the fragrance, the bug bites, the withered leaves. These individual signs were integrated to make the representation of the real object more convincing, so that even though we know that it's not a *real* flower, we're still willing to display it in our living rooms. The better we make the sign, the better the product sells. This is what we mean when we talk about the *consumption of signs*.

13

The relationship between consumption and signs has always been a topic of interest for us. Take a look at the products around you and you'll see that not only are signs everywhere, they're also highly influential on your purchasing habits. Some signs were created that way; others only became signs as they changed and evolved through the consumption process.

When we talk about signs, we're not just talking about logos. The consumption of signs is often too narrowly understood as the consumption of brand logos like Louis Vuitton, Gucci and Adidas. But here, we're talking about all forms of images, sounds, sensations, flavours and smells that carry meaning. When you smell rotten eggs in the hallway at school, you know that it's a sign of a chemistry experiment, of hydrogen sulfide, of toxicity, of having to cover your nose.

A good understanding of how to use signs allows you to create different products and experiences. A bread company makes a pastry that's shaped like a curvy woman; it makes news around the world, and the pastry becomes a huge seller. This is just a simple use of a sign. Pastries can be baked in any shape, so they can become any sign. The company makes good use of this, and it has a successful product.

A conference table is made out of particle board, not expensive original wood. But when you look at it, it looks like original wood. Why? Because it uses artificial wood grain patterns as a sign. Why is the surface of the particle-board table made to look like authentic wood? Because the people who purchase the table are willing to pay more for this sign. They know that the table is particle board, but the wood grain pattern makes them more willing to buy it.

The packaging of instant beef noodle soup always has a mouth-watering picture of a huge piece of beef, but you know that all that's inside is a pack of powder, not real beef. But the picture of the beef makes you more willing to buy. Would you buy a pack of instant noodles with a picture of powder on the packaging, instead of a picture of beef? This is what makes signs so useful.

14

The better, clearer and more appetizing the signs you use are, the better your pack of instant noodles sells.

Of course, it probably isn't even beef that makes the noodles taste so good – it's the MSG, artificial flavourings and other additives. You know this, but you don't care, because the packaging has *beef* on it, not MSG. This is what signs do. Even when we know that the sign represents something false, something hollow, we're still willing to pay for it. It's like what Cypher says in the science fiction movie *The Matrix*: "I know this steak doesn't exist. I know that when I put it in my mouth, the Matrix is telling my brain that it is juicy and delicious. You know what I realize? Ignorance is bliss."

The Coca-Cola bottle is a classic design that makes good use of a sign – the curves of a woman's body – to attract consumers. But once Coca-Cola became a widely recognized top brand, the bottle itself became a sign.

Signs are everywhere around you. Take your mobile phone – you can use it without ever looking at a manual. You know what button to press to call up the search function, how to look up your contacts, how to return to your home screen, how to answer a call and how to hang up. You know all this without any explicit instruction. Why? Because you recognize all of the signs associated with these features, and you can guess at the ones you don't. It's not that you're especially good at guessing, it's that the designers were smart. They've made it so that anyone can use these signs to figure out how to use the phone, even if they've never used the exact model before.

Take another look at your phone. The buttons for calling and hanging up probably use an image of a receiver. A mobile phone doesn't *have* a 'receiver', and yet the receiver as a sign remains widely recognized. The next generation of kids might grow up having never seen a phone with a receiver, but still they'll have passed on this sign. In a way, this is an evolution of the receiver – an evolution that has led it to extinction, leaving behind only the sign.

Signs are especially important in today's internet industry, where everything is a system of signs on a computer screen. Product development, product naming, user experience – all of these require a good system of signs.

What is a sign, anyway? Linguist Ferdinand de Saussure, the founder of semiology, said this in his landmark work *Course in General Linguistics*: "A science that studies the life of signs within society is conceivable; it would be a part of social psychology and consequently of general psychology; I shall call it semiology (from Greek *semefon* 'sign')."

Saussure speaks of 'the life of signs', meaning that he thinks of signs as a living thing, with a powerful influence on human psychology. Semiology, the study of signs, is part of psychology.

What is the relationship between products and signs?

Products carry value for the consumer. Signs reveal and reinforce this value.

Signs guide consumer activities.

Signs give products life.

THE VALUE OF SIGNS IN BRAND STRATEGY

What is communication? Communication is the giving and receiving of information and feedback through meaningful signs, whether between people or between people and society.

Communication is a process in which signs are encoded and given to the receiver for decoding.

The goal of marketing communication is to influence the thoughts and actions of consumers so that they purchase your product.

If you want to persuade consumers to buy your product, you'll need a sign to *represent* the product. This is the first function of signs – representation.

The representation behind a sign can be very simple. For example, the word 'dog' is a sign that represents a kind of animal.

However, a sign can also efficiently represent an enormous amount of information in highly condensed form. This is the second function of signs – condensation of information. Take the mathematical equation 1+1=2. '1', '+', '=' and '2' are all signs. Without these signs, we might be fine with a simple equation like one plus one equals two. Yet, something like three thousand eight hundred and fifty-two multiplied by fifty-eight thousand three hundred and twenty would be much more troublesome.

Think back on those math, physics and chemistry formulas you learned back in high school. There would be no system of science without signs. Of course, we wouldn't even have language without linguistics signs.

Greetings, rituals, games, literature, art, myth – all of these are comprised of signs. Military salutes, Boy Scout salutes, a blown kiss, a thumbs-up, a raised middle finger – all of these are signs as well. When you raise your index finger, put it to your lips, and say 'shh!' this is also a sign – a sign for quiet.

The Nazi salute, given by a hundred thousand people at once, is a sign with formidable and terrifying power. A single motion to unify the will of an empire, to suppress opposition and to bring about a genocide. Hitler's Germany was an empire of signs. In Hitler's monstrous hands, the terrible and violent power of signs came to its apex.

The third function of signs is to convey directions.

A sign is an order.

We are accustomed from childhood to rely on signs telling us what to do. Zebra-stripe lines painted on pavement tell us where to cross the street. Stoplights protect us from being hit by cars when we cross. The signs on public restrooms tell us which door to go in.

Because you know what signs mean, you know what button to press when someone calls your mobile phone. If you showed your phone to a two-year-old boy, he wouldn't know what to do with it.

One day, his father will tell him that tapping the green button will pick up the call. And when that happens, you'll find him fascinated – every time the phone rings, he'll want to be the one to tap the green button.

A child might not be able to reach the buttons in an elevator. But the moment they discover that they can push those buttons to tell the elevator where to go, they'll become obsessed. Every time they're in the elevator they'll want to be the one to push the button. They might not even want to leave the elevator. They'll be perfectly content going down to the first floor, up to the ninth, back down to the first, and then up to the eighth. The elevator never makes a mistake, the kid discovers: push the button for the ninth floor, and the elevator door will open on the ninth floor. Push the button for the eighth floor, and the door will open on the eighth, never the ninth.

And so the child slowly learns how to use signs, how to obey signs, and how to work with signs to control themselves and the world.

Signs are immensely powerful. They affect how people think and influence how people act. People obey the directions and orders given by signs. 'Stop on red, go on green' is an example of people obeying signs. Apple founder Steve Jobs used the same concept to design the user interface on his computers: the red button closes a window, the green button maximizes it.

In the above discussion, we saw that signs can convey an enormous amount of information, and that they can carry immense power and influence over people's thoughts and behaviour.

The first function of signs: to represent and identify.

The second function of signs: to condense information.

The third function of signs: to direct action.

All three of these functions are precisely what is needed in marketing communication. This is what makes signs so valuable in your brand strategy.

After the above discussion, it should be easier to understand why we say that to establish a brand is to establish a sign.

When we're building a brand, we want to find a sign to represent us; to express our brand value in a condensed way; to influence consumer opinions – so that they like us – and their actions – so that they buy our products and recommend them to others.

Action is something that needs to be emphasized here. The ultimate goal of everything is action. The basic pattern of communication is that of stimulation and reaction. A sign is a form of stimulation, but we need a reaction on the part of the audience as well. If you don't get the reaction, that means your stimulation was ineffective.

USING SIGNS TO BUILD YOUR MINIMAL MEMORY UNIT

We live in an age of information fragmentation.

People's impressions of a brand are shaped by a series of memory fragments. For example, your impression of Coca-Cola probably comes from a series of memories accumulated over years or decades.

When we study signs, we're trying to turn the smallest possible memory fragment into a sign for your brand. This allows for three things:

First, everyone will remember the same fragment.

Second, the fragment will be very hard to forget.

Third, the fragment carries the identity and value of your brand, and it can be communicated with no information loss.

It is essential that everyone remembers the same fragment about your brand. That way, you can avoid the situation described in the old Chinese story about five blind people each touching a different part of an elephant and coming away with five completely different impressions of what an elephant is like. Brand communication starts with one person and ends up reaching thousands or even millions. You don't want your message to get lost, misunderstood or exaggerated in the process. To do this, you need to build a clear and memorable sign.

When Chinese consumers think of Sanjing's medical syrups, the first thing they think of is the blue bottle that they come in – a colour that evokes purity, safety and high technology. When they think of Sunflower children's medications, they think of the little sunflower that teaches moms about children's health in the brand's most famous ad campaign. This is a brand image that is healthy, friendly, professional and trustworthy. When they think of Tianqi toothpaste, they think of how they say 'Tian-qi' when they take a photo.

When we talk about signs associated with brands, we say that they're 'minimal memory units'. They help make the memory of your brand, and the communication of that memory, more efficient and more accurate. They also greatly decrease the cost of communicating and getting people to remember your brand.

Everyone needs to have the same memory fragment, the same impression, about your brand. This is one of Hua and Hua's most important principles when designing the brand experience. You can test out your brand right now. Ask the people around you, "What do you think of when you think about Brand A?" See if everyone describes the same fragment of memory. If they do, congratulations – this is an incredible achievement.

When people talk about Gu'an, everybody thinks of the jingle: 'I love Beijing Tiananmen, 50 kilometers south'. This is Gu'an's memory fragment and most important brand asset. But to create this kind of brand asset, you need to remember one important tip:

Propoganda is repetition.

If you can repeat your message tirelessly, endlessly, for an entire decade, then your brand can become a century-old classic.

Repetition is the key to successful advertising. It's easy to say but difficult to do, because people can't control the impulse to do something *different*. That's like throwing away your goose that lays the golden eggs, but they'll say it's an 'upgrade' or 're-launch'!

New creativity is often a crime against the brand, because once you throw away the goose that lays the golden eggs, no one will know the difference anymore – it'll just be gone.

WHAT MAKES
A SIGN SUPER?

What is a super sign?

What makes a sign super, and what makes it not-so-super?

Earlier we talked about the three major functions of signs: representation, condensing information and directing action. Super signs are the signs that are maximally effective at all three.

A super sign is as strong and clear as possible in its representation.

A super sign condenses as much information as possible, in the most powerful and accurate way.

A super sign is the most effective and powerful element in influencing people's actions, and it influences the most people possible.

That is a super sign. When you use a super-sign, you can make the communication of your brand maximally efficient.

What signs are super signs? There are two major categories: *public signs* and *cultural signs*.

Examples of public signs include stoplights, traffic signs and restroom signs. These are the most powerful signs in existence, because everybody in the world knows them and obeys them. Humans are directed in every action, and every day we're directed by these signs.

Super signs are signs that everyone understands and obeys. People don't even think about why a sign is like this – they see it and obey!

Attempts to challenge these super signs can be disastrous. In China, there have been two attempts to change the meaning of the stoplight. The first was during the Cultural Revolution. Because red was the colour of revolution, leaders thought that it should represent 'go' instead of 'stop'. The meanings of red and green were reversed, but quickly changed back because of the chaos that ensued. The second was when new rules regarding yellow lights were introduced in 2012. The new rules specified that, when the light turns yellow, all vehicles that have passed the stopping line should continue forward to clear the intersection, but vehicles that have not yet reached the stopping line should stop. Drivers trying to beat yellow lights were fined and given points on their license. The new rules confused everyone and ended up unceremoniously disappearing.

Cultural signs are the archetypal signs of human culture. For example, the boat-like shape of the gold ingot is a cultural sign for the Chinese. The checkered tablecloth is a universal cultural sign.

What good are super signs? They are immensely valuable in brand communication.

Super signs can easily change the brand preferences of consumers, and they can drive large-scale purchasing behaviour within very short timeframes. They can also help an all-new brand seem like an old friend to millions of consumers overnight.

Why can super signs change the brand preferences of consumers, so that they like the brand associated with the sign? Because consumers *already* like the super sign.

Why can super signs make a new brand seem like an old friend to consumers overnight? Because the super sign is *already* an old friend to these consumers.

Super signs are archetypes that are infused with the force of human culture.

When a brand is connected to a super sign, it too is infused with this force. There is a place for this brand deep in everyone's brains. It's like the movie *Inception* – your brand has been planted as an idea deep into people's subconsciousness.

Using super signs is a game aimed at finding this place for your brand in the minds of your consumers.

Chubang Soy Sauce is a classic example of using a super sign to great success.

How did Chubang emerge from obscurity to become a heavy-weight national brand in the highly competitive Chinese soy sauce market? A major factor was its brand sign, created by Hua and Hua based on the green checkered pattern found on tablecloths. As discussed earlier, the sign was used in the packaging of all Chubang products as well as the corporate image of the company itself.

Consumers might not know Chubang, but everyone knows the green checkered pattern and what it stands for – dining tables, food, a good appetite. In one fell swoop, this green checkered pattern allows the Chubang brand to be identified and remembered, its value conveyed. The consumer's positive impression of the green checkered pattern is connected to the Chubang brand, shaping their brand preference.

Hua and Hua believes that packaging is the most important form of media you have. Packaging is the most crucial strategic tool for a brand.

How powerful was our packaging design for the Chubang brand?

First, the visibility of Chubang products was greatly increased. The green checkerboard pattern made for an attention-grabbing product display, particularly at the 45-degree angle at which consumers see bottled products on shelves as they walk down the supermarket aisle. The sides of an entire row of Chubang soy sauce form a solid block of the green checkerboard pattern. This is part of the Hua and Hua way – the goal of packaging design is to establish an advantage in the product display.

Second, brand preferences were instantly shaped. We said that a super sign can turn a new brand into an old friend for consumers. Consumers found the green checkerboard pattern familiar and friendly, so they instantly found the Chubang brand familiar and friendly as well.

Third, the packaging was tremendously appetizing. When you're selling a food product, the package needs to stimulate the appetite. What kind of visual sign would be effective in doing this? Well, one good choice was a sign representing a tablecloth.

The magic of super signs is that they can evoke *holistic* experiences in people.

Signs stimulate people with information, producing a reaction. Super signs, cultural signs, are a stimulus that brings to mind *all* experiences associated with that sign, unlocking a treasure trove of memories, emotions and experiences in the consumer's brain. That means you're harnessing the entire heritage of human history and the power contained within.

By using super signs, we're using the most effective way to provoke instinctual reactions in consumers. Signs are there deep within our brains, a cultural reflex, a direct and instinctual shortcut to reaction.

When the consumer sees the green checkerboard pattern, a visual sign, there is an instant reaction in their thoughts and even in their tastebuds. This reaction is instinctive and instantaneous. The *Force* of super signs is awakened.

When we talk of the Force, of course, we're borrowing a concept from *Star Wars*. Filmmaker George Lucas' conception of the Force, meanwhile, was borrowed from the mythologist Joseph Campbell. Lucas describes *Star Wars* as a modern myth that was created based on Campbell's ideas. What were these ideas? Campbell was one of the founders of the study of mythology, and in his works – including the seminal *Hero with a Thousand Faces* – he proposed the theory of the *monomyth*. Campbell studied the myths and legends of tribes and religions around the world, and discovered certain patterns common to all mythologies, whether they be Christian, Buddhist, Islamic, Native American or African. All of these myths revolve around the hero's journey, fashioned on the same core model. The hero has a thousand faces, each one unique to a particular group, but all of them conform to the same archetype. They are all the same hero, in the same story.

Archetypes are the images that repeatedly occur in myths, religions, dreams, fantasies and literature. Of course, these images also recur in brand marketing. Scholars of brands developed a theory of brand archetypes that was based on Campbell's work in mythology.

Campbell himself was inspired by psychologist Carl Jung's theory of the collective unconsciousness, which has been shaped over thousands of years and which Jung suggests every human is born with. The theory of collective unconsciousness was in turn built on psychologist Sigmund Freud's theory of the unconscious.

How long has the checkerboard pattern been around in human history? Probably a few tens of thousands of years. How long has the green checkerboard pattern been associated with tablecloths? We don't know the answer to this question – certainly for a long time – but what we do know is that the association is so widespread that it's practically universal. All around the world, people react to the pattern in the same way. This is the force of the collective unconsciousness. In our exploration of the theoretical basis for super signs, we've touched on George Lucas, Joseph Campbell, Carl Jung and Sigmund Freud. Super signs are a way to harness human subconsciousness to tap into the Force of human culture.

Saussure said that semiology is a part of psychology. Naturally, drilling down into the topic led us to Freud and Jung.

Let's turn to another example and look at Xibei, a successful Chinese restaurant chain.

As we mentioned earlier, Xibei's mission is to promote *youmian* cuisine all over China, and all over the world.

Youmian is a kind of oat grown in northern China. It is considered China's third most important staple crop and one of ten 'superfoods' by the United Nations. But even in China, many people don't know about *youmian* – not even how to pronounce it. Our goal is to make the Chinese character representing the grain (莜) known by every person in China, and maybe even every person around the world. But who would be interested in a Chinese lesson before they can even learn about our product? This is an enormous obstacle to our marketing efforts.

A super phrase – a kind of super sign – will help lessen this barrier. It will give *youmian* an instant path into the mind of everyone, so that everyone knows, remembers and likes *youmian*.

Sure enough, Hua and Hua found such a super phrase for this client – *I love you*. We made the connection between the *you* in 'I love you' and in *youmian*. We then harnessed a globally known

25

super sign – the I ♥ NY logo. Using these elements, we created the I ♥ You super sign.

Xibei now had a powerful system of super signs that allowed it to create an inimitable brand experience that is relevant around the world. With this super sign, a local northwestern-flavoured restaurant brand was transformed into a world-class international brand.

FIVE WAYS TO BUILD YOUR BRAND'S SIGN

How do you create signs for your brand? Focus on the five senses: sight, hearing, smell, taste and touch. Let's explore that further.

(1) VISUALS FIRST

When we talk about signs, we're usually talking about visual signs.

Most of the time, brand signs should focus on visuals. People usually remember brands based on visual impressions. We can see further than we can hear; light travels faster than sound. Words need to be translated, but pictures are universal.

That said, sound shouldn't necessarily play second fiddle.

(2) SOUND ISN'T NECESSARILY SECOND

Tianqi toothpaste built its brand around a campaign in which people say 'Tian-qi' when having their picture taken. This is a classic example of an aural sign.

Repeated pieces of music in commercials are also frequently used to give a brand an aural identity. Think of Intel's familiar jingle.

It's always better to have an aural sign than not, just like it's better to have a logo than not. You should have an aural logo in addition to a visual one. Of course, Tianqi's method of establishing an aural identity is quite different from Intel's. Intel simply repeated a short, five-note jingle so much that it became a sign to represent the Intel brand. This jingle is not Intel itself, nor does it have any intrinsic connection with what Intel does as a business. But Tianqi's campaign to say 'Tian-qi' when snapping a photo is a completely unique sign that only it can use. The sign can even double as a slogan. And of course, by having people smile and show their teeth, it also conveys the brand's identity, values and experience. That's why we say that the campaign is about creating an aural logo for the brand.

Why do we say that sound shouldn't necessarily play second fiddle? The reason is that companies don't currently pay nearly as much attention as they should to the importance of aural logos. There is a lot of potential in this space.

Sounds have an undeniable advantage compared to images: you don't need to *see* them.

Plus, your audience can only engage with visuals in one way: with their eyes. They can engage with sounds using both their ears *and* their mouth, helping you spread your message.

Customers spreading a message among themselves is what we call *propagation*. Propagation isn't going to be very effective if it's done through the eyes. You need mouths and ears. Propagation doesn't happen through visuals, it happens through sounds.

At Hua and Hua, we don't want your message to be *communicated*, we want it to be *propagated*. We want the creative work to virally spread itself. We want you to put something out there and have your audience do your work for you!

Saying 'Tian-qi' when you're getting your picture taken is a great example of putting a sign out there and having the audience do the work. It's not just the brand doing it in their commercials. Customers started doing it themselves, and so they spread Tianqi's message *for* the company every time they got their picture taken.

In the Gu'an Industrial Park example, the 'I Love Beijing Tiananmen' jingle is both a super-phrase and an aural super sign.

Visual super signs need to be unforgettable.

Aural super signs need to be familiar.

Remember: adapt, don't create. You're not *copying*, you're passing on a tradition. Traditional things, things that have been

passed down for centuries, have become signs. People are familiar with them. They're your best tools. Remember what Confucius said about his work: "I explain, I do not create." We do
not create, we adapt the wisdom that our ancestors have spent
centuries refining.

In China we're all familiar with revolutionary songs. Those
songs were also created as super signs, because they were almost
all adapted from traditional folk songs. That is what made them so
popular and well-known.

If we want to make sure our voice is heard around the world, we
need to speak in a voice that has resonated for eons – super signs.

We've talked about the importance of propagation. Visuals can
only be communicated; sounds can be both communicated and
propagated. The key to successful visual design is that your visuals
must be sound-friendly – people need to be able to *describe* these
visuals. Chubang soy sauce is a great example.

Suppose your wife wants you to run to the store and get a
bottle of soy sauce. If she says that she wants Chubang soy sauce,
you'll probably forget the moment you walk out the door. But if
she tells you she wants 'the one with the green checkered packaging' then you'll never forget. Propagation is the key. Propagation takes place with the mouth and ears, not with the eyes.
That's why being sound-friendly is the key to creating good
advertising. Your visual elements need to be able to drive sharing
through sound.

Take a look at Chubang's green checkerboard pattern design.
Certainly it's a striking visual design, but it's also a design that's
concrete, describable, and sharable through sound – "A green
checkered pattern, like a tablecloth."

What about your design? Tell me.

This is actually a way to test out your design proposals. When a
designer comes to you and says that they've finished a design, ask
them: "What's your design? Tell me." If the designer can accurately
evoke the design in your brain using only words, you know you
have a good design that will be easy to spread. If the designer says,

"I can't describe it, you'll have to come and see," then you know this design will be difficult to spread, that it will be a risky proposal, that you'll have to be careful in your decision.

Propagation over communication. This is a core part of the Hua and Hua way. When companies buy advertising, they calculate their costs using exposure rates. But propagation rates are at least ten times more important than exposure rates! Propagation rates are an important part of the Hua and Hua creative process; we'll discuss this in-depth in a later chapter.

(3) SMELLS AND TASTES AS SIGNS

Some people say that we're entering an age of 'olfactory marketing'. This seems like a new trick, but really it's just old-school common sense.

If you use new tricks without using your common sense, you'll run into problems.

What's olfactory marketing? In Taiwan's 2012 election, the candidate Tsai Ing-wen hired an olfactory marketing consultant to design a 'campaign fragrance' for her. The fragrance, called 'Loving the Wind of the Pacific' was used in campaign events to create an 'olfactory impression' that the team hoped would persuade people to vote for Tsai. The team even developed campaign-branded hand cream, seeking to create a 'tactile impression' for their candidate.

These are smells and tastes used as signs.

The problem is, Tsai Ing-wen was blindly using signs in her marketing, because her team didn't establish a connection between the sign and the product. Her attempt to capitalize on the 'olfactory marketing' trend was ridiculous. Why? Because she was not a brand of soy sauce, or a hotel chain, or a plastic flower. She was running for 'president'. Her brand had nothing to do with smell or touch. She needed to create memories of policy and character, not olefactory or tactile memory.

From this failed campaign tactic, we see a common pitfall. People often don't try to *understand* how marketing ideas and methods work. They think that anything that's new and unexpected is a winner, so they're easily misled by 'amazing' new tricks.

In your work, you must always be guided by your ultimate goal. We said earlier that the stimulation of your signs must lead to a better memory of your value and provoke a reaction. If there's no value and no reaction, then it's just blind stimulation – a distraction.

Using signs isn't just about your advertising, it's also about your products.

In China, we often call social media and other internet platforms 'self-media' – a form of media that anybody can use to put themselves out there. For companies, their products are the ultimate form of self-media for their brands. With every one of our clients, Hua and Hua emphasizes 'self-media work'. We're not talking about social media, we're talking about the client's products, packaging, plants, employees, delivery vehicles ... everything. You need to think of all of that as a form of media. You need to do the work with these forms of media before you start advertising on traditional media platforms.

Chubang soy sauce is a great example of successfully turning product packaging into advertising. Right on the neck of every bottle, there's this declaration: 'Seeing is believing. Our beans are dried for 180 days right here'. This bit of packaging design is more effective than hundreds of millions spent on television advertising.

Speaking of taste signs, Lao Gan Ma hot sauce tastes like Lao Gan Ma hot sauce – undeniably, reliably, unfailingly. It's what customers want.

Master Kang instant beef noodles uses this slogan in their advertising: 'This taste right here!' I find this advertisement to be very resonant. Sometimes when I'm eating instant noodles from another brand, I'll notice that it's similar to what Master Kang tastes like and think, "Hmm, this must be more authentic."

Hotels have been a pioneer in olfactory marketing. Every Shangri-La Hotel around the world smells like every other one.

Even for consumable products, you can develop olfactory signs. The scent of a shampoo, bath gel or toothpaste can now be embedded on scratch-and-sniff paper and used in product packaging.

We say that olfactory and taste signs are mostly used in products, because you can't smell or taste media advertisements. But of course, with scratch-and-sniff technology, the scent of your product can be there in a magazine as well.

(4) TOUCH AS A SIGN

When we talk about tactile signs, a fever is the most common example.

How do you know that a child has a fever? First, you might see that their cheeks are red, their spirits are low, their expression is pained – all visual signs. You might hear a painful moan from them – an aural sign. But none of this is conclusive proof that the child has a fever. You need to use your sense of touch, and put a hand on their forehead. One touch and you know: they're burning up!

The tactile sign of heat is the crucial sign that represents a fever.

It's actually quite common to use tactile signs in brand marketing. In fact, we took special care to design the tactile experience for the cover of this book. Think back to when you first picked this book up. What did it feel like? How did this affect your impression of the book?

Some linguists believe that touch is the first language for every human being. Babies need to be touched right after they're born, and they understand what it means to be touched.

Many people, especially women, like to touch every product they see when they're shopping. They might not make a habit of doing so in any other situation, but they need to touch the product before buying it. Same thing with buying a car, or buying furniture. And when you buy a house, you'll certainly want to touch the walls first! We talk a lot about online retail and physical retail nowadays, and being able to touch things is an important advantage for traditional brick and mortar stores.

Is there a master of tactile marketing out there? Yes! His name is Kenya Hara, and he's from Japan.

Hara has been described as an 'acupuncturist to cure visual excess, master of texture, leader in the tactile experience field, fugitive from colour, shaper of basic items'. High praise indeed for a designer.

Hara designed the wayfinding system for Umeda Hospital in Japan. All of the items used white cotton material to create a soft, clean, cozy and friendly touch. The hospital was named a 'baby-friendly hospital' by the UN and the World Trade Organization.

To sum up the above discussion, all five senses can become systems of signs to build your brand. So use them to emphasize your product's best sides. And at the very least, you can't overlook visuals and sounds.

VISUAL SIGNS ARE NOT JUST LOGOS: THE IMPORTANCE OF PRODUCT DESIGNS AS SIGNS

As we said, visuals come first. So let's talk some more about visual signs.

First, visual signs are not just logos. A lot of people think that there's not much to visual signs – they're just logos, right?

Wrong.

The first place you should look to harness signs is on your product itself. For example, Sanjing's blue bottle is just that – a bottle. That's not a logo.

Cars are a good example of how products can be signs. Every brand of car has a unique front-end design that makes it instantly identifiable. Not the logo medallion, but literally the shape, look and feel of the front of the vehicle. This design is much more important than the logo, which is too small to be seen from a distance. The sign contained in the product design can be seen from very far away.

Clothing brands are another good example.

Adidas' sign to represent itself is three stripes. These three stripes make it easy for anyone to instantly see who's wearing Adidas on the field.

The goal of signs is to lower the costs associated with the brand – the cost of discovering the brand, and the cost of remembering it.

In order to lower the cost of discovery, the sign needs to be eye-catching – for instance, Chubang's green checkerboard pattern is undeniably eye-catching.

What about the cost of remembering? Usually, concrete designs are easier to remember. The secret to a low cost of remembering is to combine visuals and sound. Signs that are easy to describe are easy to remember. Adidas: three stripes. Nike: a swoosh.

So now let's compare. Which is easier to remember – Adidas' image or Nike's?

The answer is Adidas', and it's not even close!

When you're watching soccer on TV, you instantly know what team is wearing Adidas because the three-stripes pattern reaches from head to toe. You need a close-up to know who's wearing Nike.

If you're interested, you can even put a number on how much lower the cost of spreading visual awareness for Adidas is than for Nike.

Get a few people to dress up in various brands of sportswear, have them stand in a row, and tell them to start walking forward from 100 metres away. It'll be like an eyesight test. Note how far away they are when you identify the person dressed in Adidas. Let that number be X. Then note how far away they are when you identify the person dressed in Nike. Let that be Y. The ratio between X and Y is the ratio of the awareness/recognition cost of these two brands.

This analysis shows us that many sports brands in China are trying to blindly imitate Nike. Their logos have strokes and swooshes all over the place. What use is that? It's not an effective sign, as Adidas' is. It's not easily describable, like Nike's sign. For China's sportswear companies, their logos fall into a common trap: they do not lower the awareness cost associated with the brand, they actually increase it. They don't help the consumer remember the brand;

they actually make things *harder* for the consumer by giving them one more thing to remember.

How do you explain the success of these brands, then?

The answer is that success can mask many mistakes.

This is also a good place to discuss how to learn from internationally successful companies. A lot of companies uncritically copy everything from leading international brands without realizing that the secret to success for these top companies lies in their past. The important thing is what they did to succeed when they first started, not imitating what their second- and third-generation leaders are doing.

For instance, Nike didn't start with just a swoosh. In the beginning its logo was a swoosh under the word 'NIKE'. It was a long time before the swoosh became so iconic that it could be simplified into a single visual sign.

Plus, the swoosh itself is a cultural super sign. It's a shape that's familiar to everybody. Even in elementary school, teachers essentially use the swoosh shape when marking homework, in the form of a check mark. There are companies that try to imitate the swoosh, but without basing it on such a recongizable shape. What use would that be?

Next let's discuss a fashion brand – Burberry.

Burberry's most important sign is not the equestrian knight logo, but its Scottish-inspired check patterns. Many people don't even know what Burberry's logo is, but they can instantly recognize someone on the street wearing Burberry. They might not be able to do the same with Armani, for instance.

This also explains why Louis Vuitton, with its iconic overlapping 'LV' logo, has been the most successful luxury brand. It uses signs better than anyone else.

Similarly, Chubang's most important sign is not its corporate logo, but the green checkered tablecloth pattern. It is much more easily identified than the Chubang logo.

When companies design an image for their brands, they usually start with a logo and then add a 'supporting image'. I don't know who invented the concept of the supporting image, but I think it is an absurd idea. Why does a logo need a supporting image? How does this image support the logo? Does the 'support' actually make the brand more valuable?

Is the green checkerboard pattern a 'supporting image' to the Chubang logo?

No. The green checkerboard pattern is a sign for Chubang's brand. It's the core of the Chubang brand image.

Then what's the supporting image for the Chubang brand?

We don't know. There's no such thing as a supporting image in Hua and Hua's vocabulary.

The key to using visual signs is to make your brand *instantly memorable*.

In Chinese we have a saying: "One single glance at a startled bird." It means that when a bird is startled and flies out of the tall grass, you may only manage one glance out of the corner of your eye at it – and yet you can still be awed by the beauty of the bird's plumage.

This needs to be the goal of your brand. When the customer gives one look at your product out of the corner of their eye – and sees just one bit, maybe just a shadow – your product needs to grab them! You need to let them know who you are, what your value is and what your relationship to them is.

In the 2010 Winter Olympics in Vancouver, the ski jumpers were just blips in the sky as they executed their tricks. But what country had a uniform that was instantly identifiable? The United States did.

Undoubtedly, the US had the best uniforms in the Games. If we were to give them a grade out of 100, I would give the US a 90 and no other team would get higher than 60. That's how big the gap in quality was.

Designing a uniform is like designing packaging for a product. What are the basic principles?

1. It needs to be instantly recognizable, so that one single glance allows a consumer to identify your brand.

2. It needs to harness signs. It can't just be a big loud logo, it neeeds to have its unique style and effect.

The US team's uniform was a perfect implementation of the above principles. It was instantly recognizable. You could pick out American athletes from the crowd with one look.

Why? Because it made good use of signs and details. The most noticeable parts of the uniform are taken up by the Olympic rings, so they need to make the other parts count. The uniform design covers the athlete in the Stars and Stripes – it's not only evocative of snowflakes, fitting with the winter theme, it also fills every corner with a sign representing America. The Stars and Stripes are a background for the Olympic rings, but they are much more attention-grabbing – the United States brand is centre stage.

Other countries, like Switzerland and Canada, featured the symbols for their countries prominently on their uniforms. This is a common logo-based design, which doesn't leave much room for surprise.

Team China's uniform design certainly had its strengths as well. The collar and the back made use of traditional Chinese patterns. The collar had some particularly nice touches. But these patterns did not *signify* enough.

What do we mean? The US team used the Stars and Stripes; anybody in the entire world would know that the uniform represented the US with just one look. But nobody outside of China would know that the collar pattern on our uniform represented China. The sign that China used in its uniform design was not a universally recognized sign for China. It was not self-explanatory. When it comes to design, you need to value breadth over depth. It's pointless to congratulate yourself on the 'cultural depth' of your designs. In the real world, there is no voiceover narration telling consumers how to interpret your work. When we discuss design, the focus should not be on how the design came to be, but on what effect the design can bring about. To use semiotic terms, it must be clear to all what your signs *signify*.

36

This is breadth, not depth. You need cultural breadth in order to create more value.

Hua and Hua created a design very similar to the US Winter Olympics uniform: the packaging for Yuntianhua's 'Six Stars Long-Lasting Fertilizer'. The sales environment for fertilizers is usually suboptimal. Bags of fertilizer are strewn in dirty, dark, hole-in-the-wall shops in farming villages. There's no such thing as display management in those shops. So how can we make it so that consumers can instantly pick out our brand? Like the US Olympic team, we used a star design so that our packaging is instantly recognizable no matter how haphazardly it's placed on a shop shelf. It is the most recognizable brand no matter what the setting is.

Are there any good designs that are similar to the Team China uniform? Yes, and the design is much better! In the memoir of the warlord Li Zongren, there is a photo of the general in official dress when he was China's Vice President. The collar and cuffs of his shirt featured a plum blossom design. It was beautiful and highly significant, because the plum blossom was China's national flower during the Republican period.

What was the difference between Li's collar and the collar on the Team China uniform? There is an enormous difference in their use of signs. Li's official dress used a concrete image – a plum blossom – on the collar. Anybody can see that it's a plum blossom at first glance. To put it in Hua and Hua terms, this is a visual that is *describable*, that can be *propagated*. The collar design on the Team China uniform is too abstract, too difficult to describe, has too high a cost to communicate.

There is a lesson in all this: concrete images are more easily spread and have higher commercial value than abstract ones. And yet, in practice a lot of people are unwilling to use concrete images. Designers tend to go for more abstract designs. Why? Because creative types often think that there's no *creativity* if the design is 'just' a plum blossom. They've convinced themselves that it's only 'creative' when the plum blossom is adapted and abstracted.

The problem is, the goal of the creative output is to create value. We want to use plum blossom imagery because the plum blossom sign is of value to us. If the designer abstracts it to the point where it's unrecognizable as a plum blossom, then what's the point of the design anyway?

Back to the Six Stars Long-Lasting Fertilizer example. There's more to this super sign story. This Yuntianhua fertilizer is now China's leading chemical fertilizer brand.

Yuntianhua's flagship fertilizer brand used to be called Ingdeli. This name is the combination of the Chinese names for three European countries – *Ing* for the UK, *de* for Germany, *li* for Italy. They thought that this made the brand more international.

But Ingdeli is not nearly as 'international' as they imagined. Nobody in China understood it; nobody in the UK, Germany, or Italy understood it either. This brand name was not relevant to anybody, so in fact it was extremely difficult to comunicate.

So Yuntianhua went back to its catalogue of registered brand names and decided to invest in the 'Six Stars' brand as its new flagship.

Some people say that the Six Stars name is too 'local'.

The truth is exactly the opposite. This name is extremely global. It's what an international brand name should be like. Whether you're in China, the UK, Germany, Italy, Thailand, Madagascar, Cuba or Iceland, you'll instantly understand what *Six Stars* is. The stars are right there on the packaging! This is a super sign that is recognized around the world.

By the way, we also created an aural super sign for it. We set our slogan to a chant used by Chinese folk performers: "Six Stars Long-Lasting Fertilizer – one tube lasts for half a year!"

Now when you go to Changchun, in the northeast of China, you'll actually hear performers using this little jingle in their chants to entertain the audience. Clearly, the campaign has caught on.

EMBEDDED BRANDING: MAKING YOUR BRAND PART OF CONSUMERS' LIVES

Our super sign method isn't just about connecting your brand to culture – it can also be about connecting your brand to customers' lives. We call this 'embedded branding'. This is done by embedding your brand into the daily activities of consumers. For example, the campaign to have people say 'Tian-qi' when taking a picture was a way to embed the Tianqi brand in the daily activity of taking a picture.

WHAT'S YOUR BRAND SUPER SIGN?

The super sign for the Gu'an Industrial Park is Tiananmen, and the song 'I Love Beijing Tiananmen', was also harnessed to become a super sign for it. The super sign for Chubang soy sauce is the green checkered tablecloth pattern. The super sign for Tianqi toothpaste is saying 'Tian-qi' instead of "cheese" when taking a picture. The super-sign for Sanjing medical syrup is the blue bottle that it comes in. The super sign for Intel is the five-note jingle. The super sign for Adidas is the three stripes.

Super signs are the core driver behind brand communication. They are the most condensed form of information related to the brand.

A brand is a system of signs. A brand is built with signs, and in turn the greatest brands become supersigns themselves.

What's your brand super sign?

CHAPTER 2

PERSUADING CUSTOMERS WITH ONE SENTENCE

SUPER LANGUAGE: ONE SENTENCE TO PERSUADE CUSTOMERS TO BUY

In the previous chapter, we talked about super signs. Now let's talk about super language.

First, ask yourself a question: Can you explain your business in one sentence? Pause and think about it for a moment before you continue reading.

Then ask yourself another question: Can you convince a customer to buy your product or service with one sentence? Again, pause and think about it before continuing.

The notion of explaining your company and getting customers to buy your product in just two simple sentences is what companies dream of.

How can we explain what our company does? Forget about one sentence; many companies can't even do it in 10.

How can we persuade customers to buy what we have to offer with just one sentence? Try as they may, most businesses don't come close to being able to do so.

It's hard! And so we just keep talking, trying to squeeze in as much as we can in as short a time as possible. We count on maybe *one* of those sentences moving the customer to action.

And yet we do see some companies that persuade the customer in just one sentence. Many of these companies are mocked and envied. Marketers say, "I don't care how successful we are, I'm not doing what they do." These are the companies that make *tacky* commercials. They repeat one sentence over and over again. It's annoying ... and yet it works. Their products are runaway successes. And then we have people saying, "It doesn't make sense. It's because Chinese consumers are stupid."

These are the companies that found the one sentence that works for them. If you haven't, then you wouldn't be able to appreciate what these companies are doing. Once you find that one sentence that persuades the customer, you'll realize what you've been missing and you'll never settle for anything less. (Or, in this case, anything *more*!) You could have all the time in the world and you still wouldn't be doing anything other than repeating that one sentence over and over.

PERSUADING IS NOT EXPLAINING OR CONVINCING

Let's go back to the two questions we asked you to think about at the beginning of this chapter. These questions involved two things: *explaining* and *persuading*. *Explain* what you do; *persuade* the customer to act. These two things are on different levels. To explain is a means; to persuade is an end. We explain in order to persuade.

Do we always have to explain in order to persuade?

The answer is no.

There is an enormous difference between explaining and persuading.

Explaining is subjective; persuading is objective.

You might think you've explained something perfectly clearly when you haven't. You think you've been clear, but your colleagues do not. And so you end up in an interminable argument in the conference room about how to explain what your company does.

Finally, you reach a compromise. You come to an explanation that you all agree is clear. But when you say it, you realize that a third-party listener – your intended audience – doesn't find it clear at all.

The listener might *think* that they understood it, but they didn't. Or, perhaps they came away with something that you never meant to convey. "I didn't mean it that way!" is a common problem that we all face.

No matter what, the listener will never understand what you intend to say as well as you do.

On the other hand, sometimes it's other people who have the clearest view on what you're trying to say – clearer than even your own.

Explaining, understanding – all of that is subjective and fraught with uncertainty.

Whether you effectively explained something is relative. How clear is 'clear'? This is an important question as well, because people always think that they haven't explained themselves clearly yet.

Persuasion, on the other hand, is objective and absolute. You *persuade* someone to *do* something. If they do, you've succeeded; if they don't, you've failed.

When you persuade someone, you sway their actions. Either the customer comes to your store, or they don't. Either they buy your product, or they don't. It doesn't get more clear-cut than this.

Let's take the discussion of *explaining* and *persuading* a little further.

Sometimes we speak of explaining, convincing and persuading as three levels of communication. But it should be noted that these are not three *phases* of communication. Persuading someone does not necessarily entail explaining something to them, or convincing them.

To convince someone is a difficult and complex pursuit. Don't try to *convince* your customer. In fact, the harder you try the less open they might be to convincing.

Instead, your goal should be to persuade the customer to do something. We should <u>focus on changing *actions*, not thoughts</u>.

That's why this chapter on super language focuses on *persuasion*, on changing your customers' actions in just one sentence.

SUPER LANGUAGE NEEDS TO SPUR PEOPLE INTO ACTION

Your brand's super language is one sentence that can persuade your customer.

Persuading the customer means that you cause them to take action after listening to you.

'I love Beijing Tiananmen, 50 kilometers south: Gu'an Industrial Park' is the super language for the Gu'an Industrial Park.

Let's take a look at how this particular slogan works on the levels of explaining, convincing and persuading.

What does this slogan explain? It explains the geographical location of the industrial park.

Is this a comprehensive explanation of what Gu'an is all about? I doubt anyone would think so, especially not anyone who actually works for the park. They would say this is too superficial. It doesn't convey the real value that Gu'an Industrial Park – with its infrastucture, amenities and services – delivers. Gu'an is also about this and that, they would argue.

Does this slogan convey the 'positioning' of Gu'an Industrial Park, in a non-geographic sense? Not really.

Does this slogan convince anyone of anything in particular? Probably not. People are not so easily convinced.

When we make it our objective to explain or to convince, it's difficult to focus on the real goal of persuading.

Objectives and goals are two different levels of purpose. We set out to accomplish *objectives* in order to achieve our *goals*. The goal is the key; the objectives are just ways to get there. It doesn't matter if we accomplish all of our objectives, as long as we still reach the goal in the end.

'I love Beijing Tiananmen, 50 kilometers south: Gu'an Industrial Park'. This is a slogan that persuades the target customer of the Gu'an Industrial Park – investors looking to buy parcels of land.

For these investors, this slogan is an accurate and concise summation of where Gu'an is, as well as one that engages their imagination. Fifty kilometers south of Tiananmen – this means that they can enjoy all of the big-city amenities that the Beijing megalopolis provides. Whether we're talking about commerce, lifestyle, education, healthcare, research or talent, all of China's best resources are concentrated here. In fact, you don't even need to go 50 kilometers to access all that Beijing's urban sprawl has to offer, because Tiananmen is in the center of Beijing. So why isn't the slogan '30 kilometers south of the 3rd Ring'? Because the 3rd Ring Road is not a landmark; it's not a super sign.

Once an investor hears '50 kilometers south of Tiananmen', all the transport and logistical networks associated with the location would also come to mind: Capital Airport, Tianjin Airport, the Port of Tianjin, the freeway network.

In just one sentence, this slogan conveys a lot of information.

It also conveys a lot of emotion! 'I love Beijing Tiananmen'. This would touch the heart of any Chinese investor. It triggers a deep sense of belonging, a surge of curiosity. They'll definitely want to come take a look.

A PIECE OF SUPER LANGUAGE IS A SIGN THAT CONNECTS WITH CULTURE

In the book *L'Aventure sémiologique*, literary theorist Roland Barthes has this to say about advertising: "The commercial motive is not disguised, but rather amplified by a much greater representational effect, because it allows the reader to communicate with the grand themes of humanity."

Two levels of information are encoded in the sign 'I love Beijing Tiananmen, 50 kilometers south: Gu'an Industrial Park'.

There is the commercial level: Gu'an Industrial Park is 50 kilometers due south of Tiananmen. And there is the cultural level: the song 'I Love Beijing Tiananmen'.

'I Love Beijing Tiananmen' is the shortcut to a bundle of rich memories in the brain, connected to the grand themes and cultural heritage of China.

The slogan does not obscure the commercial purpose of Gu'an Industrial Park. Instead, the commercial purpose is amplified and connected with a grander theme, with the rich treasures of China's cultural heritage.

Gu'an Industrial Park started out with no specific connection with its customers, but with just one sentence it is able to build a deep and abiding link.

Gu'an Industrial Park is a new brand with no brand equity to speak of. But with this one slogan, it taps into the enormous value that a cultural asset like 'I Love Beijing Tiananmen' represents. This value is now part of Gu'an Industrial Park's brand equity.

This is part of what makes super language so potent, but not the whole reason.

Let's go back to the word *persuasion*.

The Chinese word for persuasion is *shuodong*. This word is comprised of two characters: *shuo*, meaning to speak; and *dong*, meaning to move. The value of a piece of brand super language is not just that it moves the customer into action; it's also that the language itself is capable of moving around the world, achieving worldwide prominence on its own.

SUPER LANGUAGE NEEDS TO BE CLEAR, FAMILIAR AND VIRAL

When we discussed visual and aural signs, we said that they need to be *unforgettable* and *familiar*. When it comes to formulating your brand super language, Hua and Hua has three similar but distinct keywords: the language needs to be *clear*, *familiar* and *viral*.

The langauge needs to be clear: Gu'an Industrial Park is 50 kilometers due south of Tiananmen. It needs to be familiar: Tiananmen the landmark, and 'I Love Beijing Tiananmen' the song. It needs to be viral: it can spread far and wide without spending any money, because people are able and willing to repeat it over and over. To go back to the concepts we used in Chapter 1, being clear and familiar is about communication. Being viral is about propagation – rapidly spreading your message far and wide.

Just like super signs, super langauge is about using the memorable words passed on through our cultural heritage, in order to activate the treasure trove of memory within every customer and trigger a reflexive action. In doing so, we can make a new brand seem like an old friend to our customers, instantly establishing a brand preference.

Let's go back to something we discussed earlier, which is that persuasion is about *moving*. First, it's about moving consumers into action. Second, it's moving the words themselves: making the words easy to remember, and ensuring that customers are willing to repeat these words to people in their lives so that they can propagate our message for us.

There is a third dimension to the idea of moving: moving our employees. Do your own employees use and repeat your super language in their communication? The employees of Gu'an Industrial Park certainly say "I love Beijing Tiananmen, 50 kilometers south" all the time. The sales staff of the Peacock City development project also repeat the slogan "One Beijing, four Peacocks"

48

in their sales pitches. Back when Nokia was the leader of the cell phone industry, their employees also repeated the phrase "Connecting people."

To sum up: your brand's super language needs to be persuasive on three levels. It needs to persuade your customers to take action and buy your product. It also needs to persuade your customers to repeat your messaging to other people. And finally, it needs to persuade your employees to actively make it part of their everyday speech.

If you're not sure whether you came up with a good slogan, try seeing if your employees are willing to use it first. If your slogan can't even become part of the everyday speech of your own employees, then it won't become a piece of brand super language. This kind of slogan is, in effect, useless – if even your own employees won't use it, how can you expect customers to use it?

This brings us to our next topic.

SUPER LANGUAGE IS SPOKEN LANGUAGE, BECAUSE PROPAGATION IS AN ORAL PHENOMENON

Propogation is an oral phenomenon. We cannot repeat this often enough, because too many in this field have been destroyed by the pursuit of language that looks good written down – without ever knowing what their mistake was.

Written language is useless when we're trying to spread a message, because it's not *propagated*.

Communication without propagation is useless.

Propagation is an oral phenomenon because language itself is primarily an oral phenomenon. The sounds of language appeared far before text did. The spoken word came before the written one.

Ferdinand de Saussure urged his readers to remember the "primacy of spoken language." Spoken language is fundamental to the exchange of ideas. Saussure wanted people to overcome the stubborn instinct to treat the written word as the fundamental form of language, because writing is "useful, but flawed and dangerous."

Saussure pointed out that writing should be treated as a "complement to oral speech, not as a transformer of verbalization."

No aspect of language can be regarded as more important than how it sounds. In his book *Orality and Literacy: The Technologizing of the Word*, literature professor Walter J. Ong pointed out that only 106 languages in the history of the world have been written down, and that the vast majority of languages have no writing whatsoever. Of the approximately 3,000 langauges spoken today, written literature exists for only 78. Even today a large number of languages and dialects cannot be written down.

If spoken language is the primary form, then the primary aspect of language is its sounds.

When we start to learn to read and write, we're learning the *written* form of language, the form that makes us seem 'cultured'. So when we're asked to write 'text' or 'copy', we start thinking in terms of written language. But written language is not conducive to propagation, because people don't talk in written language. People might have no trouble reading your written words, but they won't make it part of their speech, word-for-word, and they won't repeat it verbatim to others.

In his *Course in General Linguistics*, Saussure draws a distinction between *langue* and *parole*. Translated to English, these French terms are *language* and *speaking*. Sassure argues that the study of marketing and communication needs to be the study of speaking.

SUPER LANGUAGE IS NOT 'COPY' – IT'S TALK

There are people who spend their whole lives trying to learn how to write better *copy* – the advertising/marketing industry term for written messaging – but end up losing their ability to just *talk*. I see this all the time. The corporate leaders that I talk to can all describe their own businesses in three sentences. Everyone is clear about what they do. But when you read the descriptions or profiles of their businesses that they provide, it becomes impossible to understand what they do. Why? Because when you start thinking in terms of *writing*, it becomes difficult to simply and clearly convey what you mean.

For writing assignments in school, teachers always say: you need to start with things that give you feelings. Then just write down what you see, hear and think, and what you want to tell the reader. If you pick up the pen thinking "I'm going to write an *essay*!" then nothing will come out.

SUPER LANGUAGE IS ONE SENTENCE FOR CUSTOMERS TO TELL THEIR FRIENDS

Language is based on the spoken word, but writing imprisons language in only the visual dimension.

How do we interact with language? There's listening, speaking, reading and writing. Each one corresponds to a different part of our bodies. But we can interact with written langauge only through reading and writing. Only through spoken language can we use the entire spectrum of ways to interact with language. That's why written language is far more difficult to propagate than spoken language. It's a problem of anatomy.

Written language can only be read with the eyes. (Or, of course, through Braille for the seeing-impaired.) If you hear written language read out with your ears, you'll find that you often hear it without really understanding. That's because written language is not formulated in a way that's conducive to listening. It goes in one ear and out the other, without ever really registering in the brain. When you try to spread your message using only written language, you're giving up on your customers' hearing.

Visual perception is linear. It's not even two-dimensional, because you can only focus on one point at a time.

But auditory perception is three-dimensional. Giving up on hearing is giving up a lot.

If you want your customer to see your message, then your message needs to be within their line of sight. It's much easier to get them to hear your message. Imagine a housewife who's washing the dishes or mopping the floor with the television on. When a commercial announces "180 days of brewing is what gives Chubang Soy Sauce its great flavour!" the message comes through loud and clear. However, if the commercial played a readout of written language, then it certainly wouldn't get through to the listener.

The key to spreading a message isn't *communication*, it's *propagation*. It's about getting customers to communicate your message for you.

Your brand's super language isn't about coming up with something to say *to the customer*. It's about coming up with something that the *customer would repeat to their friends*. By the same token, a slogan isn't something for your company to say, it should be something for the company's customers to repeat.

When your slogan is confined to written language, you're not just giving up on the ears, your also giving up on the mouth – the mouths of your employees, your customers, the general public, everyone.

Your slogan needs to be something that your employees are happy to repeat, something that comes to mind over and over as they go about their day.

In Chinese we say that a slogan like this is *langlangshangkou* – it "Easily comes to the mouth." When your slogan easily comes to the mouth, then it can be spread far and wide – it *propagates*. Otherwise, you're just communicating without propagating, because nobody wants to do it for you.

SUPER LANGUAGE IS FORMULAIC

It's not enough that your brand's super language is in spoken language, it also needs to fit a *formula*. To explain why, we need to delve into academic research on the history of language. From what linguists and communication experts have discovered about Homer's epics, we can tap into the most powerful and primal forces of language.

Academics studying Homeric epics – the heroic tales of ancient Greece – had long been puzzled by one thing: without writing, how did long-ago poets create and remember works that ran tens of thousands of lines? Did people back then just have much better memories? Were they all amazing savants?

Professor Milman Parry of Harvard University asserted that the epics were not memorized. The bards of ancient Greece were not *writing* poetry, Prof. Milman suggested, they were 'sewing' their poems together using a variety of pre-composed parts. (Incidentally, the word *rhapsodize* comes from a Greek word meaning 'to sew together'.) He postulated that the thousands of lines that make up Homer's epics were pieced together using a series of 'modules' – descriptions, titles and names, events, themes, settings, and so on.

The theory holds that Homer's poems were woven together from all of these pre-existing pieces of language. Rather than a poet creating something new, Homer was more like a worker on an assembly line, fitting together various components.

The concept of pre-existing, modular language formulas is crucial to the propagation of your ideas. The slogan 'I love Beijing Tiananmen, 50 kilometers south: Gu'an Industrial Park' that we've discussed again and again is anchored in the pre-existing 'I love Beijing Tiananmen'.

These pre-existing formulas aren't just important for propagating your creations, they're crucial to the act of creation itself. We're all familiar with art and literature that uses and incorporates known formulas. For example, every James Bond movie is an assemblage of classic lines, names, plot events, themes and settings. And people love it! This secret of success was already well known by the bards of ancient Greece nearly three thousand years ago.

These pre-existing formulas are where the power of language lies.

So the act of finding your brand's super sign and super language is the act of *mythmaking* for your brand. By mythmaking, we don't mean exaggeration or excess. We mean using the formulas that enable you to tap into the power of myth.

In oral cultures, known facts must be frequently repeated so that they are not forgotten, because there is no way to write them down. A way of thinking based on repetition and known formulas is necessary for smart and effective management.

The way of thinking used in oral cultures is a way of thinking based on human nature. Creations that use the formulas of oral cultures are creations that can speak to human nature. Human language has existed for tens of thousands of years, writing only a few thousand.

Have you ever read stories to a child? Children's storybooks often consist of sentences that are designed to be read out loud, sentences that are repeated over and over. Children demand the same story over and over again for months, even years. You might think that the child already knows the story by heart, that they must be sick of it already, but they are just as excited as they were the first time you read the story. But it's true, they do know the story by heart: get one word wrong and they'll instantly correct you.

Oral formulas are a way to remember, to learn. We must emphasize that oral formulas are an important way for humans to store knowledge in their memory. In the time before writing, formulas were the only way that knowledge could be passed down through the generations. People who grew up in rural areas might still remember old sayings about predicting weather, or about the best time to plant crops. These sayings are a way to store knowledge in a highly condensed form, so that it could be passed down. And so, every child in the village could predict the weather based on past experience.

Does your brand need this kind of formula to store its unique knowledge and value, so that they can be passed down? This formula is your super language.

Oral formulas are *memorable!*

Oral formulas enable you to *pass down knowledge!*

Walter Ong rightly praises oral formulas as strengthening the rhythm of language and aiding memorization. Oral formulas are set patterns that are easy to spread through word of mouth. The emergence of these formulas in oral cultures was no coincidence: they rapidly increased in number and formed a base of knowledge and thinking.

A friend once told me: "I heard your slogan for Chubang Soy Sauce on television, and I could never forget it. I didn't even see the commercial, I just heard the slogan, but it was right there in my memory."

I replied: "That's right. That's what oral cultures are all about. Oral formulas are the oldest, most primal, most instinctual, and strongest way to remember, store, spread and pass on knowledge. From our ancestors to our own childhoods, from ancient history to language learning today, these patterns are perfectly suited to our natures."

DRINK IT AND THRIVE

SUPER LANGUAGE AND PROVERBS

We've talked about the physical aspect of brand super language. Now let's discuss the psychological aspect.

Super language needs to break down the psychological barriers your customers put up. Without these psychological barriers, you can win acceptance and trust. At Hua and Hua, we believe that proverbs are the quickest way to break down barriers.

'THE EXPERTS SAY' VS. 'THEY SAY'

Have you ever noticed that there are two kinds of declarations that are impossible to argue with? 'The experts say' and 'They say'. In modern society, science is a religion and the experts are the high priests. There are experts for everything, and 'Experts say' is the incantation that stops any opposing arguments.

But now there are so many so-called experts that people have grown resistant, even mocking.

Luckily, there is a much older idol that humans also worship – the ubiquitous 'They'. 'They say' is a much older source of authority than 'Experts say'. Folk sayings are the most powerful words there are.

That's why we need to use the power of 'They say'. We need to speak in proverbs – the kind of sayings that are impossible to refute or argue against.

In the previous chapter we said that brands are either derived from signs or become signs themselves – or both. Along the same lines, your brand super language must be derived from a proverb or become a proverb itself.

That's why Hua and Hua's advertising slogans make use of rhyming or set rhythmic patterns, like proverbs do. These are devices that humans instinctually react to!

180 days of brewing is what gives Chubang Soy Sauce its great flavour!

One Beijing, four Peacocks.

Six-Star long-lasting fertilizer. One shot for half a year.

Xibei Youmian Village. Close your eyes and order: you can't go wrong!

Xinhe Wealth Management. We do what we say.

For the best quality hotpot ingredients, go with Haidilao!

We always use formulas and sayings that roll off the tongue, because this formulaic language is the best match with how the human brain works. This is the essence of communication.

SUPER LANGUAGE IS A STATEMENT OF FACT OR A CALL TO ACTION

We've discussed how super language needs to be spoken language that uses the power of oral formulas and proverbs to roll off the tongue ... not bookish written language. The next thing to remember is that super language needs to be a statement of fact or a call to action, not empty platitudes or pretentious verbiage.

Let's use some classical Chinese literary theory to explore this further.

Wang Fuzhi, a philosopher of the late Ming dynasty, believed that good poetry arises from *xianliang* – a phrase we might translate as 'direct perception'.

What does he mean? He argued that poems should be composed based on what is seen and experienced. You just need to write down what you see and what you do. A good poem should be real and natural, showing no sign of artifice. The poet's subjective feelings should be a direct response to the objective happenings around them, with no process of reasoning in between.

In short, poetry should come out plain and direct, with no extra flourishes.

Wang Fuzhi's favourite line of poetry was "The spring grass grows in the pond," by Xie Lingyun. This is certainly an immortal line in the Chinese canon. "The spring grass grows in the pond." I look at the pond and I see spring grass growing in it. That's what my poem says. There's simply no way to make it better.

No fancy rhetoric, but there isn't a single word you can change.

On the other hand, another famous line of Chinese poetry is "The monk knocks on the door under the moonlight," by Jia Dao. Legend has it that Jia Dao spent countless hours debating with himself whether the monk in the poem should 'knock on' (*qiao*) or 'push open' (*tui*) the door. The story is so famous that in modern Chinese 'push or knock' (*tuiqiao*) has become a word meaning to spend a long time deliberating between two options. However, Wang Fuzhi had little regard for this poem. He said that all the time spent debating between *pushing* and *knocking* was empty speculation on nothing more than a fantasy.

What did the poet really care about? If the poet was really able to place himself in the scene and the feelings it evoked, then there was no need for all that deliberation. The choice would have been clear. So why shut himself in an empty room and try to choose between two equally imaginary options?

Harsh words, but necessary ones! What did the poet care about? Did he really care about whether the monk pushed or knocked? No, he cared only about the composition of his own poem and which word would sound better.

Often in this industry we see people working all day to polish a line of copy. But all this effort is not going toward the ultimate goal that the copy is meant to achieve, but rather toward making themselves look good as a copy writer. They care little about the goal at hand; they care endlessly about how they appear to others – whether they can appear cultured and creative and clever.

But if you want to create useful content, you must be *selfless!* You need to stop caring about making yourself look good to others.

The only thing you should care about is solving the problem.

In contrast to the empty fantasy of "The monk knocks on the door under the moonlight," Wang Fuzhi gave the example of "The circle of the setting sun falls over the river," which arose directly from what the poet saw; and "I ask a woodcutter across the water," which arose directly from what the poet experienced. Neither is the result of the poet's fancy or imagination. This is the *xianliang*, or direct perception, that he speaks of.

Another noted literary theorist, Wang Guowei of the early 20th century, made a similar argument with what he termed *buge*, 'no barrier'. He said that perceptual barriers between the poet and the subject are what make poetic descriptions ineffectual. These barriers make it impossible for the description to resonate with the reader; there is always something in the way. What kind of poetry can avoid this kind of barrier effect? Just like Wang Fuzhi before him, Wang Guowei likes lines like "The spring grass grows in the pond," and "The mud from birds' nests falls from empty beams."

We can explain Wang Fuzhi's concept of direct perception from three perspectives: the present, the immediate and the real.

The *present* means that the poet should focus on what is in front of them, and what they feel about what they see, instead of filtering the present through their memories of the past. Lines that Wang favours, like "The spring grass grows in the pond," and "Butterflies fly in the south garden," describe here-and-now scenes that resonate with the poet's here-and-now feelings.

The *immediate* means that the poet should write down the feelings directly evoked by the here and now, the raw emotions instantly triggered, instead of putting them through any kind of abstract thought process. "The circle of the setting sun falls over the river," and "I ask a woodcutter across the water," are both good examples.

The *real* means that poetry must reflect the true nature of things, without doubt or speculation. Wang emphasizes that the creative process should go beyond superficial observation to perceive the substance of things. He also believes that poets should be faithful to the full range of their aesthetic experiences regarding their subject matter, instead of distorting these experiences with their subjective judgments.

Commenting on a classic of ancient China, Confucius said: "To sum up the three hundred poems in the *Book of Odes*: there is no impropriety of thoughts." Wang Fuzhi interprets this quote in the same vein as his idea of direct perception: the poems in the *Book of Odes* arise from what is directly experienced and felt, with no deliberation or hair-splitting.

This is also the central tenet of *Zhong Yong*, which can be translated as the Doctrine of the Middle Way. The text of *Zhong Yong* emphasizes sincerity: "He who possesses sincerity is he who, without an effort, hits what is right, and apprehends, without the exercise of thought; he is the sage who naturally and easily embodies the right way."

We often make the mistake of thinking too much. It's true that 'think thrice, then proceed' is a quote from the *Analects*, but people always forget that Confucius' response was, "Thinking twice is sufficient." Three times is overthinking it! Twice is enough! And our ultimate goal should be to act without needing to think, to react in the right way and fight for the quick victory.

Your brand's super language needs to be a statement of fact, or a call to action.

You brand's super language needs to be clear and concrete. State the facts – better yet, state just one fact! But what you absolutely must not do is say nothing at all. Say clearly what you want the audience to do. Don't be wishy-washy and unsure.

'One Beijing, four peacocks' is a statement of fact as a slogan. It's also a brand strategy and a marketing tactic. This is the theme that the entire promotional campaign for the Peacock City development is based around. And this is the promotional campaign that vaulted Peacock City from a regional brand to one of the top-20 real estate players in China.

'180 days of brewing is what gives Chubang Soy Sauce its great flavour!' is also a statement of fact and a brand strategy. Another soy sauce brand, Haitian, has made the brewing process part of its advertising for a decade now. But they used all kinds of ways to try to 'convey' the fact that their soy sauce is brewed, without ever coming out and just saying so. It was only when Chubang emerged as an unexpected force in the market that Haitian realized it was going about it all wrong. So they started running television ads right after Chubang's, saying: "We brew more than 180 days!" This slogan was all over the airwaves, and they changed the packaging design to be more like Chubang's as well. They say imitation is the sincerest form of flattery.

Chenguang stationery uses the slogan "New items at Chenguang every Monday." This is a statement of fact and also a guide to behaviour. Now customers know to visit stores every Monday to see if anything interests them, and retailers know that they need to arrange for new shipments every Monday.

'I love Beijing Tiananmen, 50 kilometers south: Gu'an Industrial Park'. Again, a statement of fact.

'Golden wine for the elders'. 'Want to play games? Come to 51.com'. These are calls to action, telling people what you want them to buy.

For advertising, the *immediate* aspect is crucial: raw emotions instantly triggered, with no abstract thought process. The Hua and Hua way is this: a slogan isn't something for your company to say, it should be something for the company's customers to repeat.

The best slogans are the ones that are immediate, raw, with no thinking involved. So your creative elements need to be concepts that can be *understood without thought*. This is another concept from the *Zhong Yong*:

"It is only he who is possessed of the most complete sincerity that can exist under heaven, who can give its full development to his nature. Able to give its full development to his own nature, he can do the same to the nature of other men. Able to give its full development to the nature of other men, he can give their full development to the natures of animals and things. Able to give their full development to the natures of creatures and things, he can assist the transforming and nourishing powers of Heaven and Earth.

Able to assist the transforming and nourishing powers of Heaven and Earth, he may with Heaven and Earth form a ternion."

The best kind of creative work is the kind that flows from you, without thought.

Language that flows from you without thought can be remembered by the listener without thought, and spread to others without thought. This is the most efficient way to spread a message.

We often think in terms of 'packaging' our message. But in fact, it's much better to simply say what you mean. When Barack Obama was running for re-election, he faced unclear prospects in Ohio, a crucial state. His team had a simple and direct pitch for Ohio voters: "Ohio, I need your help."

Sure enough, Ohio helped him and he won the state ... and ultimately the presidency.

CREATIVITY NEEDS TO BE ABOUT PROPAGATION

The Hua and Hua way evaluates advertising along three dimensions: reach, transmission and ritualization.

In the media, advertising reach is calculated in cost per thousand exposures. Hua and Hua does not think of reach as particularly important. Let's say it accounts for 24% of the pie. Transmission is 51%. The key to spreading a message is propagation, and propagation needs to be the focus of your entire creative process. The remaining 25% is ritualization. This is an aspect that's often overlooked, because people are locked into their pursuit of reach. They think that all that matters is that their mesage *reaches* an audience. A commercial on the CCTV network is ritualized; an internet pop-up ad is not. They have very different levels of influence.

Hua and Hua advertises its services in airlines' in-flight magazines. This was an effort to increase our reach. Later, we bought a billboard in the most expensive place for outdoor advertising in China: along the Beijing Capital Airport Freeway. This was to improve our ritualization.

Your slogan and your audience's sense of hearing are the key to improving your transmission.

The sun, the moon and the stars are the only things that everyone in the world can see. Besides these exceptions, people hear about much more than they can see. Hearsay happens all the time, at no cost whatsoever.

Let's think back to the example of brewed soy sauce. Chubang's slogan about brewing soy sauce for 180 days is much more effective than CCTV network commercials showing people putting soy sauce under the sun. Think of another memorable slogan: "Open up a Remy Martin, and good fortune will follow." A great slogan is all it takes to spread awareness of your brand.

No creative element can rival a powerful slogan. A great slogan doesn't just spread around the world, it can end up in history books. We talked about reach and transmission. Visual elements can only *reach* audiences. You need to engage the sense of hearing to *transmit* your message. You need a good slogan to propagate your message.

Why do people talk about *word-of-mouth*, but never *word-of-eyes*? It's interesting to point out that the Chinese term for word-of-mouth is 'mouth monument'. People say word-of-mouth is important, but the real question is not whether your word-of-mouth is good, it's what your word-of-mouth *is*. When people talk about you, what they say should never change – just as the words carved on a monument never change. It should be the same thing for 50 years or even 500 years. That's what word-of-mouth is all about.

The key to word-of-mouth is to have a few simple words that don't change. Just like that indelible inscription on a monument. People may die, but the monument still stands.

What's written on your monument?

CHAPTER 3

USING WORDS TO START TRENDS

WORDS CAN CONQUER
THE WORLD

We've talked about super signs and super language. Now let's talk about super words.

We're discussing super words in a separate chapter from super language because words and language operate on different levels. In this chapter, we're going to tell you how to summon the power of words.

We say that language is power. But the power of a single word or phrase works on an even higher level. One word can be much more powerful than one sentence.

Note that we're asking more and more of ourselves. We're no longer content with moving people with one sentence; we want to move people with one word. Conquering the world with one sentence isn't enough anymore, we want to conquer the world with one word.

Can this really be done? In the previous chapter we talked about how Barack Obama won Ohio with one sentence. Now let's take a look at how he won America with one word.

HOW OBAMA
CONQUERED AMERICAN
WITH ONE WORD

The battle between Barack Obama and Hillary Clinton for the Democratic presidential nomination in 2008 was a classic example of a battle fought with the power of a single word. Obama's key-word was *CHANGE*. He said that change was what people needed. Clinton's keyword was *EXPERIENCE*. She said that Obama was too new to national politics to be president, and touted her own political experience.

Clinton's first mistake was that she took her eyes off the customer, and focused solely on her opponent. Obama focused on his 'customers', the voters: Voters need change, and I will bring change. Clinton focused on Obama: Obama is inexperienced, I bring more experience to the table than him. So every time Clinton talked about her message, she handed over half of the exposure to her opponent: "I am more experienced *than Obama*."

Clinton's second mistake was that she was unable to make full use of her keyword's power. This is an enormous waste. On a visual level alone, wherever Obama went he would wear a CHANGE sticker. When he spoke, the CHANGE slogan was always visible somewhere.

Obama completely took ownership of the word 'change' and made himself the standard bearer for change. But what was in front of Clinton's podium? Nothing except her name! In essence, she wasted a prime advertising slot and failed to take advantage of the biggest outlet for her message. She didn't have her own *word*. The theme of her campaign, experience, still partially belonged to Obama, because her experience was only meaningful in comparison to Obama's lack of it. Without Obama, there was no power to this word.

Obama made the word 'change' into his most powerful weapon. He convinced the public that he would bring change. And he succeeded.

Words are actions. Language calls people to action. Obama's 'change' keyword was both an action and a call to it. Clinton's 'experience' was neither. And so she was unable to convince the public to take action for her.

Obama is a wizard with words. After winning the presidency with the word 'change', he chose another powerful word for his re-election campaign: FORWARD.

Obama used this word to cut through his opponent's attempt to drag him down into a mudslinging contest. The word told the public, "There's no use slinging empty words, let's just go forward! Continue!"

And that's what they chose.

WORDS CAN CHANGE WHAT PEOPLE THINK AS WELL AS WHAT THEY DO

The example of Obama's political slogans shows us the power of words. Words don't just *say* things, they can also *do* things. Words can drive people to action. Words can change what people think.

The great 20th-century thinker Friedrich Hayek made an interesting argument about how words determine thought processes. When we think about a problem, he said, we must use neutral words. Most words imply a certain set of positions and arguments; simply using the word represents an acceptance of these positions and arguments. Without choosing your words carefully, it's impossible to think independently. Your conclusions are already predetermined by the words you choose.

This argument came into play in Hayek's discussion of planned economies versus market economies. He said it was inappropriate to use the word 'planned'. Once that word is used, the discussion focuses on whether 'planning' is good. It's impossible to argue against the notion of *planning*. Why use a word that defeats discussion?

That's why Hayek chose to use two neutral terms in his analysis: collectivism and individualism. By using these two words, the discussion is refocused on whether to allow individuals to pursue their own development. Hayek's conclusion was that if society did not allow such individual pursuit, then such a society was sure to collapse.

In our thinking, we need to use neutral terms to prevent bias in our thought process. On the other hand, terms strongly associated with certain positions and arguments are exactly what we need when we're trying to spread a message. Think again of the movie *Inception*. Using the right word allows us to plant the seeds of an idea in the audience's subconscious.

People think using words. Using words to plant ideas is even more effective and direct than using dreams. Obama used words like 'change' and 'forward', words with strong associations and positions, to plant the idea of supporting him in voters' minds. And so people chose to stand with him.

Many philosophers have thought deeply about the relationship between language, speech and words. The Austrian linguist and philosopher Ludwig Wittgenstein said: "Our thinking is always misled by our words. I often feel that, when I am speaking, I need to remove the words from our exchange, clean them, then return them to our exchange."

Wittgenstein proposed the idea of 'language-games'. In his view, the rules of the language game are constantly established and change during play. It's a highly complex process.

Take a look at newspapers from a few decades ago, and you'll see how the rules of language have changed.

That's why Wittgenstein says that we need to use signs in simpler ways, using the most primal forms of language – the forms of language used by children who are just learning to talk. In this raw and simple form, the fog of obfuscation that surrounds our daily use of language disappears. We see the clear and accurate lines drawn between action and reaction.

This is what happens with blunt and direct slogans like '180 days of brewing'. There is no fog of obfuscation, just plain clarity.

A lot of people try to shroud their language with obfuscation, but they end up confusing themselves instead of convincing anyone else.

The German philosopher Martin Heidegger, in his *On the Way to Language*, has this to say about the power and dignity of the word: "Only through a word can something show what it is, and therefore exist."

A word is the means through which we summon something. If the word is absent, the thing remains unknown.

Language is the world. Words are the home of existence. Words are what makes things exist – what we say is what is, what we cannot say cannot be.

Language is not simply a tool to express yourself. Language is not only expression, nor is it merely a human activity. Language *says* and *does*. Language is a strong driver of action. Language creates and rules the world.

It is difficult for people to control language, but easy for language to control people. Language controls thought much more than the other way around. Language is not just a vessel for thought, but also a driver of thought and a demarcation of what can be thought.

The power gained through language is far greater than the power gained through violence.

Naming something is not just labeling through the use of a word. To name something is to summon the word for it. Naming is summoning.

Language speaks. The authority of language is ancient.

The study of the power of words often draws on poetry as the research subject. Just as we used Wang Fuzhi and classical Chinese poetry in the last chapter, let's begin our discussion with a poem. This is a very philosophical poem by the German poet Stefan George, called simply *The Word*:

Wonders from dreams and from abroad
I carried to my country's port,
But for the names I had to wait
Which in her depths were searched by Fate.
Then I could hold them in my hand
And now they blossom in this land ...
Once I returned from such a tour
With a small treasure rich and pure;
She searched for long but had to tell
That no such thing slept in her well;
At once it vanished from my hand
And ne'er this wealth entered the land ...
So, sadly, I became aware
That things are not if words aren't there.

In any study of words, this poem is worth reading and thinking about.

What is 'my country's port'? It is the limit of our knowledge, the boundary of the world. What we know is the world; what we don't know is beyond it.

The world is knowledge. To know is to classify. To classify is to give names and labels. Names and labels are words and signs.

What is the one thing the poet needs at the port of his country?

He needs a word. A name.

And once he gets the name ... his treasure will blossom in his land. Why?

Let's come back to Chinese philosophy. Laozi's *Daodejing* answers this question: "Having no name, it is the Originator of Heaven and Earth; having a name, it is the Mother of all things."

In the beginning the world was only chaos and confusion, because there were no names for things. The world came into existence only after they were given names. When we say *every thing*, what we really mean is *every name*.

Did the chicken or the egg come first? Did existence come before naming? Some say it's obvious that existence came before naming. But let me ask you, *what* existed before it was named? If you can't name something, then that thing cannot be said – and by extension, it cannot exist in the world shared between you and me. Later in this chapter, we'll talk about a method of product development that puts naming before existence.

But back to the poem:

Once I returned from such a tour
With a small treasure rich and pure;
She searched for long but had to tell
That no such thing slept in her well;
At once it vanished from my hand
And ne'er this wealth entered the land ...

"No such thing slept in her well." As it cannot be named, the treasure might as well never have existed:

> So, sadly, I became aware
> That things are not if words aren't there.

Heidegger said that this is the end and the beginning of *The Word*: "things are not, if words aren't there." This isn't a difficult concept to grasp for Chinese people like us. When we were young, we had no concept of the *Republican era* in China's history. Why? Because the word 'Republic' never came up in our history classes. There was only the 'old society', and the 'era before liberation'. Chinese history went: Ming dynasty, Qing dynasty, era before liberation, era of the new China. The concept of the Republic is forever lost to our minds, without the word to summon it. This is the power of the word.

Heidegger said: "The poet experiences a power and dignity of the word, and there is no higher or grander way to conceive of this power and dignity. But at the same time, the word is also a treasure that the poet relies on and gazes upon in an extraordinary way."

The word is power. The word is a treasure.

Next let's talk about how you can unlock the power and wealth contained in the word.

NAMING: COST, CALL, INVESTMENT

Companies constantly have to face the problem of naming: what to name the company, its brands, its products.

What is the primary principle of naming? The answer is cost. You need low-cost names.

What do we mean by this? A good name can be communicated, propagated, used and marketed, all at a low cost.

Take a look at your own name, and compare it to other people. Is your name low-cost or high-cost?

A lot of parents in China like to name their children with obscure characters they find in dictionaries. It's as if they're trying to make things harder for teachers. The teacher looks at the student roll and sees that they know only one character out of three in a student's name – they'll never call on the student, that's for sure.

If a student is rarely called on to answer questions, then they have far fewer opportunities to learn and improve.

The best illustration of the problem of a high-cost name is when you're at an airport. We have a colleague in our company whose name uses a character so obscure that it can't be typed in most computer systems. When she's on business trips, often she'll have to make a special detour to the security office when everybody else has already passed the security check. Another colleague's name is even more infuriating – it can't even be typed in bank computer systems! There's all kinds of trouble associated with transferring money to him, so he needs to be paid in cash. The high cost of his name isn't just his own problem, it's a problem for our accounting department as well.

Simple and common names give people better opportunities. Sociological studies show that people with simpler names have better chances for success. Think of how a former American president *and* one of the richest people in the world are both named Bill.

You must have experienced this personally as well. If you make a new friend named Li Yong or Zhang Li, you'll remember the name with no trouble at all because it's so familiar. Simple names like this – Li Yong, Li Zhiyong, Zhang Li, Wang Yan, Chen Bo – are super words. They are the most common and memorable names for Chinese people.

Super signs are shared cultural signs that have been repeated for centuries and millennia. Super words are shared cultural words that have been repeated for just as long. So much value has been invested in them. Go ahead and use them!

Let's take a look at what companies call themselves. This is a good way to compare low-cost and high-cost names.

Apple is a low-cost super word. Dell is not.

Whahaha is a low-cost super word. Lebaishi is not.

Take note of names like Alibaba and Whahaha. They're not just culturally rich words, they also have repeated sounds that make the names even easier to remember and spread. Alibaba's naming connects to the shared cultural heritage of the *Thousand and One Nights*. The most memorable part of the Alibaba story, 'open sesame', is also emblematic of Alibaba's mission: to open up the doors to wealth by making it easier to do business. Whahaha's name uses a children's song everyone in China knows by heart: "Whahaha, whahaha, smiles on every face."

A low cost is one key to naming. Another key is whether the name constitutes a call to action.

Does your name have a strong point to it? Is there a clear call to the audience?

Heidegger said: "Naming is not labeling or using words. It is summoning words. A name is a call. This call summons the thing near. The summoned thing responds as a matter of course."

Here's an example of poor naming: Toyota China.

A few years ago, Toyota changed all of its brand and product names in China. The Lexus, the Land Cruiser, the Prado and the Camry all originally had localized names that were easy to remember in Chinese. But Toyota changed them all to sounda-likes of their English names, random strings of characters that were impossible for the Chinese population to remember.

This was a clear mistake. Names that were low-cost and clear calls to action were changed to high-cost names that compelled the audience to do nothing.

In its news releases, Toyota claimed that the reason behind the name change was 'globalization'. They said that the new names sounded like the names in English and French. So when a Chinese gentleman and a French gentleman were to meet, the argument went, they would immediately know that the other drove a Lexus, even though they have no common language.

The news releases never explained how two people with no common language could even start a conversation about their cars.

Of course, there was a limit to the mass renaming – Toyota kept its original company name in Chinese, without trying for an awkward phonological rendering. But perhaps this too would come in a misguided future phase of the 'globalization' strategy.

A complete misunderstanding of globalization is common among Chinese companies. The case of Toyota is a reflection of a problem with Chinese companies around the globe. It seems that this is a Chinese problem.

You speak Chinese in China, English in the UK, Japanese in Japan. This is what globalization is. Speaking English in China is not globalization, it's not knowing your market. True globalization is being able to adapt yourself to every local market, not enforcing a mechanical uniformity.

The call is where the power of the word lies. A good word evokes the value of the brand. The name *Land Cruiser* evokes what the brand is about, and calls out to the customer. A random string of characters does not.

The cost of a name is the cost of remembering it, transmitting it and understanding it. Land Cruiser is a low-cost name. A random string of characters is a high-cost name.

And finally, a name is an investment. Once you decide on a name, you need to invest in it long-term. Toyota invested many resources over the years in the name Land Cruiser, but it took only one leadership change to flush all of that down the drain in China.

DON'T LET
TRADEMARKS LIMIT
YOUR THINKING

Looking at the names of cars on the Chinese market, you'll quickly notice that all of them are hard to remember, and different brands all have annoyingly similar names for their cars. For most car commercials, you can slap a different brand or product name on it and the creative elements still work. All of these ads are interchangeable. Why? Because there's no personality to any of the names. They're jumbled-together combinations of nice-sounding, nice-looking Chinese characters. This is so the name can be registered as a trademark. In this day and age, trademarks that haven't been taken are very rare. What do you do if all the good names have been taken, or your name is too common to be registered?

You need a trademark for your brand, but you can forget about it for your product. Just use the common word. Don't bother registering it with the trademark office, register it in the minds of your customers. Names like Land Cruiser, like AK47 – just use them. Why register them? If you don't use a good name because you can't register it, that's just throwing the baby out with the bathwater.

NAME FOR THE EARS, NOT THE EYES

We're making this point again because the principle remains the same. Messages spread through spoken language. You need to engage the sense of hearing.

For a name to constitute an effective call, and to be spread at low cost, companies must choose names that appeal to the ears. It's not enough that a name can be idenitified at first sight, it also needs to be identifiable at first *listen*.

Land Cruiser's original name in Chinese could easily be understood even if you only heard it once. When it turned into an approximation of what 'Land Cruiser' sounded like in English, confusion ensued.

THE TELEPHONE TEST

There's an easy way to test whether a name is low-cost and easily understood. Try seeing how long it takes to tell someone what the name is over the telephone.

Take a look at two weekend-home communities in Shanghai's western suburbs. One is called West Countryside Estates. It's easy to say this over the phone. The other is called *Lan Qiao Sheng Fei* – and no, it doesn't make much more sense in Chinese either. In English, you'll have to spell out this incredibly long name: *L* as in lemon, *A* as in apple, etc. In Chinese, the process is no less tedious, as the way to describe a character is to give an example of a word the character is used in. Chances are, the poor delivery man who's trying to find your community would have forgotten what the first character was by the time you're finished.

In the first chapter, we said that the cost for visually identifying Nike's logo is higher than that of Adidas', and that the difference can be quantified simply by looking at the distance from which the logos remain identifiable. In the same way, the difference between the auditory cost of the names 'West Countryside Estates' and 'Lan Qiao Sheng Fei' can be quantified by measuring how long it takes to tell someone the name over the telephone. It takes maybe one second for West Countryside Estates; it could take 30 for Lan Qiao Sheng Fei. The difference is even more stark when you consider that West Countryside Estates contains so much more information – it tells you that it's a housing community and its approximate location. Lan Qiao Sheng Fei tells you nothing. With no additional information, people wouldn't even know what it is. It could be a coffee shop. It could be a fashion brand. It could be anything.

Names were invented to be heard, not to be seen. You can see this even in the construction of the Chinese character that means 'name', 名. According to the classic of Chinese philology *Shuowen Jiezi*, the character can be deconstructed into two constituent parts, 夕 and 口. The top part means 'evening' while the bottom part means 'mouth'. In early human history, people could identify each other in the daytime using their appearance. But at night, when it's impossible to see, people could identify themselves to each other only by calling out their names.

Names are meant to be called, not to be seen.

One more point. The people who live in those fancy communities with the fancy foreign names are the people who best know what it means to have a 'high-cost' name. They're the ones who need to repeat the name over and over again to friends, delivery drivers and milkmen. If you really want a fancy name, try something like California Sun Gardens. There's a nice foreign ring to it, but it's still understandable to Chinese people.

THE NAME COMES
BEFORE THE PRODUCT

Think back to the *Daodejing* quote at the beginning of this chapter: "Having no name, it is the Originator of Heaven and Earth; having a name, it is the Mother of all things." Do things come first, or do names come first?

When it comes to product development, our view is that names come before things. Words come before products.

What we call product development is really a process where we think of a good name, then turn it into a real product.

A friend called me when I was writing this chapter, inviting me to visit him in Ergun, a city in Inner Mongolia. He was preparing to open a hotel there, to be called the White Birch Hotel.

I couldn't help it. I said: "You should change the name."

My friend said that everyone liked the name. The white birch is the official tree of Ergun City. It is an important tree in the ancient cultures of the area.

But the problem wasn't whether the name was *good*, it was what the name *does*.

The power of words is not in telling, but in doing.

What does the name White Birch Hotel do? To me it sounds like a call to plant a forest of white birches.

Wouldn't it be better to have a call to do something else ... like schedule a stay at the hotel?

I suggested that he call it the Ergun Bonfire Hotel. Associate it with lighting a bonfire.

Instead of a fountain, put a bonfire site in front of the hotel. Light a fire every night, and have performers play traditional Mongolian instruments and sing Mongolian songs. All the guests can gather around.

The bonfire is a product for the hotel. It's a part of the guest experience. And it's a great piece of outdoor advertising.

The hotel should feature suites with fireplaces. The lobby and restaurants should also have them, so that guests can relax in front of the fire and let the day's worries melt away. That's an experience you'll never have in Beijing or Shanghai.

What is a product? It's how you make a super word into something you can touch.

The word comes before the product. We use the word to summon the power. The word is our weapon. When you're marketing a hotel called the Bonfire Hotel, the word *Bonfire* does all the talking.

THE AUTHORITY OF
THE UNCHANGING WORD

Suppose my friend doesn't take my advice, but does take my idea. He offers the bonfire experience, but still calls it the White Birch Hotel. The advertising goes like this: "Enjoy the bonfire experience at the White Birch Hotel, every night at seven." If that's what he does, then the marketing would be much less convincing and efficient than if he'd just called it the Bonfire Hotel. The most important reason is that it will be much more difficult for the hotel to be seen as *the* authoritative bonfire experience.

Suppose Buick is launching a high-spec commercial vehicle with this slogan: "The all-new Buick. Luxury experiences in a commercial vehicle." A better way would be to simply call it the Buick Luxury, or something similar. This is a much more authoritative statement. Such a vehicle would seem more valuable and have much higher price potential.

If you can actually say the product's value in its name, then don't wait to say it in the slogan.

If the name conveys the product's value, then you don't have to worry about how long it is.

A long name that conveys value is much better than a short name that conveys nothing.

'Sunflower children's coughing and wheezing oral syrup' is an awfully long name, both translated and in Chinese. But it clearly states what the medicine is for. Shorten the name, and you'll just end up making it less clear to the customer what the medicine can be used for.

Names are authoritative. Slogans are less so.

Why?

Because names don't change often. As for slogans, who knows? You might say one thing today and another tomorrow. You might say one thing to me and another thing to someone else. There's always going to be a psychological difference between the name and the slogan.

Sometimes you have a killer slogan but can't find a decent name. In that case, don't be afraid – use the slogan as your name!

A young man in New York had a great idea for a business. He knew that women liked to carry around luxury handbags, but handbags can be very expensive – it's much easier to have a closet of designer clothing than one of designer handbags. So he set up a business that rents out luxury handbags. Customers can have a new bag every week, always the latest fashion. He had a great way to sell this service: 'Bag, borrow or steal'. And that's what he called his company. 'Bag, borrow or steal' doesn't have to be a tagline under the company's 'real' name, it is the real name. It's everything: a name, a slogan, the brand's value, the brand's experience, the brand's fun.

One long name meant that marketing and spreading awareness of the brand was much easier.

Prince George of the United Kingdom was born when I was writing this chapter. All of the major papers in the UK were jostling with each other to have the best, most attention-grabbing headline for the royal arrival. In my view, the winner was *The Sun*. It went as far as to change its name for the edition covering the prince's birth – in big letters, there it was: *The Son!*

EVERY COMPANY NEEDS A CORPORATE DICTIONARY

You need to define your products before you can position them.

When you're formulating your market strategy, you first need to settle on how you position your company, your brand and your products. But there's one even more fundamental thing you need to do before you think about your position: You need to *define* your company, brand and products.

The act of defining is a way of thinking. It's also a way to *express*. Suppose the names of your company, brand and products were to be added to the dictionary. How would you write the definition for them?

Try doing this exercise. List out all the names your company uses. Think of how your company will define them. Then ask your colleagues to give their own definition. Do you have the same definition in mind?

If everyone gives a different definition, then that means you don't even understand the words used by each other in meetings. You might be speaking the same language, but you are still stuck in a linguistic Babel. The language is the same, but you don't understand each other's words! This makes communication very costly, and all but ensures that your meetings are pointless. Even if you reach some kind of 'conclusion', there's no guarantee that everyone is on the same page regarding the conclusion. That's why 90% of meetings are highly ineffectual.

So try to compile a corporate dictionary. Define the words your company uses. This is a very fundamental task. If you can't even communicate clearly among yourselves, then there's no hope in spreading your message outside the company.

The first three chapters of this book all focus on one common theme: lowering the cost of spreading your message. The Hua and Hua way is a way to lower costs using creativity.

All of our thinking is along two dimensions: cost and investment. This is a very business-oriented way of thinking.

In the next chapter, in discussing the concept of *branding cost*, we're going to delve into a more creative-oriented way of thinking.

Accounting has given us the concepts of standard costs and operational costs. So now let's talk about 'creative costs' and how to use creativity to lower these costs.

CHAPTER 4

CREATIVE ELEMENTS ARE THERE TO LOWER MARKETING COMMUNICATION COSTS

BRANDS REPRESENT RISK MITIGATION FOR CONSUMERS

Things exist because we need them. We have brands not because companies made them, but because society needs them. If society and consumers didn't need brands, no amount of effort from companies could bring them into existence.

How do brands work on a societal level? Let's start by listening to economists instead of brand experts.

Some economists explain brands from a game-theory perspective. They say that brands are a mechanism for companies to engage customers in repeated games. And by giving customers an opportunity to punish companies, brands create a worry-free choice for consumers.

No trust can be created in a one-time game. Why do tourist traps offer such poor quality for high prices? Because it's a one-time game. Shops and restaurants at tourist destinations know that you're unlikely to come back, and they don't expect you to. On the other hand, the restaurant right around the corner – which also caters to year-round residents – provides great service and quality, because they're counting on repeat business from satisfied customers. If you don't like the restaurant, you can punish it by never visiting again. A neighborhood restaurant relies on customers from nearby. It can't survive if it's alienated them.

In the US, McDonald's doesn't allow franchise locations near highway rest stops. All McDonald's locations in rest stops are directly owned and operated by the corporation. That's because stopping at a McDonald's right off a highway is a one-time game for that specific location. It's only a repeated game from the perspective of the company's national headquarters. And so, McDonald's maintains ownership of these one-time game locations to ensure the quality and service that its brand is known for.

That's why we say brands are a social mechanism to mitigate risk for customers when they purchase goods and services.

THE ESSENCE OF BRANDING IS LOWERING COSTS – FOR COMPANIES, CONSUMERS AND SOCIETY

What does all of this have to do with cost?

We must learn to look at all corporate management problems from the perspective of cost. All problems can be reduced to the question of how to reduce costs – production costs, marketing costs, management costs, communication costs, development costs, personnel costs, strategic expansion costs, etc.

Brands are also a mechanism for lowering costs. First, they lower marketing costs for companies. When a company creates a successful brand that customers actively seek out, then the cost of the company marketing to those consumers is lowered. Without branding, marketing costs are high.

Second, brands lower the decision-making cost for consumers. Consumers pay a decision-making cost every time they buy something. They don't know which product to buy, which one is guaranteed quality. So what do they do? Simple, they buy the brand they're familiar with. Now customers don't need to spend time gaining in-depth knowledge of how to tell good products from bad. They just need to find the brand they trust.

Third, brands lower the cost to society of monitoring companies and products. If there's a problem with a certain brand's products, it's easy to spread the news so that all of society can watch to see if the problems are solved. Without branding, it would take a lot more time and money to ensure that products are safe.

Why does the government prefer the business of a given industry to be concentrated among a limited number of major players, preferably no more than a few thousand? Because it's easier to monitor and regulate that way. It's easy to keep a few dozen CEOs in line but much harder to do the same with thousnads of companies. But of course, this is government logic, not market logic. In truth, society regulates companies not through centralized government and policy management, but through market competition that eliminates the poor performers. In highly concentrated industries, laws and brands work hand in hand to regulate what companies do.

THE LOWER THE COST OF CHOOSING YOUR BRAND, THE MORE CUSTOMERS MAKE THE CHOICE

To lower your company's marketing cost, you need to lower the customer's cost in choosing your brand and society's cost in regulating it.

The cost perspective in understanding branding is crucial to mastering what we call the cost-centric creative approach. This understanding allows every part of the creative process to be oriented toward lowering costs. All of the design and creative work that goes into a brand needs to be done with the aim of lowering costs. This aim applies to formulating the brand strategy, naming the brand, selecting the brand logo, packaging the product and designing advertising campaigns.

The cost-centric creative approach starts with lowering the cost for customers to choose you. The lower the cost, the more customers will choose your product.

In addition to lowering the cost to customers, you also need to lower the cost to society of regulating your company. This is the key to a brand that lasts. You must keep this in mind! Companies often try to increase the cost of regulating them, out of instinct. But at the end of this chapter, we'll discuss how companies that increase society's regulatory cost fare against companies that actively work to lower the cost of regulating them.

Now let's look at the cost-lowering potential of brands and the cost-centric creative approach.

YOUR BRAND NAME'S MARKETING AND COMMUNICATION COST

I was once asked: "Is it better to have one brand or multiple brands?"

"Why do you ask?" I replied.

He said: "I don't want to put all my eggs in one basket. If I only have one brand, then I'll be finished if something happens to it. If I have two brands, there will be something to fall back on."

This is a ridiculous way of looking at it, but it's also a common one. This way of thinking centers on the essence of branding: the question of cost. My interlocutor wanted to increase the cost to society of regulating his company.

I asked another question: "Do you think it's better to have one house or several?"

Of course it's better to have multiple houses, but this question overlooks one basic precondition: if you want to have multiple houses, you need to *pay* for multiple houses. You can probably only afford to put a down payment on one. In that case, what's the point of discussing the benefits of multiple houses? If I were a soft drink maker I'd love to have two brands on the level of Coke and Pepsi. The problem is, if I can't even create one top-tier brand, how could I ever have two?

Building a brand takes an enormous investment. Having one unified brand greatly lowers the cost of that investment.

Peacock City is a classic example of using a unified brand to lower the costs of marketing and communication. By focusing their advertising investments, they were able to become one of China's top-20 property developers in just four years.

The concept behind Peacock City is to develop a series of low-density residential towns targeting the Beijing market, all within one hour of the city. Their pitch is to give residents a chance to see the sky, to touch the ground, and own a garden, while living the so-called '4+3' or '7+3' lifestyle.

For high-income urban residents living in the concrete jungle, this is a chance to have a home where they can step out to see blue skies and walk on dirt and grass in their own yard. The '4+3' lifestyle refers to living in a city apartment four weeknights, then spending Friday to Sunday in a Peacock City development. Similarly, '7+3' refers to having parents move into Peacock City, so that the entire family can be together on weekends, when the urbanites arrive, without the day-to-day inconvenience of having three generations under one roof.

These are all typical needs for a high-income urban family. Many people want to own a house like this and live a life like this, so they'll look at the choices the market offers them.

But the cost of choosing for these customers is high. There are many projects around Beijing catering to this customer segment, so which one is the best for their family? Which developer can they trust? No one would buy a house without seeing it in person, so what projects should they drive to for a look? How many projects do they need to see before they make their decision? There's a Chinese saying that you should 'compare the goods of three shops' before you make a purchase, but how many housing projects can you compare without going crazy? Three? Thirty? Three hundred?

No matter what you're selling, you need to think about how to get yourself into the customer's range of choice. The business that can lower the cost for the customer to choose them is the business that can lower their own marketing costs.

From the start, Peacock City planned four projects with a unified brand strategy. All four developments were named Peacock City. And then the famous slogan: "One Beijing city, four Peacock Cities!"

The subtext here is that customers have the chance to choose between four options. What are the customer's choices for a weekend house in the suburbs? Well, here are four Peacock Cities for them to choose between. This slogan is also an example of super language, because the slogan turns a new real estate brand into an authoritative, leading chain brand the moment it's introduced.

But brand names for real estate projects are like place names. Doesn't it create customer confusion to have four places called Peacock City around Beijing?

To address that issue Peacock City used geographical modifiers to differentiate between their four products. All four developments are named after nearby natural features or landmarks: Peacock City Yongding River, Peacock City Grand Canal, Peacock City Chaobai River and Peacock City Badaling. All of these modifiers have concrete references that immediately come to mind for a Beijing resident.

Suppose they had named the four developments using abstract concepts: Peacock City Luxe, Peacock City Comfort, Peacock City Sky, Peacock City Elegance. *That* would certainly have caused confusion. This is the cost difference between concrete naming and abstract naming.

Naming represents costs. Naming is summoning. Naming is an investment.

Peacock City uses a concrete noun for its overarching brand name – everybody knows what a peacock looks like. It's immediately understandable and familiar. As we've said, for the names of individual projects the developer also invoked the names of nearby landmarks. These names represent the value of each project. The names engage with the imagination. The names *are* the reason to make the purchase.

There was some back-and-forth over the naming of Peacock City Badaling. The development is actually on the shores of Guanting Lake, at the foot of the Badaling hills. So should this project be named after Badaling or Guanting Lake? Our criterion for making the decision was to choose the name with the lower cost. Badaling is the world-renowned site of the Great Wall, but only people who live in Beijing know Guanting Lake. So we chose Badaling.

Naming is an investment. The Peacock City naming system means that every investment we make in advertising these projects is also building up the Peacock City brand. Fifty years from now, we'll still be reaping the rewards of every cent we spent to promote this brand.

Naming is an investment, not just for the company but for the customers as well. In real estate, one day the buyer will also become a seller. If every project had a different name, then the propagation of the name would end by the time the project sold out; the name would have no more presence in the market. If one day an owner wants to sell their house, then there'd be no influential brand name that they can advertise under. With one unified brand, every owner can share in the value brought by the investment into the Peacock City brand.

A coherent naming system lowers the advertising investment cost and makes the investment more efficient.

'One Beijing city, four Peacock Cities' represents a brand strategy as well as a marketing and advertising strategy. Every advertisement using the slogan is promoting all four Peacock City projects. Every dollar spent in advertising the brand is like four dollars spent advertising individual projects – and even more effective. If the four projects were separately branded, then not only would the company have to spend four times the money, the campaigns would also have been far less memorable.

'One Beijing city, four Peacock Cities' is also a low-cost slogan. The slogan meant that Peacock City was more than an ordinary residential project from the start; it was a strong brand with products all over the greater Beijing area.

This slogan is also a good example of the power of words, which we discussed in the previous chapter. The power of this super language means that the commercial case for the brand is not obscured, but rather magnified and brought together with the grand narratives of humankind. Peacock City is now tightly linked with the idea of *Beijing*, meaning that it makes use of the city's brand power.

In terms of marketing, this slogan also borrows from the shelf-space strategy we see in selling fast-moving consumer goods.

An important point in marketing fast-moving-consumer goods is that the more shelf-space a product takes up in the store, the higher the possibility that the customer will see the product and purchase it. That's why consumer goods companies would develop multiple products belonging to the same range, or even pay for shelf space, just so their own brand would occupy as much of the shelf as possible.

Every purchase is a choice. Marketing is all about how to design the choice by manipulating selection criteria or even the range of options. 'One Beijing city, four Peacock Cities' offers the Peacock City as a criterion *and* 'four Peacock Cities' as a range of options.

On the figurative 'shelf' of low-density residential developments in suburban Beijing, we've launched four products to net the biggest display area of all. To borrow another analogy, it's like having four stalls in a market, all of which are owned by us. The question is no longer which residential development to choose, but which *Peacock City* to choose.

YOUR BRAND LOGO'S MARKETING AND COMMUNICATION COST

Every company and every brand needs a logo. But at least 70% of logo designs we see are mistakes. They only cause trouble for the customer. Logos are a solution to the problem of identifying, remembering and propagating brands. Most logo designs not only fail as solutions to the problem, they actively cause new problems.

Why? Because people don't know the ultimate purpose of the logo: lowering costs. Lowering the costs of identifying, remembering and propagating your brand.

Just like names, logos are there to lower costs.

The idea of the 'brand' came from cattle herders. The word originally referred to designs 'branded' onto cowhide with a hot poker, so that it was easier to tell whose cattle belonged to whom. This was the forerunner of the concept of logos and of branding.

So what are the cost differences between logos and names?

Logos have lower costs. The goal of the logo should be to lower the cost of the name.

The original brands were words: 'Steve Jobs' Cow'. 'Bill Gates' Cow'. These were the first brands that made it possible to distinguish one herder from another. But this was a high-cost solution. It was hard reading a bunch of words from a distance, and it caused a lot of unnecessary pain to the cows to brand them with such long messages. So to lower costs, these words were replaced by shapes: a square, a circle. This was less trouble for everyone.

No to mention, far fewer people could read back then. For people who couldn't read *Steve Jobs* and *Bill Gates*, this was a very ineffective solution. But everyone knew what a square was, what a circle was. So the shape designs were a lower-cost approach.

But that's all history. Now things are different.

In the modern age we have a lot more things we need to idenitfy. There simply aren't enough basic shapes to use (circles, squares, triangles) so logos became more and more complex. And at the same time, literacy rates are now much closer to 99% than 1%. In light of all that, are shapes still the lower-cost solution, or are words?

Why do we want a logo for our brand? One, we want to lower the cost of identifying and remembering our brand. Two, we want to convey our brand's values and spirit. But in practice, 90% of logo designs *increase* the cost of identifying and remembering the brand. These designs make the customer's job harder.

When you're designing a logo, the focus should be the *name* of your brand. The focus should not be on designing an image that turns the name into part of the background. When the image takes the focus, then the rightful place of the name is usurped.

Some brand logos use highly complex or abstract images with 'deep meanings' that are only clear to the designer. The meanings are so deep that nobody else sees them, not even the designer's assistant – and you can forget about the customer. Then these brands end up promoting the logo instead of the brand. It's all a waste of time, energy and money.

Customers have one job: remember the brand name associated with the logo. You should design your logo to help your customers succeed in doing so. You should *not* turn this one job into three jobs: remembering the name, remembering the logo, and remembering that the name is associated with the logo. If you do this, you're increasing the cost to your customer.

Now take out your business card and look at your company's logo. Are you making the same mistake?

If the 'meaning' of your company's logo is the topic of an internal training course, or even a quiz, how can you expect your customers to get it?

Here at Hua and Hua, we refuse to write 'logo explainers' for our clients.

The very idea of a 'logo explainer' is ridiculous. Logos *are* for explaining. Is there anything more ludicrous than writing 300 words to explain a logo you designed for a one-word brand name?

The Hua and Hua way is to never explain.

If you come up with a slogan and have to formulate another sentence to 'explain' the slogan, then you should throw out the slogan and just use the explanation. If you design a logo and end up needing an explainer for it, then you should throw out the logo. What use is it if it can't even explain itself?

Wittgenstein said: "If an explanation is not the final explanation, if it hangs in mid-air without another explanation, then what does it explain?"

There is one simple standard for a low-cost, high efficiency logo that fulfills the essential value of logo design: it must be clear at first sight.

Remember our rules for super language? *Clear, familiar* and *viral*.

These principles create the lowest costs for propagation. When you're designing a logo, your goal is to create a super sign. So once again, the foundation of everything is that it must be clear and understandable. Only then can it be familiar and viral.

Note that we're adding one conditional to the 'clear' rule: understandable. Can your logo be *understood* at first sight?

What do you want the viewer to understand? First, who you are. A John Smith logo needs to be immediately understood as a John Smith logo.

Remember, it needs to be understandable at *first* sight.

We're spending a lot of time emphasizing this, because this is where a lot of mistakes in business management come from. Everyone thinks from the perspective of the top global companies that they're familiar with. They think in the context of a Fortune-500 company. The vast majority of companies are very different from Fortune-500 companies, but business schools design their courses around a Fortune-500 context. I emphasize the importance of understanding *at first sight* not from the perspective of a well-known brand that's already been around for 50 or 100 years, but from the perspective of a new brand in its infancy. We'll talk more about this later, when we discuss television advertising. We need to convince an audience member in 15 seconds to buy a product they've *only just heard of for the first time*.

Back to logo design: the easiest way to let the viewer know they're looking at a John Smith logo is to literally have the words 'John Smith' in the logo. This is our logo design philosophy: use text as much as possible. Make the name clear at first sight, and design the logo around the text.

Here are three examples of logos designed by Hua and Hua: Yibai Pharmaceutical, Northeast Pharmaceutical and the Haidilao restaurant chain. All three logos are designed around text. Yibai's logo is the number '100' designed to look like a pill ('yibai' sounds like '100' in Mandarin). The logo for Northeast is the Chinese word for 'northeast' inside of a pill shape. Haidilao uses the English word 'hi', a homonym for the first character of its Chinese name.

Why did we use pill shape designs for both pharmaceutical companies? This is another aspect of being clear: what your brand *does* needs to be clear at first sight.

You need to let people know what you do right when they see your logo. If you're a food company, your logo needs to look like that of a food company. It's the same if you're a pharmaceutical company, a bank, an airline.

People say: Doesn't it show a lack of creativity if every drug company uses a pill in its logo?

I don't agree that there's a creativity problem with this aproach. Your creativity needs to be in service of a solution, not in service of 'being creative'.

Merck uses a pill in its logo too. You could also use a benzene ring, like Roche does. Or you could use a pill bottle, a beaker, a test tube. Anything that brings medicine to mind.

Your logo needs to differentiate your brand from brands in different industries. To give an example, what do I want to differentiate Yibai Pharmaceutical from when I'm designing its logo? Northeast Pharmaceutical, you might say. That's true, but first I need to differentiate Yibai from the Bank of China, so that when customers see the logo they know that it's a pharmaceutical company and not a bank. When Pepsi designed its logo, were they thinking of competing with Coke? Sure they were, but fist they needed to make sure they weren't competing with Dulux paint. When Pepsi customers see the logo, they need to know that it's a soda, not a paint.

A lot of logo designs try to set themselves apart from their industry competitors, because designers think that it's not creative enough if the logo looks too much like other companies in the field. Then why don't these companies remove words like *pharmaceutical, airline* or *bank* from their names? Won't that set them even further apart from their competitors? People know that you won't do that, for all the right reasons, so why do they think it's fine to have a completely random logo? The only reason is because the harm that a bad logo does to a business is more subtle.

The first job of a logo for a bank is not to set it apart from other banks, but to set it apart from, say, restaurants, so that pedestrians on the street immediately know that there's a bank up ahead. Some people mock Chinese banks for all using the 'coin' motif in their design, but it's really they themselves who should be mocked.

The industries that seem backwards or outdated in their branding and marketing are often the ones that use the best design principles. That's because they don't know anything about marketing *expertise*, they just do everything based on *common sense*. There are too many people who have just enough 'expertise' for it to be dangerous. These are the people who fall into the trap of counterproductive creativity.

We talked about two aspects in which a brand's logo must be immediately clear: the name and the industry. There is a third aspect to clarity – when you're designing with imagery, the image must be clear and concrete.

If your brand is Peacock City, your logo needs to be immediately identifiable as a peacock. You might use the silhouette of a peacock, or a peacock head, or a peacock tail pattern. Whichever you choose, you need to let the viewer know at first sight that it's a peacock. Don't try to stylize the image too much, and end up requiring careful observation to see that it's a peacock. Your customer doesn't have the time for careful observation.

All of the brand imagery that we design is used on streets and in malls, so that people can idenitfy it immediately in a visually cluttered environment. The images are not museum exhibits that take up an entire wall, with carefully designed lighting, mounted for people to fly in from around the world just to see it. A lot of the time, designers think of their logos as museum pieces. And that leads them down a road that's the opposite direction from where they should go.

THE COST OF CHANGING A LOGO

We often see news about companies 'rebranding' or 'reimagining' their logos. Our principle is simple: Unless change is absolutely necessary, unless it's the only way to save the brand, then you shouldn't change a logo.

Why not? When we talked about names, we talked about names as a cost, as an evocation, as an investment.

The same thing applies to logos. A brand logo carries the investment of years, decades or even centuries.

Why would people think that a logo change is necessary to convey a new attitude or new ideas about the brand? Why not just change the name of the brand itself? Because people know that names shouldn't be changed without a very good reason. So why do they think logos can be changed whenever they like?

After merging with Amoco, BP wanted to reposition their brand as a healthier, safer, green energy company instead of just an oil company. So they changed their original logo from the letters BP in a shield design to a stylized sunflower image with the lower-case letters 'bp' in the top-right corner.

Was this really necessary? In my opinion, a shield was a much better representation of a healthy, safe, green company than the flower. And of course, the letters BP inside the shield design were much easier to idenitify than the tiny letters next to a huge flower.

This logo change threw away a brand image that BP had accumulated over the course of nearly a century. One could argue that the cost of switching out BP's logos around the world ultimately totaled several tens of billions of dollars.

But people thought it was a positive change. They thought that there was little brand value lost, and that the new logo made the public aware of BP's new strategy.

But people didn't become aware of BP's new strategy because the company changed the logo. They became aware of it through the enormous PR and advertising campaign that came with the change. The company probably wouldn't have gotten so much free press without the logo change.

That makes more sense. But does this mean we need a new logo with every new strategic direction?

Coca-Cola has not changed its logo in more than a hundred years. Meanwhile, Pepsi has changed its logo several times. That's why Coke is a super sign whose power stretches across all of human culture, and Pepsi is not.

Here's one more issue with logo changes. We discussed earlier how a brand's products are the most effective medium to communicate the brand. Similarly, a company's most effective medium is itself. Every company is its own media source.

People say that this is the age of *we media*. Everyone is part of the media nowadays, and the most important media source for any company is itself. Every major global company is also a major media source. Everything a company like BP does is global news, so by changing its own logo it can create a major news story that allows it to communicate its new values. If your company can't make it on to CNN by changing its own logo, you shouldn't look to BP as an example.

The Chinese sportswear brand Li Ning also won plenty of free press for changing its logo. It wanted to bid the old Li Ning farewell and welcome a new Li Ning – but after it said 'out with the old', it never managed to achieve 'in with the new'.

The real estate developer Vanke went through two logo changes. First it changed its text design to an abstract image. This caused a huge increase in their brand communication cost; it was a completely counterproductive move. It's now changed its logo back to text. They admitted their mistake and returned to common sense.

When companies change their logo, it's usually due to one of six situations.

The first is when a new owner takes over. The new boss wants to put their mark on the company, like when PCCW bought Hong Kong Telecom.

The second situation is when there's no new owner, but there's a new CEO who really wants to change things up. The rationale is that nothing changes things up like a new logo.

Third is when a company makes an important acquisition or wants to go in a new strategic direction, like BP in the example above.

Fourth is when a company *wants* to go in a new strategic direction or to make a big move, but doesn't manage to actually do anything. Then they do something with their logo so it seems like they're doing something. This is very common. Yahoo did it again just recently.

Fifth is when they're feeling anxious. This is also very common. The business is in turmoil and they don't know what to do, so they find some busywork, and there's nothing else to do but change the logo.

Sixth is when they want to be 'creative'. This is nothing but a 'creative' impulse.

Should your company change its logo? You can answer that question using our marketing communication cost metric. If your current logo has no meaning, no value, no brand equity associated with it, then you're not really *changing* your logo, you're *creating* one from scratch. But if your logo has been on the market for years, if it's familiar to customers, then you should absolutely hold on to it! A logo is a cost. It's an evocation. It's an investment.

The Hua and Hua way emphasizes the perspective of your brand assets. Take a good look at your brand and identify your assets and liabilities. Don't throw your assets away, and don't do things that won't help you create new assets. Minimize useless work and eliminate counterproductive work. Even BP's logo change was useless and counterproductive; it did little good and plenty of harm. It's just that BP is a big enough company that even when it's shooting itself in the foot, there's barely a flesh wound.

THE MARKETING AND COMMUNICATION COST OF PACKAGING

What is the point of packaging?

The most important thing about packaging is not the product it's wrapped around, but the *information* that it conveys. Every package is a blast of information! And these bits of information compete with other information on store shelves, whether physical or online. The one that can stand out and attract the customer's attention, the one that hits the customer's sweet spot with its appeal, is the one that creates a purchase.

We've said before that your products are your company's most important communication medium. And a large part of that is in the packaging. Good packaging design can greatly lower the cost of marketing and communicating your brand.

What costs can good packaging reduce? First, the cost of being noticed on a store shelf. We've said it before, and we'll say it again: the goal of a packaging design is not to be shown in a museum under bright lights. The goal is to attract customer attention in the visual clutter of a store shelf and convince customers to buy the product.

Naobaijin is a major health supplement brand in China, widely derided for their ugly packaging. But if you walk into any supermarket, I guarantee you that Naobaijin packaging will be the first thing you see. This is the exact point of product packaging – gaining the upper hand on the store shelf.

Again, gaining the store shelf advantage is the goal of packaging design.

Some would say: You're right, we can't make good designs. We need to make tacky and loud designs, because Chinese consumers have bad taste. The tackier a design is, the more they like it. That's how China is.

This is a ridiculous thing to say, just as ridiculous as saying Chinese people don't deserve democracy and human rights.

Why are Naobaijin products so successful? Because customers *buy their product*, not because customers *like ther packaging*. People mix up these two ideas all the time. As I'm writing this chapter, Nielsen has just issued a report on 'accurately tracking consumer attitudes toward advertising'. This is the entirely wrong approach. Never study consumer attitudes toward your advertising; study consumer attitudes toward you product. Once you start from the wrong question, everything you get will be wrong. If we try to study 'why consumers like Naobaijin packaging', then all of our conclusions will be wrong. We'll be reduced to insulting an entire nation's taste.

Naobaijin's packaging succeeds not because it is 'ugly' but because it is eye-catching. Why focus on how ugly it is instead of how eye-catching it is? Why mock its shortcomings instead of learning from its strengths?

Going to a store and looking at its shelves should be your first step to designing your packaging, because packaging design is not about a single product, it's about an entire shelf. Most of the shelf has already been designed by other people; there's only one little corner that's up to you. So you need to use that little corner to make your product stand out. You don't necessarily need to read any of your reference materials, but you *must* take a look at the shelf your product will be sold on. If you don't know what 99% of it looks like, how will you even start designing the 1% that's yours?

You should not be measuring yourself against the fancy designs you see in books. You should be measuring yourself against the designs you see on the shelves of your local supermarket. Too often, those 'great' designs immortalized in books would never survive on a supermarket shelf. Nobody would ever see them except in a book. The things you see on the shelf are the true winners.

Here's a question for designers: Would you rather have your works featured on a supermarket shelf or in a design yearbook? My guess is that nobody has ever asked this question, but most designers already know the answer. They want their work in the design yearbook.

The design yearbook represents recognition from one's peers – one's competitors in the design world bubble. But surviving a supermarket shelf represents recognition from the market and from customers.

Craving recognition from competitors instead of from customers is a common trap to fall into. We'll have more to say about this when we discusss corporate strategy later.

The goal of packaging design is to gain the upper hand on *store shelves*. The e-commerce age has brought new meaning to the term store shelf. Nowadays shelves are screens: computer screens, phone screens, tablet screens, even smart-TV screens. Designs like Naobaijin's have an even greater advantage in the e-commerce age, because one principle rules all in online shopping: your product photos needs to be clear even in thumbnail form.

In the e-commerce age, you need to design so that customers never need to click the thumbnail. It doesn't matter how 'good' your design is. It's useless if nobody clicks.

Packaging is a product in itself. Packaging design is product design.

You need to approach packaging like you approach product development. The packaging design process is a product re-design process.

Why do we say that packaging is a product? Because that is the perspective and context of the customer. When we treat packaging and product as separate, we're looking at things from the business perspective. When customers are browsing store shelves, what they're looking at (to them) is a series of *products*, not *packaging*.

We'll have a discussion dedicated to product development later. Right now our point is that you need to consider how your product packaging fits into your product as an overall *sign*.

Every product on the shelf is a sign. The first order of business is not to make your message stand out on the packaging, but to make your product stand out on the shelf. That's why we say you need to make sure your packaging fits into your product as a sign.

For example, we've talked about how our design for Chubang soy sauce uses the checkered green pattern instead of emphasizing the Chubang logo. An entire row of green-checkerboard packaging stands out on the supermarket shelf.

Making your product stand out on the shelf is your first job. Your second job is to organize signs and information on the package itself to communicate your sales appeal more efficiently. This is an important way to lower marketing costs through packaging design: make your product speak for itself!

Previously we noted that you should treat advertising space as shelf space. With product design, it's the other way around: you should treat shelves like billboards, and your packaging like a poster. Your product is your most important communication medium, the one media source that your company is 100% in control of.

On every Chubang soy sauce bottle, we print this slogan: 'This is Chubang's drying field for soybeans. Seeing is believing. Our beans are dried for 180 days right here.' Printing it right on the bottle is more effective than any TV campaign that costs a hundred million.

Hua and Hua is dedicated to using packaging design to lower the cost of marketing products and to create interactions with customers, maximizing the value of the packaging.

When we designed packaging for Zhenshiming eye drops, which has improving eyesight as a major appeal, we designed the entire box as an eye chart. This design allows the product to speak for itself, conveying the functional value of the product. It also has practical use for customers, who can put the box on the table and conduct a quick and simple eye test.

When it comes to product design, we have one simple, core idea: even without advertising, even without anyone having heard of our brand, our packaging can speak for itself and communicate with customers so that our products sell themselves on the store shelves. And on a shopping website, our packaging does all of this even at thumbnail size!

In doing this, we're maximizing the value of packaging and using packaging to lower marketing costs.

That's why when you're designing your packaging, you're also creating your biggest marketing campaign.

THE MARKETING AND COMMUNICATION COST OF SLOGANS

Why do we need slogans? Again, it's an issue of cost. How did the Communist Party convince 400 million Chinese people to join in the revolution? None of them would have any idea what a *Soviet* is. But with one slogan – 'Overthrow the landowners, divide up their land' – revolution became a reality.

Does your slogan have this kind of power? Does it lower your marketing and communication cost?

Try to apply this standard to your own company's slogan. You'll find that most slogans say nothing – they're utterly meaningless.

Slogans have to convey the value of your brand and call the audience to action.

We said a lot about this in the previous chapter on super language. We talked about how a slogan is easier to spread than almost any other kind of information. 'Open up a Remy Martin, and good fortune will follow!'. This is a simple, ten-syllable, rhyming slogan in Mandarin. The low cost of spreading the slogan, the broadness of its reach, and the positive sentiment that it evokes are all unparalleled in the history of Chinese advertising. Now let's take a look at another slogan: 'I don't care about eternity, I care about this moment'.

This slogan is not a positive role model. I've asked people about the slogan on many occasions, and barely 1% of people can even remember what kind of product this slogan was for. Most people think it's a diamond commercial, because of the mention of 'eternity'. Only a small minority know that it's a watch commercial. True to its word, the appeal of the slogan lasts barely 'a moment'. Remi Martin's slogan is the one that is remembered for eternity.

A lot of brands spend a lot of time thinking about product placements. They want their brands in movies and TV shows. But many of these companies never think of placing their brand name in their own slogan.

You should try as much as possible to include your brand name in your slogan. If you miss this opportunity, you're driving up the cost of marketing your brand, because you're not letting it come out to play.

When you're evaluating the cost of your slogan, you need to focus on lowering the cost of discovering it and remembering it.

When you want to lower the customer's cost of making a purchase decision, you need to create an impulse to buy.

When you want to lower the cost of using your product, you need to evoke a user experience. 'Open up a Remy Martin, and good fortune will follow!'. That conjures up a very clear experience of using a Remy Martin product.

You need to lower the cost of propagating your slogan, because a slogan isn't about talking to the consumer – it's about creating something that your customer will repeat to other people. We've already talked about this principle at length, so we won't repeat it here.

THE MARKETING AND COMMUNICATION COST OF TV AND VIDEO ADS

Note the term 'video ad' in the title of this section. In the past, the vast majority of video content that people saw came through their television sets. Now we have countless outlets for video advertising: TVs, movie theaters, PCs, tablets, phones. But the underlying principles and methods are still based on the practices of TV commercials, so that's still our main focus.

When we talk about the cost of a TV commercial, we need to start with the literal cost of buying airtime. The cost of buying airtime for a 15-second commercial is three times that of a five-second commercial, and a 30-second commercial twice that of a 15-second commercial.

Remember, this is the age of the 15-second commercial.

Why 15 seconds? Because it costs only half as much to put on the air as a 30-second commercial. The cost of airtime could go from 100 million to 50. So if you need 30 seconds to communicate your brand, then that's an extra 50 million to spend – too much!

TV commercials started out as one-minute spots, a format that survives in Super Bowl commercials in the US. Later, the 30-second commercial became the standard. Companies wrote their commercials with the 30-second 'full version' in mind, cutting that down to 15- and five-second versions. But it's a problem if your commercial needs 30 seconds to tell the full story. You need to think of the 15-second version as the full version, and come up with a 15-second solution.

STOP USING THE WORD 'STORYBOARD'

We've spent a lot of time talking about the power of words. Words affect how people think. When an ad agency develops a TV commercial for a client, it usually starts with a 'storyboarding' phase – the proposed scenes are literally drawn up and laid out as cartoon-like panels. The very word *storyboard* implies that you must create a story in the commercial. And so, people think that a story is the only possible creative element, that in order to be creative there must be a good story. You've probably heard people say, "I've come up with something really creative!" And then they launch into a long story they thought up.

I've often heard people in advertising say, "We're not in the advertising business, we're in the content business." They want to say that their creations are no less valid and entertaining than a movie.

Of course there's nothing wrong with being entertaining, but entertainment should be incidental to a commercial, not its reason and purpose. When you're trying to entertain the masses with your commercial, what really happens is that your forget about selling and your audience forgets about buying. They see the commercial and forget about it.

A TV commercial should not be about telling a story. It's about playing tricks. It's about putting on a performance, starring your product.

If we're to replace the word 'storyboard' with something else, I would recommend the words 'trick' or 'performance'. And these words don't apply just to TV commercials: packaging design and promotion campaigns are also about playing tricks and putting on performances.

What is a trick? A trick is something that the audience will give their full attention to, so that they receive every bit of information you convey, so that they're predisposed to accepting your conclusion.

Tricks are not just about the whole, but also about the details. Only a true master of the art can know exactly what moment, what line, what image, what expression, what look was the one that sold your product. Sometimes you'll find that the actor was much more important than the story. Some people are naturally able to command a camera. They can say anything and people just listen and believe.

Your tricks need to have truth, goodness, beauty. They need to stand up to scrutiny. You're selling to 1.3 billion people, and you want annual sales of 1 billion RMB. The bigger your business, the bigger your responsibility and your moral risk. It's serious business convincing consumers to give you their money, particularly when you're selling food or medicine. So you need to be serious *and* engaging.

A TV commercial is a performance your brand puts on, so you need to make your product your hero. You don't need a 'creative director'. You need a person who can convince people in 15 seconds to take out their wallets and buy a product they've only just heard about for the first time.

Doing a TV commercial is harder than putting on a segment for a Chinese New Year special! Chinese New Year TV specials are a big deal in China. People say it gets harder to pull off every year. Now you need a punch line every ten seconds; that regular stuff just doesn't excite audiences anymore. There are only a select few in China who can actually pull off a Chinese New Year special. But TV commercials aren't just about convincing the audience not to change the channel, they're also about getting the audience to pay money for something. That's much harder, right?

So here are the technical requirements for a 15-second TV commercial: In a 15-second performance, grab the audience's attention – and convince them to buy a product – that they've only just heard of for the first time.

This is very important: always assume the audience is hearing about your product for the first time!

Hua and Hua operates in the emerging Chinese market, so we have many new companies among our clients. We've definitely helped a lot of all-new products that no one knew of to establish their own brands.

But even when our clients become better known, we still assume throughout the creative process that people are hearing about the brand for the first time. This is the secret to our process.

We've noticed one successful international brand that always makes people think it's new: the *All New L'Oreal Paris*. It's always the *'all new'*. They know the secret.

People are always interested in new things.

Here is Hua and Hua's checklist for creating a 15-second TV commercial:

1. Have people remember what the brand name is.
2. Have people remember what the product looks like.
3. Give people a reason to buy and an impulse to buy.
4. Establish the brand's sign and the company's strategic advantage.

Take note of these four items. The first two are minimum requirements, and the first one is essentially a prerequisite. The last two are a higher bar. But our standard is that every 15-second commercial needs to do all four.

Let's start with the first item. This is the most important and most fundamental requirement, but it's also the most overlooked. That's why we need to emphasize it here.

Having people remember your name is the prerequisite for everything. It doesn't matter how good a job you do – if people don't remember your name then it's all for nothing.

Remember this item. This is not just a *necessary* condition for success; if you do it well, it can also become a *sufficient* condition. If enough people remember your name, then you're bound to succeed.

Let's take the example of the wool company Heng Yuan Xiang. They made an infamous series of commercials that started with the slogan 'Heng Yuan Xiang. Sheep, sheep, sheep' and then went through all the other animals of the Chinese zodiac. Now, I'm sure someone will complain that I'm going with the tackiest example possible again. But still I say: ignore the things about other people that you don't like; focus on the things that you could learn from.

Ridiculing successful people for things they're not good at is use-less. You can only improve and grow by learning from what others do well. So don't look at these commercials from the point of view of a critic, look at them from the perspective of a consumer.

You may say that consumers hate the slogan too! Right – and also wrong. That's because consumers interact with this commercial in two separate contexts. The first context is when they see the spot on TV. Heng Yuan Xiang. Sheep, sheep, sheep. Heng Yuan Xiang. Monkey, monkey, monkey. Chicken, chicken, chicken. Ugh, what a ridiculous assault on the senses!

The second context is when they're at the mall looking at sweaters. And that's when they remember Heng Yuan Xiang. The brand that annoyed them so much. The brand that advertised on CCTV. *Well, I guess I'll buy that.* They've never even heard of the other brands, so go with something you know, right?

This is what we mean when we say that brands lower the mar-keting cost for companies, decision-making cost for consumers and monitoring cost for society.

Economics also gives an account of this issue. Economists say that an information gap exists between companies and consum-ers; consumers don't actually know what companies really do, or whether companies are really reliable. Companies need to *signal* to consumers in order to bridge this information gap.

There are many ways for companies to signal. Advertising is one way; opening stores in expensive locations is another. For exam-ple, if a new brand opens up next to the LV store in Shanghai's most upscale mall, then it can sell its products at similar upscale prices and customers will naturally think of it as an upscale brand.

What makes for an effective signal? Economists say that signals must be sufficiently expensive. Cheap signals are ineffective.

This can easily be understood through common sense. Peo-ple know that it costs a lot of money to advertise on CCTV, so advertisers on CCTV must be rich companies. If a company is rich, lots of people must be buying its products; if lots of people are buying a company's products, then the company's products must be good; if the company's products are good, then maybe people should try them.

Heng Yuan Xiang took the name-recognition strategy to the ultimate level. They gave the strongest signal possible. In previous chapters we talked about advertising as ritual. Heng Yuan Xiang's Chinese zodiac commercials are an embarrassing spectacle, but they are undeniably an engaging brand ritual.

Some people say that Heng Yuan Xiang isn't building a *brand*, they're just building *sales*.

There's a lot to unpack with this.

You could even argue that Nike isn't building a brand, but there's no way you can argue that about Heng Yuan Xiang. Heng Yuan Xiang is nothing *but* a brand business.

Nike has a brand business, but it also does product design and sales. It outsources only its manufacturing and logistics. How about Heng Yuan Xiang? It doesn't do product design, or sales, or logistics. Its entire profit model revolves around its brand and its brand licensing. The design, manufacturing, logistics and sales are all outsourced to other companies. All Heng Yuan Xiang does is brand licensing, brand services and brand management.

You might not *like* Heng Yuan Xiang's brand, but you can't deny that it's a brand business.

Heng Yuan Xiang's model is to dial up its brand recognition to the max. And its unsubtle way of going about it means that it can also minimize the cost of its advertising.

Name recognition needs to be the first priority of a brand. Too many commercials are ineffective in making the viewer remember the name of the brand being advertised. Too many commercials don't even clearly *tell* the viewer the name of the brand. They just tell their stories, then flash the logo. This kind of commercial is 90% useless.

Not only should your brand name be repeated over and over, you also need to say it early! Especially for online advertising, your name should be the very first word. Viewers will be looking for the big X as soon as they hear the first word, so it better be your name.

Another problem with advertisements is an unwillingness to show the product packaging. This is an even bigger problem in print advertising. You have a beautiful image full of deep meaning ... and the actual product tucked away in a corner, barely visible. Why not emphasize the product packaging more? Because the designer thinks that it gets in the way of the 'creativity'.

There is a rule for this 'sound and sense' dilemma in poetry. The sound must *support* the sense. You shouldn't sacrifice the meaning of the poem for a pretty rhyme.

What is the purpose of putting focus on the product? So that people know what it looks like! So that customers can *find* your product in the store. How can they look for your product if they don't even know what it looks like?

Your product should always have the starring role in your commercial.

The product is the star; everyone else is only supporting it. Without the product the commercial is nothing. What does it mean to be the *star*? It means being the focus of everything and having the most screen time.

So your creative stuff can't upstage the product. You're investing in a commercial to sell products, not to entertain the masses.

The same goes for your celebrity spokesperson. You're paying the celebrity to sell your products, not so you can worship the celebrity.

Back to the checklist. Items 1 and 2 tell you that the viewer needs to remember the brand name and what the product looks like. These are basic requirements that are fundamental to successful marketing, but these requirements are also the most frequently overlooked in advertising. Why? Because people are learning from the wrong companies. This is a problem we've talked about several times in this book: People think about new brands, brands just starting out, in the context of globally famous, mature brands. Companies want to be Nike or Coca-Cola, without realizing that their position in the market is not remotely similar.

Item three on the checklist is to give people a reason to buy. You must trigger an instinctual impulse like we talked about in previous chapters, so that the viewer will be spurred into action. Driving the customer to action is more valuable than any kind of unique appeal. 'Have a problem? Here's the solution' is always going to be an effective call to action.

Item 4 is the highest-level priority, and it's really a two-part priority: First, establishing your brand sign, and second, establishing your company's strategy, or strategic advantage.

Is it really possible to satisfy all four items on the checklist in a 15-second commercial? Let's take a look at one of Hua and Hua's commercials as an example: the 15-second spot for Sunflower children's coughing and wheezing syrup. Here's the script for the commercial:

Class is in for the Sunflower School for Moms!
A persisting cough in a child is usually a lung fever.
What can we do?
Use Sunflower children's lung fever coughing and
wheezing syrup.
It clears up the lung fever and stops the cough.
Every mom needs to remember this!

The scene is a group of moms in class at the 'Sunflower School for Moms', taught by the company's sunflower mascot. The sunflower says: "Class is in for the Sunflower School for Moms! A lingering cough in a child is usually a lung fever." This is accompanied by an image of a fire burning in a human lung. One mom asks: "What can we do?" The sunflower shows off the product and says: "Use Sunflower children's coughing and wheezing syrup. It clears up the lung fever and stops the cough." And the fire burning the lung goes out. Finally, the sunflower stands in front of the product packaging and says: "Every mom needs to remember this!" The commercial ends with a freeze frame on the packaging.

Let's talk about how this 15-second commercial with just 49 words checks off every item on the Hua and Hua checklist.

Have people remember the name, both the Sunflower brand name and the coughing and wheezing syrup product name.

The commercial features the sunflower mascot, the 'Sunflower School for Moms', and repetition of the Sunflower brand name in the script. There's no problem with the brand name.

The difficulty comes from the 'coughing and wheezing syrup' product name, which is quite a mouthful. This commercial solves the problem by introducing a simpler phrase, 'lung fever'. With repeated emphasis on this key phrase, the viewer will remember 'Sunflower, kids, lung fever'. This is a simpler thing for viewers to remember.

Have people remember what the product looks like. This commercial does everything it can in this respect. First, the design of its entire brand image, packaging, and this TV commercial were done together to ensure strategic consistency. Every frame in the commercial – except the one line with the mom asking, "What can we do?" – includes either the Sunflower mascot or the product packaging, plus two images that show the 'before' and 'after' of taking the syrup. In other words, the entire commercial is dedicated to conveying the product's image and information. By doing this, the viewer will remember this product even if it's the first time they've heard of it.

The *reason to buy* comes across clear, strong and undeniable. A child's persisting cough – usually lung fever – use Sunflower children's lung fever coughing and wheezing syrup – clear away the lung fever – cure the cough. It's a simple thought process.

Of course, the most important part is the last item – *establishing the brand's sign and the company's strategic advantage.*

In terms of building the brand's sign, the very first thing you see in this commercial is the sunflower mascot. In terms of building the company's strategic advantage, the very first line – "Class is in for the Sunflower School for Moms" – conveys Sunflower's strategic advantage.

The Hua and Hua way emphasizes your company's *ambition* and your company's *opening move*. Sunflower's ambition is to become China's top brand for children's medicine and health with its sunflower mascot. So its opening move is to invest in a creative template for its commercials – the Sunflower School for Moms. In the future, all of Sunflower's children's products can be advertised through the Sunflower School for Moms. The Sunflower School for Moms is also a platform for Sunflower's education and PR campaigns, a core of its integrated messaging. Through continued investment in the Sunflower School for Moms creative template, it's establishing a way to be heard and a strategic advantage from the company.

'Class is in for the Sunflower School for Moms!'. This is a slogan that the company can use for the next 50 years. And every time the slogan is repeated is a further investment and accumulation of brand value. This investment will continue to pay off for 50 years. This is strategy.

CULTURAL ARCHETYPES AND THE COST OF A CARTOON

Since we just talked about Sunflower, let's talk a little more about cartoon mascots.

This is still a discussion of brand costs. A cartoon mascot is a character representing the brand. Its purpose is to lower the cost of propagating the brand. So the basic principles of super signs still apply. The best way is to find a cultural archetype – something that already exists in human culture, something that people already like.

The Sunflower mascot is a good example. It's a smiley face in a sunflower. This is an image everyone likes and everyone is familiar with. It meets Hua and Hua's key criteria: understandable, familiar, viral.

Why? Because archetypes are low-cost. Without leveraging cultural archetypes, we could never afford the cost of building up a new cartoon mascot.

People often try to design mascots without knowing why or what to do. This became very clear to me when I participated in the discussions around designing mascots for the Beijing Olympics.

There were three groups of experts there who all agreed: The best choice is the Chinese zodiac.

I said that we could create the biggest group of Olympic mascots ever – the 12 Chinese animals. Why the zodiac? Because that's what the Olympics are about. Why did China want to host the Olympics? Because it was an opportunity to spread our culture around the world. Only when our culture, lifestyle and knowledge are known around the world can we sell our brands and products around the world.

It was not to be, but suppose we had tapped into the Chinese zodiac for our mascots. First, everybody would then be encouraged to discover their own zodiac animal – they'll learn one piece of Chinese culture. Then we could have the best-selling Olympic mascots ever. We just need to hand out tables for everyone to look up their birth year. Then everybody could buy a little souvenir with their own zodiac animal. That way, every Olympic spectator will be helping us spread Chinese culture.

The Chinese zodiac is a cultural archetype. Cultural archetypes are a shortcut to success. You must remember that people only accept what they've always accepted, remember what they've always remembered, know what they've always known. You should not gamble by introducing something new. A character becomes a cultural archetype maybe once per century. An archetype as powerful as the Chinese zodiac comes around less than once per millennium. Why not use it?

Judging by the standards of super signs cultural archetypes, there weren't many good choices for the Beijing Olympics mascot: the Chinese zodiac, the giant panda, maybe Sun Wukong the Monkey-King. And 2008 was the Year of the Rat, so having a rat-bride and rat-groom in reference to the Chinese folk tale would have been a good choice, because it is very much in the Olympic spirit. The folk tale has the rat trying to find a suitable groom for his daughter, and he wants her to marry the strongest thing in the world. So they ask the sun, but the sun says it can be covered by the cloud. They go to the cloud, but the cloud says that it can be blown away by the wind.

They go to the wind, but the wind says it can be blocked by the wall. They go to the wall, but the wall says it can be dug through by the rat. So finally, the rat's daughter married another rat. The moral of the story is to be confident in your own strength!

The point is, we need to have a clear purpose: to propagate our culture and our values.

Four years later, I knew as soon as they were revealed that the dual London Olympics mascots were doomed to fail. Why? Because they didn't engage with any cultural archetypes. Nobody knew or cared about those two bizarre aliens. There was no emotional connection.

Has there ever been a successful mascot for a sporting event held in China? Yes! Her name was Pan-Pan. The 1990 Asian Games were not a particularly important event, but they left behind a cultural legacy – Pan-Pan the Panda. We still have Pan-Pan brand food, Pan-Pan brand safety gates. She is still a commercially valuable property.

Pan-Pan had a clear image and a good name. As we've said, for the 2008 Olympics we could have chosen such culturally resonent symbols as the Chinese zodiac, or the giant panda, or Sun Wukong. But we didn't choose any of that, because people thought they weren't 'creative' enough. Everybody knew them! What was the point?

People didn't realize that the *point* was that everybody knew these things. Don't you want to have a mascot everybody knows? Why throw away something that was already famous? It bears repeating: creativity should not be in service of 'being creative'. It needs to be in service of a solution.

Hua and Hua loves to create mascots for brands. If the mascot is successful, then every cent we invest in it will pay off for the next hundred years!

The majority of successful commercial mascots of the 20th century were created in the US. My hope is that the 21st-century hall of fame for commercial mascots will have several entries from Hua and Hua. The Sunflower mascot is one of Hua and Hua's most successful commercial mascots. And in my view, our 'god of fortune' mascot for Xinhe Wealth has potential too.

THE COST OF BRAND CULTURE – LEVERAGING HUMAN CULTURE

People talk about 'brand culture' a lot. But as with cartoon mascots, people don't think through why or what to do.

What is 'brand culture'? Let's talk about what *culture* is before we talk about brand culture. Culture refers to the sum total of material and spiritual wealth created by humankind throughout history. Sometimes it's used to refer exclusively to spiritual wealth. So how can we create a brand culture that lowers costs for us? By leveraging human culture, by using the wealth that humankind has accumulated over the generations.

This is what we were referring to when we talked about super signs, super language, super words and mascots. This is all brand culture: turning human culture into signs, and hitching a ride with these signs to propagate and sell your products, so that your business can become embedded in the grand narrative of our species.

Brand culture can lower the cost of a brand. That's why one kind of brand makes the best investment – what Hua and Hua calls 'cultural heritage brands'.

Cultural heritage brands are those that are tied to an entire group's cultural heritage. In other words, an area's cultural heritage brands are the cultural heritage that the people of this area have built up over the years.

What are some cultural heritage brands? Maotai liquor is one. Yunnan Baiyao toothpaste is another. So is Dong-e Ejiao pharmaceuticals. Why is Yunnan Baiyao toothpaste so successful? How does it command such high prices? Because it links itself to a well-known piece of cultural heritage through the perfectly chosen medium of toothpaste.

Another toothpaste brand that leverages cultural heritage well is Tianqi. Tianqi is a traditional Chinese medicinal plant whose value is well-known. So it is a cultural heritage brand not only in Guangxi Province where it originated, but all across China.

What makes cultural heritage brand so special? If you screw up with it, consumers will still be willing to give it a chance. They'll think it's just a temporary setback. They'll blame the execution, not the brand.

Cultural heritage brands have deep roots. Even if you kill it, it's still there in the ground. If someone else comes along to water it and give it some sun, it can spring forth anew.

One more thing makes cultural heritage brands valuable: when a nation becomes more prosperous and more confident, its people become more enthusiastic for its cultural heritage brands. In the past, Chinese people would disparage our own tableware, saying that a locally made china set is worth only a few hundred RMB but an English-made set might be a few thousand. But now that China has become richer, even a small pot could cost in the six figures if it's well made. In the past we thought of wine and coffee as 'high-class' drinks. Now even the most expensive Blue Mountain coffees are much cheaper than the best Chinese teas. This is the value of Chinese culture.

Cultural heritage brands are the most valuable brands we have. When you're building a new brand, your goal should be to make it into part of global culture. Look at Coca-Cola: it's an important part of the cultural heritage of the entire planet.

THE COST OF PRINT ADVERTISING – DIRECT DECISION-MAKING COSTS

The key difference between print and TV advertising is that print has a much larger information capacity. To put it another way, in print you have a choice to provide more or less information.

My suggestion is, the more information the better. In print, make the copy as long as you can. The more information you provide, the more customers will buy. The purpose of print advertising is to provide the information the consumer needs to make a decision up front. It needs to offer guidance, instead of just attracting attention. Leave the job of attracting attention to your billboards.

If a real estate advertisement has no price information, then the consumer won't be able to make a decision – the decision-making cost has increased. When people buy property, they have to settle on a price range first. They set a budget, then make a choice based on this budget. If you don't list your price, then your customers would have to call and ask you before they even start their decision-making. Most people would never make the call.

We used Peacock City as an example earlier in this chapter. In that case, clearly stating prices was an important step in driving sales.

In our newspaper ads for Peacock City, we showed off our beautiful houses with clearly marked prices. When customers saw the great houses and the great prices, the *ka-chings* began.

Then we took an even bigger step. We included the full price chart in our ads, showing the price for every house type.

There was a secret to this price chart!

Why include the chart? Because we wanted to lower the decision-making cost for our customers. What did our customers base their decision on? On the price we were selling at. So the price chart was sorted by price range. The four Peacock City projects were all mixed up. The house types that fell into each price range, regardless of which project they were in, were listed together.

This tactic was inspired by my experiences with shoe shopping. I have small feet, so it's difficult for me to buy shoes. Often I find a shoe I really like, but the salesperson has to go in the back to see if they have it in my size. A lot of the time, they come back after 15 minutes to say that they don't. I don't blame them – I have small feet, so it's naturally harder to buy shoes.

Then one time I was in the US and I walked into a shoe shop, and I discovered that there was no reason that I couldn't find five pairs of shoes in my size in just five minutes! That's because this shop arranges the displays by size, not by brand. Think about it: the right size is a *requirement* when you're buying a pair of shoes.

Price and brand are *factors* in the decision, but not requirements. In this shoe store, there are signs hanging from the ceiling with numbers representing sizes. The shelf under the number six were all size-six shoes, and the next shelf was all size seven, all the way to size 12 and more. The customer just needs to go to the shelf for their size, where there could be a hundred pair of shoes, all of which fit your feet. You can leave with a pair you like in minutes. This is what I mean by low decision-making costs.

At that time Peacock City offered homes from half a million to four million RMB. We listed them all, grouped by price range, so that customers could choose the best one for their budget.

The next day, a line of cars formed in front of the sales office for Peacock City Yongding River, stretching all the way to the freeway. The highway police had to be deployed to maintain order. That was when the sales for Peacock City launched into the stratosphere.

LOWERING MONITORING COSTS FOR SOCIETY IS THE FOUNDATION OF BRANDING

The Hua and Hua way is a way to lower costs with creativity. You want to lower your own marketing costs, and you want to lower your customers' decision-making costs. But the very foundation of branding is to lower society's monitoring costs. So this is the note we'll end this chapter on.

I'm sure some people are very confused by this entire concept. Isn't it better for monitoring my company to be as costly as possible? Why even try to lower this cost?

When companies talk about having a single brand, there's one frequent worry: We'll lose everything if something happens. We shouldn't put all our eggs in one basket.

This way of looking at things is common, but completely wrong.

It is imperative for Chinese companies today to fully understand the fact that societal monitoring is the very essence of branding. This will significantly lessen confusion and mistakes.

What if something happens to our brand? The answer is this: The entire point of a brand is that something will happen to it. If nothing can happen, then there's no need for branding.

No one in the world is immune to making a mistake. No company in the world is immune to making a mistake. Even the sun can be blotted out by an eclipse. Mistakes are inevitable for any company. It's just a matter of time and the size of the mistake. Catastrophic mistakes are also inevitable – again, just a matter of time.

Of all the mistakes a company can make, none can be as horrifying as a plane crash. But there's no such thing as an airline that is forever crash-free. It's going to happen, but airlines don't go out of business just because of one crash.

What's important is, how do they prevent crashes? And what do they do *after* a crash?

Society invented brands to *prevent* companies from making mistakes, and to help them *deal with* mistakes. Brands have two major functions in human society:

One, brands lower the chance of a mistake.

Two, brands make it easier to punish a company for a mistake.

Companies think that they came up with the idea of branding. Wrong! Brands emerged not because of companies, but because society needs them. If society didn't need brands, no amount of effort would have made it happen.

Brands are a *cost* mechanism, a *risk* mechanism, a *social* mechanism.

In terms of cost: brands lower the cost of decision-making for consumers. Brands present options they can trust.

In terms of risk: brands are the result of a game. Economists say that companies create repeated games through branding, giving customers the chance to punish them. That's the point of branding.

As noted earlier, restaurants that are tourist traps either have terrible food or terrible prices, because their transactions are one-time games. You'll only ever eat there once, so there's no chance to punish the establishment by not choosing them the next time. Brands create repeated games. There's always a next time – multiple next times in fact. So you have a chance to punish them.

Pay very close attention to this: The essence of branding is a social mechanism to lower the costs for consumers to monitor the company, so that consumers can punish companies that make mistakes.

The bigger the brand, the lower the cost to monitor and punish it.

If brands try to get away from monitoring and punishment, then they've lost the essence of branding. The brand will lose a great part of their value.

If a brand willingly accepts punishment after making a mistake, even helping to make the punishment greater than customer expectations, then the brand becomes more valuable.

Brands are not killed through punishment; they grow when they are easily punished. Brands live on through punishment.

So when 'something happens' to your brand, this is a chance to prove to customers that they can *punish* your brand. Take it willingly, and pay the price honestly. Then your brand becomes more valuable. These are the rules of the game. If executives try to skirt responsibility to avoid punishment, that's when the brand suffers real damage.

In a wave of anti-Japanese sentiment in 2012, many Toyota and Nissan vehicles were destroyed across China. Toyota and Nissan were not blamed for this, but they still compensated their customers for it – you bought our car, and it got destroyed, so we'll pay for repairs.

These companies needed to protect their brands.

Leading brands are always at the forefront of scandals. When news broke of tainted baijiu liquors, Maotai quickly became involved even though it wasn't their baijiu that was tainted. And of course, KFC is the perennial subject of food safety 'exposès'. Has this sunk KFC? Of course not. In fact, people *trust* KFC because it's always under fierce scrutiny. Society has it under the microscope.

Johnson & Johnson has gone through countless product recalls, but it's still one of the most reputable brands in the world, the top of its field. Why? Because it's willing to *do* recalls. J&J's Tylenol poisoning case is a textbook example of how to do it right, and emerge stronger than ever.

A lot of companies in China won't honestly admit their mistakes and take responsibility when something goes wrong with their products. They delete negative social media feedback. They try to silence people. They blame others, they try to 'minimize their losses'. These companies are wasting their money on their PR advisors. A problem with your products is not a scandal. Trying to *cover up* the problems is the scandal. A product recall is nothing to be ashamed of, it's something to be proud of. Don't get spooked by critical press. Remember that the media can't sink a company through words. Consumers are not idiots. They know that a company that's criticized all the time is a company they can trust. The only thing that can sink you is *yourself*.

When something goes wrong with your product, you need to take responsibility and accept punishment. That's what branding is all about.

It's the difference between what's *right* and what's *best*. Companies that try to blame others for their mistakes often think that they're right. But these companies don't know what's best for them. You say you're right, but nobody believes you. If you want to do what's best for you, then you should face up to your mistakes, pay what you need to, and end the controversy.

Confucius said in the *Analects*: "The benevolent are comfortable in benevolence; the wise take advantage of it." Kindness is a natural state for kind people. They respond to everything with benevolence. But the wise know that kindness is what's best for them, so they act benevolently too.

Another Chinese saying goes: "Those worthy of pity must have something worthy of dislike." Bad things are for the stupid.

WE MADE A MISTAKE.
NOW WHAT?

Here's a theory I'm proposing so that Chinese companies under-stand what branding is all about: The theory of brand failure.

Through branding, companies create repeated games to give customers a chance to punish them. Branding is a risk mechanism to protect consumers. When a brand makes a mistake, the brand is effective only when customers can punish it. If the brand tries to escape punishment, then the brand has failed.

When you've made the mistake, this is the *best* time to prove the value of your brand. When a mistake happens, it's like you've lifted up a heavy boulder. You can move it out of your way, or you can try to escape punishment – the equivalent of dropping the rock on your own foot.

Don't let your brand fail.

Let's go back to the *Analects*:

"Zi Gong said: 'The faults of the noble man are like the eclipses of the sun and moon – everyone sees them. But when he corrects them, everyone looks up to him'."

When your brand makes a mistake, make it a noble one.

CHAPTER 5

HUA AND HUA'S CORPORATE STRATEGY METHODOLOGY

YOUR CORPORATE SOCIAL RESPONSIBILITY IS YOUR MISSION AND YOUR STRATEGY

What is a company, really? It's a social mechanism to divide labour.

In the previous chapter on branding, we said that branding is a social mechanism. It's a way to strengthen social monitoring, improve the efficiency of decision-making for customers and mitigate risk. If society didn't need brands, companies would never have been able to create them.

In the same way, corporations are also a social mechanism: a way to divide labour.

If we think of all of society as one company, then each corporation can be thought of as an employee. This 'employee' has a job in the company that is society, so they need to do their job well, always improving and always staying among the best performers, so that they can become an irreplaceable core employee. This is how the 'employee' proves their value to the 'company'. If the corporation is of value to society as a whole, then it will never lose its 'job' and the corporation will stay in business. If the corporation is of no value, then it will eventually lose its place.

The essence of a corporation is its societal value. This is the role of corporations in society, and this is the mission for every corporation.

Management guru Peter Drucker has a lot to say about this.

"A business enterprise is an organ of society," he said. "Business enterprises – and public-service institutions as well – are organs of society. They do not exist for their own sake but to fulfil a specific social purpose ... They are not ends in themselves, but means."

"An institution," Drucker said, "exists for a specific purpose and mission, a specific social function."

"Psychologically, geographically, culturally, and socially, institutions must be part of the community."

In the above quotes, Drucker touches on the core essence of business: any corporation survives only because it fulfills a specific need or purpose in society.

Society is the master of any company, and the company is a servant, at society's beck and call.

Many companies have 'mission statements'. But many of them turn their missions into establishing some kind of corporate culture, instead of using the mission to direct their business strategy. Their mission statements turn into meaningless, empty talk.

As a company, your mission and your social responsibility should be the *start* of your business strategy, not the endpoint.

Regardless of business models, companies survive because they are useful to society. They become an integral component of how society works, so society allows them to survive. If they don't, society will leave them behind.

When we look at companies through the lens of divison of labour, we get a methodology for formulating a corporate strategy. This is the Hua and Hua formula for corporate strategy:

Corporate social responsibility = Mission = Corporate strategy

To explain this formula, we first need to redefine corporate social responsibility.

Here's a common definition: Corporate social responsibility (CSR) refers to a company's responsibility to its employees, consumers, community and environment, in addition to generating profits and its legal responsibilities to shareholders. The concept of CSR demands that companies go beyond the traditional view that profits are its sole goal. CSR emphasizes human values in the production process, and contributions to consumers, to the environment and to society.

I find this definition unacceptable. I often say that the term *corporate social responsibility* was invented by someone who never wanted to take any responsibility in the first place. If you say to a girl, *I'll be responsible to you!* that means you never had any intention of being responsible. You would never say something like that to your wife, because responsibility is never a question there.

CSR is not a company's *obligations*. It's the company's *business*.

Mengniu Dairy's social responsibility is not to its 'community' or the 'environment', it's to *milk*. It should be making sure that there are no problems with its milk, not being distracted by pledges to give out milk to children, or proclamations about funding schools in disadvantaged areas. Its responsibility should be to give Chinese consumers a dairy brand they can trust. So what happened? A tainted milk scandal. The company took on plenty of false 'obligations', but it failed in its business responsibilities.

Sunflower Pharmaceuticals' social responsibility is not a responsibility 'to its employees, consumers, community and environment, in addition to generating profits and its legal responsibilities to shareholders'. That's for companies that do evil. For companies that do good, none of that should be an issue. The real responsibility for Sunflower should be to *provide safe medications for Chinese children*. This is an enormous responsibility! When all of your products and services are developed around this core responsibility, *this* is when you fulfill your CSR and become a 'social enterprise'. This is what corporate strategy should be all about. This is the kind of corporation that is useful to society.

People talk about the 'invisible hand of the market', but the invisible hand is controlled by an invisible body – society. In a mature market, companies in every industry are able to find their own position in the industry. Behind this is a division of labour – every company is shouldering some part of the industry's social responsibility.

The best way to ensure that your corporate strategy is forward-thinking is to think about what problems your company can solve for society. Some people think that only big companies should think about this issue, but they are wrong. Even a college student running a video store on campus should be thinking about what problems they're solving for teachers and students as a starting point for their strategy.

In 2013, Hua and Hua began working with 360, a major Chinese internet security company. Just like with Sunflower, we used the 'Corporate social responsibility = Mission = Corporate strategy' formula.

360's corporate social responsibility is to protect internet security in China.

Its mission is to protect internet security in China, just like it's the mission of the police to protect the safety of civilians, and the mission of doctors to cure patients of illness. 360's mission is to protect China's internet security.

What is a mission? A mission is a job that is never finished. No police force could ever say that their mission is done, that no crimes will ever be committed again. No doctor can say that their mission is done, that no one will ever get sick again. Once you've found a mission that can never be completed, that always needs to be worked on, then you've found a sustainable business.

This is very important! To understand why a company needs a mission to last, you first need to understand what a mission is. Many companies' mission statements are full of empty talk that has nothing to do with their own business. These companies don't create value for society, so they end up having no idea what they should actually do. In a few years they start thinking about 'pivoting'.

Your CSR is your mission: the problem you want to solve for society.

What about your strategy, then?

Your strategy is your solution for this problem.

360's strategy was also its business portfolio and product structure: a solution for internet security in China, including national, corporate and personal-level solutions. All 360 products are developed under this strategy. The 360 brand represents internet security in China.

In addition to redefining CSR, we also need to redefine public relations. Both terms have been poorly defined for too long.

What is public relations? Again, here's the usual definition:

Public relations (PR) is the science of building positive social relationships between an organization and the environment that it survives in, the segment of the public that influences its survival and development. Through PR, an organization can build good relationships between internal and external personnel and with other organizations in service of a specific goal. Early 20th century public relations pioneer Edward Bernays defined PR as "a management function ... executing a program of action to earn public understanding and acceptance." PR management is a conscious management activity. Building good public relations requires the planning of good PR activities.

This is an awful definition. To paraphrase the philosopher Chuang Tzu, you should do good things, not things that make other people think you're a good person. The latter is the way a hypocrite thinks.

I dislike the idea of 'corporate image' advertising and PR campaigns. Your image is what you do. You should not do things just for your image. What do you want to do to help society? Just go do that!

So here's a new definition of PR:

PR is a company's social service product.

It's like voluntarism: Do what you're good at to serve society. PR is a product that consists of social service. You should do PR from a product development standpoint. Develop 'PR products' that are part of your business portfolio and product structure, that help you solve the social problem that you identified in your strategy and mission. Through that prism, 360's PR product will also be an internet security solution for China.

And so we developed the ultimate PR product for 360: the China Internet Security Conference.

Just like the free antivirus program it used to provide, the China Internet Security Conference is a product that 360 provides to society free of charge. It is the biggest, highest-level, most influential professional internet security conference in the Asia Pacific region. It brings together ideas related to cutting-edge issues like national network security, mobile security, cloud data security, corporate security, web and app security, software security, targeted hacking attacks, emerging threats, industrial safety and cybercrime. This is a free social service product, so we can focus on how to maximize the benefit to society instead of turning it into a one-company show for 360. We were able to get the top companies in every field to participate.

The first China Internet Security Conference, in 2013, attracted more than 10,000 participants, and every breakout session had more than 1,000 people. Every internet security-related stock on the Chinese stock exchange went up on the day the conference opened. A CCTV report on the conference referred to 360's "position as a market leader in the internet security field." In terms of 'brand image' this was a huge coup for 360. But we didn't do this by setting out to 'improve our image'. We did it by doing honest work.

Let's go back to the formula. CSR = Mission = Corporate strategy.

360's corporate strategy – that is, its business portfolio and product structure – is to provide internet security solutions for China. That means   protecting internet security for China as a whole, for Chinese businesses and individuals. So let's look at 360's products to see if they can really solve the problem.

At that time, 360 had no business-to-business (B2B) traction. Everything they did was business-to-consumer (B2C). Having established its social responsibility and mission, 360 began acquiring companies based on its new strategic roadmap and founded its enterprise security group in 2015.

A fate would have it, the user base and user data that 360 accumulated through its PC and mobile products allowed it to establish a whole new security concept and model in the following three years. In one fell swoop it became the one of the world's biggest and most advanced internet security companies.

THREE LEVELS OF CSR: KILLER PRODUCTS, AUTHORITATIVE EXPERTISE, DREAMS COME TRUE

We've established that a company's social responsibility is its core business, the way it solves social problems. The Hua and Hua way organizes CSR into three levels:

1. Killer Products
2. Authoritative Expertise
3. Dreams Come True

These three levels are a framework upon which to formulate your strategy. They also form a systemic marketing and communication tool.

KILLER PRODUCTS

Your killer products are the products that are the best at solving problems.

So now ask yourself: What are your company's killer products? Do you know the answer off-hand? Do your customers?

Apple's killer products are the iPhone and iPad. Everybody knows that.

What is the key connection between a company and its customers? The answer is the company's products. For any company, it is critical that customers can immediately think of their products and services. If the link between the company and its products is unclear, that is very bad news for the company's health. The products that immediately come to mind when people think about your company are your company's killer products.

Killer products are 'killer' not just for the company, but for society as well. They represent the best of the company, the best for society.

Think of it from the perspective of your mission. What is your mission to society? Former Chinese President Jiang Zemin said that the Party has 'Three Represents' – it represents "the requirements for developing China's advanced productive forces, the orientation of China's advanced culture and the fundamental interests of the overwhelming majority of the Chinese people." A company, then, represents China's advanced productive forces.

So you need to think of your company this way: you represent society's most advanced productive force in your field. A consumer who wants a product or service in your field should buy it from you. When they need help, they should come to you. This is your responsibility. When you take this responsibility, everybody will become your customer.

So now ask yourself another question, a more advanced version of the killer-product question: In what way does your company represent society's most advanced productive force?

If you are advanced, then you will not fail. If you are behind, then society will leave you behind. In formulating your strategy, you must think of how to maintain an advanced productive form in your field.

Products are the first and most important part of your responsibility and your strategy, because products are any company's foundation. A company is its products. So ask yourself:

1. What are my company's killer products?
2. Are my company's killer products widely known and recognized by customers and society?
3. Does our company represent the most advanced productive force in the field of our products?
4. Can we solve problems for our customers and for society?
5. Can we preserve our leading edge over the next ten years? How?
6. In what field are we ensured of a continued advantage, and how?

Earlier we used Apple as an example. Apple's answers to the first three questions are clear. Whether they can answer the last two well enough will be the key to its future strategy.

What we discussed above applies to your marketing as well as your strategy. How can you make it so that your products come readily to mind, so that customers all agree that your products are the best?

AUTHORITATIVE EXPERTISE

We're all familiar with the concept of expertise. We talk about how such-and-such brand is an *expert* or an *authority* in a field. Why do brands want to be authorities? Because they want customers to listen to them for their expertise. That's the goal of marketing, isn't it?

Here's a term to help you think about your brand's expertise – *Chief Knowledge Officer.*

Every company needs to become society's Chief Knowledge Officer for their field.

What is the job responsibility of the Chief Knowledge Officer?

To store and discover knowledge for society.

The first part of your responsibility, to *store* knowledge, means that people will come to you for knowledge in your domain. As the Hua and Hua way puts it: "Make society accustomed to you and reliant on you." This is an enormous strategic and marketing advantage.

If people rely on your knowledge, they will absolutely rely on your products.

The second part of your responsibility is to *discover* new knowledge. How will humankind progress in your field? It's up to you to explore the frontier.

Often the cutting edge of knowledge in society is not in the government, universities or institutions, but in companies.

Only companies have the resources and motiviations to discover new knowledge. If you do not, or cannot, take on this responsibility, you will never become a great company. This is, again, one of the 'Three Represents' – representing advanced culture.

All industries are consulting industries; all companies are consultants to their customers. We talked a lot about the internet security consultant 360. The government, other companies, individuals – anyone can take their internet security problems to 360, and 360 will give answers, develop solutions and offer products to solve them.

If you're a toothpaste manufacturer, you are also a consultant – an oral health consultant. If you're a fertilizer manufacturer, you're an agricultural productivity consultant. This goes double for B2B-focused companies, because sometimes they're even involved in developing new products for their clients. New toothpaste flavours are usually proposed by flavouring manufacturers, not by toothpaste manufacturers themselves. The flavouring company invents a new toothpaste based on marketing research and sells the toothpaste to the toothpaste company so that the toothpaste company will keep buying its flavourings. So being a *consultant* to clients – offering marketing advice, developing new products – is the key to being a successful B2B company. The advice is free, but it's a crucial part of making a sale.

When you think like a consultant, you'll have a whole new view on your products. You offer *information* to your customers as well as products.

So what is the relationship between products and information?

Most people think of information as subordinate to products. We offer information *about* our products, such as usage instructions. But if you're thinking like a consultant, then there's no subordinate relationship – products and information are equal. Information is not centred on your *products*, it's centred on your *customers*. You provide the products your customers need and the information that your customers need, not just information about your products. For example, a fertilizer company shouldn't be offering advice just about fertilizer, but also about crops.

So when you're providing information and advice, what you're looking at is a product that is every bit as important as what you're putting on the store shelf. When you think of information as a product, you'll take a whole new approach. When you train your salespeople, you'll be training them not just to talk up your products, but to become capable consultants to your customers.

Every company needs to learn to offer the product that is *advice*. There may not be an immediate financial return on such a product, but it is a key part of any company's strategy. It's an important tool to retain customers and expand your business.

As mentioned earlier, we often talk about the 'stickiness' of customers. A good product experience creates stickiness, but making customers rely on you for information makes them even stickier.

Another important notion is that you must become a trustworthy speaker. Do your long-term strategic plans involve becoming a trusted speaker in your area of expertise?

Widespread consumer panics are common in China nowadays. The panic might be over nothing at all, but with the media fanning the flames, companies are finding it impossible to fight back and consumers have no idea who to trust. They end up blindly believing everything they read. The reason behind all of this is that no one is trustworthy. Companies really brought the situation on themselves. If you don't take your responsibility as a provider of knowledge seriously, you won't get a shot at explaining yourself against accusations.

Remember, you reap what you sow.

DREAMS COME TRUE

Every brand, every company, is a maker of dreams. Every top company represents a dream for the future. The companies that represent the dreams of *all* humanity are the best companies in the world.

When Bill Gates wrote his book *The Road Ahead*, Microsoft represented the dreams of humanity for the information age. Gates was the Chief Knowledge Officer of the world for the new digital era, the personification of that future. That made him the world's top entrepreneur. The future then passed into the hands of Google, Apple, Facebook. Microsoft is just a second-string company now. Why? Because it no longer represents the dreams of humanity. Perhaps that's why Bill Gates has turned his attention to being the world's top philanthropist instead of its top entrepreneur.

What companies represent the dreams of humanity right now? Google is certainly one of them. To understand why, take a look at the automobile industry. The companies that represent advanced production and advanced culture should be the companies like Mercedes-Benz, BMW, Audi and Volkswagen. But these aren't the companies that I dream of when I dream about the cars of the future. Google is the company I dream of, because they're the ones doing work in smart cars, smart roads and self-driving cars.

Who will be the ones to guide the culture of the automobile in the future? One of them will certainly be Google. When that happens, Google will represent advanced production, advanced culture and the dreams of the future in the domain of automobiles. Half of today's car companies will be gone.

What do you get by having killer products, authoritative expertise and dreams come true? You get much lower marketing costs, because society is now accustomed to relying on your company for advice. When you represent humanity's dreams for the future, everything you do will be the target of attention. You will become your own biggest media source.

Think about it. What will our next generation of smartphones look like? Where would we go to find out? Certainly not a research institution or media outlet. We'll go to Apple or Samsung and try to learn what the next product they launch is going to be like. Why? Because they have the authoritative expertise when it comes to smartphones. Because, in the smartphone domain, they represent our dreams come true. When they announce a new product, it's not a new step for their company, it's a step for all of human-kind. They take over the headlines. If Nokia were to announce a new product tomorrow, they'd never get that kind of attention, no matter how much they spent on advertising.

In the context of your industry and market, you can think about your company's value to society on these three levels: killer products, authoritative expertise and dreams come true.

What kind of expertise does 360 want to bring? What dreams does it represent? 360 wants to be an authority when it comes to internet security, and it wants to represent the dream of a safe internet. Its killer products are its internet security services. Security is crucial for all four major current internet technologies – cloud computing, big data, mobile connectivity and social networks. Security is now a fundamental service for all internet businesses. 360's business portfolio is an all-in-one solution for internet security. It is taking on the responsibility of storing and discovering knowledge related to internet security. That's why it organizes the China Internet Security Conference. There is no profit in organizing this conference, but it is the company's social responsibility and value to society. For 360, its social responsibility is not an *obligation*, it's part of its *business*.

THE BEST-RUN COMPANIES ARE THE SUSTAINABLE COMPANIES

Business people talk all the time about wanting to build 'hundred-year companies'. But a hundred years of what? A hundred years of growth? A hundred years of development? Or a hundred years of survival?

The key should be survival, so the company will be alive and kicking in a hundred years, passed on across generations. This is the ultimate achievement in business. As for a hundred years of growth – well, no company has yet managed to do that.

Most public companies see their strategy as being entirely dictated by growth. Balance sheets, income statements and cash flow statements are cranked out every year. And so, we've gotten to the point where public companies can't even look beyond the current year in their 'strategic vision'.

Now let's talk about development.

What is development? Growth means more money; development means more *capabilities*. Development is the process of gaining the capability to survive in the future.

When a company's revenues reach a peak, it could very well be the eve of its destruction. Why? Because this year's success is the result of inertia from the past. If you don't develop the ability to continue to survive next year, you might be gone by then. If you have piles of cash on hand but your company faces the risk of failure, that shows you don't have a scientific outlook on development – all you're focusing on is growth. This was Nokia's problem.

Many business people, the most successful ones, often say that their companies are 6-18 months away from failure. These people are said to be 'always focusing on the next crisis'. Sometimes they're accused of faking it to keep their employees in line. But it's really none of these things. They are not guarding against sudden crises, they just have a clear understanding of how companies survive and develop – everything a company has today is the result of good decisions yesterday. But if good decisions aren't being made today, then the company won't survive tomorrow. It's a cause and effect dynamic.

What's an even higher achievement than development? Survival.

When we talk about building a 100-year company, we don't mean the company is going to *grow* for 100 years, we mean the company will still be around in 100 years. The ultimate achievement in business is *sustainable operation* – the company always survives and never disappears. How do you do this? By always having new cards in hand. If you never want to be left behind by society, you need to be always useful to it so that it keeps you around. You have to always think about your killer products, authoritative expertise and dreams come true for the next year, next five years, next decade. This is the foundation of our strategy.

BE CAUSE-AND-EFFECT-ORIENTED, NOT RESULTS-ORIENTED

When you are focused on your company's social responsibility, you are focused on cause and effect. The Hua and Hua way is cause-and-effect-oriented. Every issue we examine in this book we examine through cause and effect. Every effect has a cause, every cause creates an effect.

There is a lot of results-oriented thinking in corporate management. People accept results-oriented thinking because they want results. But results-oriented thinking is bound to miss something, because results are always hypothetical before they happen. Causes are determined by effects. Effects determine causes. Results are only one half of cause and effect. Results-oriented thinking makes you point fingers at other people. Cause-and-effect-oriented thinking encourages you to think about yourself.

Management is like life: it can take a long time for karma to get you. In Chinese we say that you should care about the sowing, not about the harvest. This applies to companies as well. Results-oriented evaluation puts companies in a state of constant tension. This is just as bad for a company as it is for a person. You need to pick only the battles that you can win. When it comes to strategy, your goal should be to leave others in the dust after just one step, succeed beyond imagination after just a few years. That's the mark of a true strategist.

The military classic *Wuzi* said: "When the world is consumed by war, those who win five battles find disaster, those who win four find difficulty, those who win three become hegemons, those who win two become kings, those who win one become emperors. Among those who achieve many victories, few conquer the world; many descend into ruin."

You must focus your spirit and remain committed to your goal. Be quick, but do not rush. Engage only in battles you have *already won*, and let one battle end the war. Don't plunge yourself headlong into skirmishes and think you'll always come away with victory.

HOW ARE COMPANIES BUILT TO LAST?

We search fruitlessly for answers, often because we have not even found the question. When we find the question, we often find the answer in it.

The value of a good question is immense. How are companies built to last? The book *Built to Last: Successful Habits of Visionary Companies* asks a fantastic question: If your company was gone tomorrow, would society feel like it has lost something?

A good question instantly clarifies a lot of things. We can ask this question about any company:

If Google is gone tomorrow, will I feel like I've lost something?

If Nokia is gone tomorrow, will I feel like I've lost something?

Compare Apple with Nokia. One could argue that losing Nokia wouldn't be much. Conversely, losing Apple would be really losing something.

Asking this question allows you to really see the essence of a company.

One more test: Which one disappearing would make you feel like you've lost more, Apple or Google?

Without Apple, we might be okay with a Samsung. But without Google, we wouldn't have just lost a search engine – the whole of humanity's progress would slow down.

So ask this about your company: If your company is gone tomorrow, will society feel like it's lost something? You can even ask it about yourself. If you're gone tomorrow, who will mourn you besides your family? Maybe other people would have already forgotten you before your family's tears are even dry. This is a mirror that shows you your own value to society.

A CORPORATE STRATEGY ROADMAP – THE HUA AND HUA WEIQI MODEL

What is a strategy?

The Prussian military theorist Carl von Clausewitz gave this definition in his classic *On War*: Strategy means 'the combination of individual engagements to attain the goal of the campaign or war'. So to formulate a strategy, you need to set targets that will allow you to accomplish the goal of your campaign. That is, you need to formulate a war plan. Next, you need to link each action you take with this goal – to plan out each engagement and deploy your resources for the battles within them. All of this can only be done based on expectations that may not fit the actual situation, and many details cannot be planned out ahead of time. So it's clear that strategy requires you to go onto the field so that you can handle the problems that are sure to crop up, while changing your plans as necessary. Strategizing is a job that never ends.

Clausewitz's idea of strategy can also be seen in his idea of the 'culminating point of victory' – all engagements are for the purpose of reaching this culminating point, so it must be ever present in your mind. This is what is meant when he said that strategy is 'the combination of individual engagements to attain the goal of the campaign or war'.

Then you need to arrange for a series of engagements – connect the actions you take to accomplish the goal with the goal itself.

We call your ultimate goal your *strategy*, and the engagements you plan to achieve the goal your *roadmap*. This forms your strategic plan. At Hua and Hua, we like to conceptualize this through the Chinese strategic game weiqi (better known in the West under its Japanese name 'go'). This roadmap is like the corners, sides and middle of the weiqi board. At the beginning of the game you start out from the corners, because that's where it's easiest to launch your moves. Then you take the sides, and eventually victory is decided by the amount of territory you get in the middle.

The corners are your base – your core business, the fort you hold against your competitors. The sides are the product lines and business portfolios that you establish around this core business or core product.

The game board is the market you've defined for yourself, and your territory is the share of the market your brand is eventually able to cover. When you start taking over the corners and sides of the board, you'll be able to gain the advantage in the game and cover as much territory as you can.

So our strategic roadmap is like this:

1. Define the board – the company's value to society.
2. Design the company's business portfolio and product structure.
3. Decide the order of launching and expanding each part of your business.
4. Carry out the launch and execution based on your plan.
5. Achieve coverage of the market.

It's like the founding of the People's Republic. The Party started from the first 'corner' in Jiangxi, then marched north, to the north of Shaanxi – the second corner. In the midst of that they also grabbed several more bases in enemy territory. When the culmination point for victory came, it started from a very valuable corner – the Northeast – and then the PLA took all of China in three major battles.

Next, let's use Sunflower Pharmaceuticals as an example for how to apply our theory of social value and our weiqi-model strategic roadmap to a real business situation.

SUNFLOWER PHARMACEUTICALS: A STRATEGY CASE STUDY

Companies are the organs of society. They exist to solve society's problems. Every problem in society is a business opportunity. If you want to start a business, first you need to see what problem you can solve for society and what responsibility you can assume.

Sunflower discovered a problem: a problem with safe pharmaceuticals for China's children.

Remember when we were young, and adults would take pills meant for adults and cut them in half for us when we got sick? A lot of medication still have instructions for adults, followed by the words 'lower dosages for children as necessary'. What does that mean, 'as necessary'? And precisely how does one measure out an appropriate, safe and effective lower dosage? It means that parents are on their own. Isn't it absurd to have detailed dosage instructions for adults, but leave it entirely to chance for children?

Now we know that drug dosages for children should be calculated based on their weight. And so, medicines for children now come with a table telling parents how much a child should take based on their weight.

But there's one more problem. Most medications have a variety of active ingredients. A dosage appropriate for a child might not be the same percentage of the dosage for adults. Children might need a different ratio of ingredients. So the lack of guidance and protection when it comes to children's pharmaceuticals remains a problem faced by Chinese society. Chinese society has a desperate need for specialized medication for children.

Does specialized medication for children exist in China? Yes, but not nearly enough. China even has a few pharmaceutical companies that make products only for children, but they're small companies with a narrow range of products. They don't have much to spend on R&D or marketing, so they're not well-known in the market.

What business opportunities arise from this problem? What value will a leading children's pharmaceutical brand bring to society? Coming at it from the cost perspective, such a brand will lower the decision-making cost for parents buying medicine for their children, lower the monitoring cost for society regarding children's medicine, and concentrate the knowledge resources related to children's pharmaceuticals.

And so Sunflower's children's pharmaceutical strategy was born. It was developed starting from an insight on a societal problem – insufficient safety in children's pharmaceuticals – that established a mission – provide safe medications for China's children and protect their health.

The mission decides the strategy. The company's business portfolio and product structure were the comprehensive solution to this problem.

Sunflower's business portfolio and product structure were the solution they developed to provide safe medications for China's children and protect their health. And so Sunflower established five business units: children's over-the-counter drugs; children's prescription drugs; children's health foods; children's personal care products; children's hospitals. Under this strategy, Sunflower decided that it had to become more than a pharmaceutical company. It had to expand into food, cosmetics and health care.

Is this a 'diversification' strategy? No, it is a specialization strategy. Sunflower is specializing in children's health. This is a philosophical question about *categories*. If you categorize the industry into pharmaceuticals, food and cosmetics, you would think this is 'diversification'. But if you think of it as the children's health industry, this is specialization. If you can clearly understand the question, you'll be able to eliminate 90% of unnecessary arguing.

The product structure is the corporate strategic roadmap.

There are three levels to the product structure:

First, the structure itself: what businesses to expand into, what products to develop.

Second, the strategic role and mission of each product.

Third, the strategic order: which businesses to launch first, which products to develop initially.

This structure and order is the weiqi board in our model. In deciding the structure, you'll be deciding what your 'corners' will be, what sides you'll be able to take over from these corners, and what businesses will form the territory you'll eventually conquer. In each business, you'll also need to identify your corners, sides and territories within that sub-category.

Think of yourself as a general. Your businesses and products are your troops. In battle, the commander must focus all of their wisdom on deciding in what order the troops will enter the field, so that the battle may be won at minimum risk and with minimum casualties.

The idea of the order is that the success of the first product must create a favourable environment for the second. The theory of the famed PLA General Su Yu emphasized the relationship between the first battle and the second and third battles. He said that he first battle must create favourable conditions for the second.

What is the purpose of your ultimate victory, then? Well, we've already established a valuable brand for children's pharmaceuticals and care. So now I can sell any product and service related to children's health. This is now about achieving coverage, taking territory. Once you have the corners and sides, the risk and cost associated with taking territory is much lower.

When we designed the distinctive blue pill bottle for another pharmaceutical brand, Sanjing, we said that the idea was 'a red ocean in a blue bottle'. The product isn't just about the medicine inside (very much a red-ocean product) but also the blue bottle outside. Once the blue bottle brand is successful, it can hold any red-ocean product and turn the ocean blue.

When we do things, we need to think about failure before success. The best way is to establish a brand, and then sell things that people use a lot with a brand premium. This is the best strategy.

Warren Buffett said that he would never invest in Apple. He didn't want to invest in a company that had to beat its opponents in technological innovation every day just to stay ahead. He was happy to invest in Gillette; it made him sleep well every night, thinking that every man in the world quietly grows more facial hair as he sleeps.

So what was Sunflower's structure and order? What was their roadmap?

Their first corner was their over-the-counter drug business. The specific product was the children's lung fever coughing and wheezing syrup.

Here is the stratgeic role and mission of the over-the-counter drug business and the coughing and wheezing syrup, and the sequence in which it was launched:

Over-the-counter drugs can be advertised in China, so the product needed to establish a beachhead for the Sunflower brand. The children's lung fever coughing and wheezing syrup was the first product to be advertised, so its mission was to become a sales success and establish Sunflower as a children's pharmaceutical and health care brand.

That's why the very first line in the commercial for the syrup was: "Class is in for the Sunflower School for Moms!" It wasn't enough that it won a victory for itself; it had to create a solid base for all future Sunflower children's pharmaceutical and health care products.

When the results came in, the children's lung fever coughing and wheezing syrup completed its mission to perfection.

The syrup successfully established the Sunflower School for Moms in the children's pharmaceutical world. From this corner, we launched dozens of over-the-counter drugs, including coughing granules, the painkiller paracetamol and children's digestion syrup.

The second corner was the prescription drug business.

Once we'd established a brand in the over-the-counter business and established ourselves as an authority in children's drugs, we were able to leverage that to help our prescription drug business in hospitals.

But Sunflower's prescription drug business was very small at that time, so it had to use a series of acquisitions to help it expand into the field. When it began the strategy, it had only 12 pediatric products. It's now expanded to 69 and growing, and Sunflower is now China's most comprehensive, best-selling, most influential children's pharmaceutical brand.

And so, Sunflower now had the favourable environment to expand into two new corner businesses: children's health foods and children's personal care.

Once we established a leadership position in these four businesses, we were able to drive development in related products to cover the whole of the children's health industry, taking as much territory as we could. The red ocean was tamed by our blue bottle.

This is the roadmap. This is the weiqi model – Hua and Hua's business portfolio strategy model.

EVERY ENTERPRISE IS A SOCIAL ENTERPRISE

Two new terms have become very prominent lately: *social enterprise* and *social entrepreneur.*

A social enterprise is not a pure business enterprise or a regular social service. Social enterprises operate through commercial means, generating profit to help society. Their profits are used to help disadvantaged groups, promote community development and invest in the enterprise itself. These enterprises consider social values more important than maximizing profits.

Social entrepreneurs view social problems from a business perspective, solving problems using the rules of business. The goal of a social entrepreneur is not solely profit. Social entrepreneurs are often founders and operators of charitable organizations. Examples include Jeroo Billimoria, who founded Childline, a 24-hour hotline for children at risk in India, and Fábio Rosa, who helped rural Brazilians access solar power.

These are two very feel-good definitions, certainly, but they are mistaken in dividing companies into 'enterprises that are for society' and 'enterprises that are for profit', and making the same distinction for entrepreneurs.

My point is, helping society is not the purpose of an enterprise. *Society* uses the enterprise to help *itself*. The survival of a company is a choice made by society. The basis of that choice is whether the company can help society achieve its goals. All companies must be and necessarily are social enterprises. All entrepreneurs must be and necessarily are social entrepreneurs. Once you realize this, you've opened up yourself to whole new avenues of thinking.

A corporate strategy is not something implemented from above. It must be embedded within every action taken by the company. Every action must be strategically meaningful and valuable, and help the company accumulate strategic assets or establish competitive positions. For example, the Sunflower commercials that begin with "Class is in for the Sunflower School for Moms!" are of immense strategic value.

Corporate strategy also does not cleanly fall into formulation and implementation stages. As Clausewitz said, strategy is something that never ends. Business people must imbue every one of their actions with strategic meaning, and re-think and adjust their strategies every day. That's because every strategy is based on assumptions, and assumptions do not always come true.

A Chinese saying goes that changes always happen faster than plans do, but this is mistaken. Changes are what make plans necessary, just as a good manager's spending might not map exactly to their budget allocation, but you still need to have a budget.

There's more!

Do not assume that companies only pursue profit maximization. Drucker said that the biggest misunderstanding of business enterprises is that they want to maximize their profits. Companies want to minimize their profits! Profits are resources that the company uses to compete with other companies. What companies really want is to eliminate their competitors with the lowest profits possible. This is what 'negative competition' is. Maximum profits can only happen in a monopoly situation. Adam Smith already made it clear:

"The price of monopoly is upon every occasion the highest which can be got. The natural price, or the price of free competition, on the contrary, is the lowest that can be taken, not upon every occasion, indeed, but for any considerable time together. The one is upon every occasion the highest which can be squeezed out of the buyers, or which, it is supposed, they will consent to give; the other is the lowest which the sellers can commonly afford to take, and at the same time continue their business."

So what do companies pursue? Only to 'continue their business'. Only to survive. Survival is the ultimate pursuit. Survival is sustainability. Survival is building to last. It's like a ruling party. Is there a higher goal than to rule forever?

CORPORATE POLICY IS MORE IMPORTANT THAN CORPORATE STRATEGY

Let's discuss the idea of social responsibility from another perspective.

For this discussion, we'll start with a quote from a master of strategy who's as revered as Clausewitz, Antoine-Henri Jomini: "The art of war, as is generally conceived, is divided into five purely military branches: strategy, grand tactics, logistics, the art of the engineer and elementary tactics, but there is an essential part of this science which has, until now, been improperly excluded from it. It is the policy of war."

Jomini introduced policy into his theory of war. He argued that although policy seems like a government rather than military matter, policy is quite important for a commander even if it may have little to do with a junior officer. The reason is that policy is deeply connected to the plans and actions that may be taken in war.

And so Jomini identifies six levels of strategy:
1. Policy.
2. Strategy, the art of commanding the army on the battlefield.
3. Grand tactics used for battles and campaigns.
4. Logistics, the application of the art of moving troops.
5. Engineering, the art of building strongholds.
6. Elementary tactics.

These six levels are very helpful to companies. They offer a framework for thinking about your corporate strategy:
1. Corporate policy: your policies toward society and consumers; the responsibilities and obligations you take.
2. Strategic roadmap: where you are, where you're going, how you'll get there.
3. Grand tactics: your operational methods, including your core technologies, manufacturing processes, marketing models, etc. Toyota's manufacturing process is an example of a unique grand tactic. There are also grand tactics for R&D, marketing, and so on. For Hua and Hua, the super sign is our grand tactic.
4. Corporate resources: the art of commanding resources such as capital and personnel.
5. Procedures, plans and toolboxes: processes and standards that help address specific problems.

Policy is extremely important to a company. Many problems, particularly ones related to consumer safety and social impacts, are poorly handled by companies because they have no policy and thus no principles when dealing with a situation. When deciding whether to launch a product or whether to keep a business, you shouldn't be looking at sales metrics. Look at your policy and decide if the action will affect your social responsibility.

A GOOD STRATEGY LOWERS YOUR COSTS AND INCREASES YOUR COMPETITORS'

Policy, politics, social responsibility: will this all increase your costs?

The cost methodlogy is the unifying theme of this book. We've discussed branding and creative work from the perspective of cost, and now we'll discuss corporate strategy from this perspective. Simply put, a good strategy can both lower your costs and increase those of your competitors.

As we continue to invest marketing resources in the Sunflower School for Moms, the cost of entering the children's pharmaceutical, food and personal care markets becomes lower and lower. Continued investment may even make the cost of us entering a new business lower than the cost of an incumbent in that business to defend their position. And when others try to expand into our businesses, they will face a stronghold that becomes stronger every day.

In this process, we're creating a value structure and a product structure. These structures are your strongholds against your competition. They are what makes your costs lower and your competitors' higher. You can chip away at your competitors while they don't even know where to start attacking you. Why? Because they're throwing individual soldiers at you while you've already built up an entire value structure. When you have your corners, sides and territory, you'll be able to get any part of the board you want. It's just the marginal value for your brand. But when your competitors try to attack you, they get nothing. This is the difference between having a structure and lacking one.

Adam Smith said that a monopoly brings high prices. A product structure brings some of the effects of a monopoly. As for how companies pursue monopolies, maybe that's something for the next edition of this book.

If you can plan out your strategy based on your responsibility, and make good use of the 'corners, lines, territory' structure and roadmap, your performance will be completely beyond your competitors' imagination.

KEEP YOUR EYE ON YOUR CUSTOMERS, NOT YOUR COMPETITORS

When we talk corporate strategy, we can't avoid the topic of competitive strategy. Hua and Hua's opinion on competition is that it is an illusion. Your industry peers are pure assumption. This is what we call our theory of non-competition.

What is the theory of non-competition? It's our antidote to the tendency in the business world to put your competitors on a pedestal. When we hear Nokia or Lenovo talk about wanting to beat Apple, they've succumbed to this trap of worshipping their competitor – worshipping Apple.

Never talk about who you want to beat. When you do that, you're telling the world who you're placing on a pedestal. What happens when you put your competitor on a pedestal? First, your competitor will be all you talk about. You end up living a fantasy of constant battle with your competitor. Second, you'll decide what you do based on what they do. You probably don't have just one competitor; you might have ten. If you're acting in response to all ten of them, would you have time to do anything for yourself? Third, you'll end up launching products aimed solely at harrassing your competitor. You see one of their products sell well, so you make something similar and try to sell it at half the price. This is a very shallow understanding of competition. The kind of company that does this will never find their true selves, so they never last.

The theory of non-competition states that the essence of competition is to keep your eye on your customers, not on your competitors.

When you want to ask a girl out, you keep your eye on the girl.

You keep your eye on the girl, not her other admirers. Even if you beat the other admirers in a fight, that's no reason for her to fall in love with you. Not to mention, there are ten or 100 other men trying to win her. Can you fight all of them? No, the entire line of thought is unnecessary. You need to focus on the girl.

In 360's battle with fellow internet company QQ, QQ made the decision to force its users to uninstall 360 products – the equivalent of fighting off the other men and hurting the girl in the process. Naturally, the girl lost interest.

When we talk about competition, it's not about me trying to fight you. It's about me baiting you to fight me.

This is what Laozi said in the *Daodejing*: "Only he who does not fight, will no one under the heaven be able to defeat him."

If Sunflower spends all the resources that it can for years or decades to provide safe pharmaceuticals for China's children and solve their health problems – taking the responsibility seriously, building solid business portfolios and product structures, and establishing the brand's expertise – then no one would ever want to fight it. When other companies realize that they'll have to copy what it does for years or decades, can they even do it?

Competition is an illusion, and industry peers are pure assumption. Keep your eye on your customers, not your competitors. When you're truly focusing on your customer, you won't even care what other companies are doing.

Industry peers are pure assumption. Sunflower was a pharmaceutical company, but once it expanded into the food and cosmetics businesses, its peers changed. Sunflower's peers are not fellow pharmaceutical companies, but fellow children's health companies.

That's why at Hua and Hua, we say that market share is meaningless. It doesn't tell you anything useful. Market share is calculated by assuming a total market, then calculating your own share of that market. It's inherently a self-limiting way of looking at your situation. If you redefine the whole pie, then your slice of it will naturally change. And of course, market share is a results-oriented, not cause-and-effect-oriented, way of thinking.

People have such a narrow view of competition for two reasons: human nature and philosophical roots.

One flaw of human nature is that people only care about who *takes away* and not who *gives*. People always ignore the people who love them, and intensely care about people who hate them.

The philosophy of corporate strategy was developed on the basis of military strategy, so philosophically it was deeply influenced by military thinking. Hua and Hua's own corporate strategy philosophy was influenced by the likes of Sun Tzu, Clausewitz and Jomini.

But there is one essential difference between military and corporate strategy. Military strategy necessarily involves an enemy; there is no enemy in corporate strategy. Military strategy is about fighting for territory in a limited geographical space, while corporate strategy is about creating value in an infinite market space.

The market is not only infinite, it's also multidimensional. Every company can carve out a space for itself. Why do I say that market share is meaningless and industry peers are pure assumption? Because every company can define an industry for itself. Competition is a race, not a fight. There's you and the customer. There are no opponents, no enemies. It's like what the philosopher Mencius said about archery: "When a benevolent man shoots an arrow, he first rights himself then shoots it; if he does not hit the target, he does not protest to those who perform better, but only looks to himself." The customer's heart is the target you're shooting for, and your product is your Cupid's arrow. Shoot when you're confident, but don't blame other people if you miss. Just adjust yourself for your next shot instead of wasting your smarts on interfering with other people.

'When you do not succeed, look to yourself' is a Confucian idea. Sun Tzu had much of the same idea. He emphasized that one must be sure of victor before engaging in battle: "The good fighters of old first put themselves beyond the possibility of defeat, and then waited for an opportunity of defeating the enemy. To secure ourselves against defeat lies in our own hands, but the opportunity of defeating the enemy is provided by the enemy himself. Thus the good fighter is able to secure himself against defeat, but cannot make certain of defeating the enemy. Hence the saying: One may know how to conquer without being able to do it."

You need to make yourself undefeatable, and then wait for the enemy to make himself defeatable – in other words, wait for a mistake. Making yourself undefeatable is entirely within your own control, but the enemy can only make a mistake of his own accord. So the enemy's defeat is due to himself, not due to me. I only received victory. What company has ever failed by being 'beaten'? How can you 'beat' another company? So don't trap yourself by thinking in terms of a fight. You do what you do, and let them do what they do. None of it concerns the other.

We can sum up Hua and Hua's theory of non-competition in two sentences:

First, keep your eye on the customers, not your competitors.

Second, let your social responsibility be your guide; keep your eye on society, not the market.

Behind every business opportunity is a societal problem. Never forget that society is what allows companies to survive. View your business from the perspective of social values, not profits. That is how you can build yourself to last. Thinking about problems from the perspective of what benefits customers and what fulfills your social responsibility is the foundation of success. A narrow view of competition is both unkind and stupid. It is not the way to any kind of success.

Your social responsibility as a company is also the source of your corporate spirit. Companies are spiritual creations. Business is not purely rational, it is also emotional. Emotions can create much more than rational thought. If all of your employees have high ideals regarding society and true love for your customers, then they can truly put themselves in your customers' shoes, think creatively, work diligently while resisting temptation, and honestly work to serve society. This is what will make your company great for society.

That's why any business needs a mission, an emotional rock. This will make every employee's work meaningful, guide every employee in their actions, and give every employee the spiritual power they need.

If you have emotion, then you'll do good. This emotional connection is your company's connection to the air of the greater world.

In Chinese, we say that the biggest influence in your life is destiny, followed by fortune, feng shui, karma and diligent study. The value of a company is given by society. So, the company needs to accumulate good karma and keep learning, on the basis of its destiny, fortune and feng shui.

Destiny is the heavens' plan for you. Destiny is your company's social responsibility and mission. If you don't know your destiny, you'll never run a great business.

You must always be guided by your customers and by society, not by competition. Some say that the customer-oriented era is over, that we're in the competition-oriented era. I say that is simply not the way the righteous would look at things.

CHAPTER 6

CUSTOMERS BUY YOUR PRODUCT FOR THE PRODUCT

THE HUA AND HUA
VIEW ON R&D

Everyone agrees that R&D is important to companies. But what is R&D? The best way to answer that question is to break it down to the *R* and the *D*.

R stands for research. Research is a technology issue. D stands for development. This is a marketing issue.

Does R come before D, or the other way around? Does technological innovation about new products, or product-related creativity, inspire technological innovation?

In our marketing way of thinking, development should come before research. Steve Jobs had the idea for the iPod. He told his technology people: find a way to fit 1,000 songs into a device this big. And they went to Research to find a way to do it.

In fact, if you read a lot of science fiction, you'll find that many 'new' products had already been conceived of 50 years before they were invented.

DEVELOPING A PRODUCT IS
CREATING A REASON TO BUY IT

What is a product? Most conceptions of products focus on function or value. Marketing textbooks use this example: a consumer wants a hole, so they buy a drill. What they really wanted was the hole, not the drill. If there exists a more convenient or cheaper way to get the hole, they might not get the drill. This is what is known as an *alternative* in marketing, as opposed to a competitor. In the example, other drills are competitors. Alternatives are not drills, but rather other ways to get holes.

This might be illuminating, but it's not very useful when applied to real-life business.

Our approach is this: the essence of a product is the *reason to buy it*. The process of developing a product is the process of coming up with a new reason to buy, writing it down, and handing it to technical people to turn it into reality.

Hence the Hua and Hua way: create a new advertisement and packaging, *then* develop the product. Here's an example involving the Keke brand cough drop that we developed for Baiyi Pharmaceutical.

Baiyi's Keke brand was a series of cough medicines. The idea was to develop a cough drop as a fast-moving product that could build up our brand equity. Cough drops are very popular consumer products that sell in huge amounts.

The problem was, there was already an enormous number of cough drop brands. It was a clear example of a red ocean market. With so many existing well-known brands, what reason did consumers have to choose Keke? We needed to create a reason, otherwise there was no point in developing the product.

Hua and Hua did some market research on the user experience for cough drops. What did we discover? We found that people used cough drops because their throats felt funny, and the cooling effect of the cough drop relieved their discomfort. But ten minutes later the cough drop would dissolve and their throats would start itching again. People needed a longer-lasting cough drop, so we set a target at 30 minutes. Thus we came up with a reason to buy: a cough drop that lasts for 30 minutes.

Why 30 minutes? Did our research show that consumers needed a cough drop that lasts exactly 30 minutes? No, we came up with the number ouselves. We'll devote a full chapter later to the topic of market research.

And so we crafted an advertising slogan: 'Keke cough drops. Long-lasting relief for 30 minutes'.

This is a good time to review the ideas we discussed in the chapter on super words: the power of words is stronger than the power of language.

It's not enough to have a *sentence*. It's best to have a word or a phrase, a *name*. The authority of a name is undeniable, far stronger than that of a sentence. So we named our product the Keke 30-Minute Relief Cough Drop.

The next step was to go to the technology people to make the product.

How could we make a cough drop last 30 minutes? There were two ways. Either we could make the cough drop harder so that it dissolved more slowly in the mouth, or we could make it bigger. So now we had a reason to buy and a real product, and the market accepted it.

From the example above, we can see that the essence of a product is the reason to buy it. The reason to buy it could be one sentence or even one word. Developing a product is coming up with a new reason to buy, and then making a product that provides the reason. Or we could say it's coming up with a word and making a product to fit the word.

The word comes before the product.

THE CASE OF M&G STATIONERY

We're not finished with product development yet. Now let's discuss the example of how M&G Stationery, as a pen manufacturer, reconceptualized the pen.

What is a pen? The easy answer is that it's a writing tool.

A *writing tool* is the identity that many pen manufacturers have established for their brand. It's not a wrong idea, exactly, but there's nothing in it to guide their work. There's no method that flows from the concept.

Your concept decides your methods. You need a concept to work in a systemized, meaningful way.

What is a writing tool? When Shakespeare dipped his quill into his inkwell and wrote *Hamlet*, he was holding a *writing tool*. 'Tool' is a stone age term. Once pottery came along, those pots and bowls weren't purely tools anymore – they were crafts.

There was skill behind them. When the fountain pen and the ball-point pen were invented, we entered the era of *writing crafts.*

Nowadays we have people spending thousands of RMB for a Montblanc fountain pen just to display it in their chest pocket. This kind of pen is a *prop* to aid the customer in their performance of their role and class. This brings us back to semiology – consumers use their purchases as a sign to define their own roles.

What about M&G's core product – those colourful pens in little school supply shops, that kids love so much? Those are *toys.* For a lot of children, these are the toys they feel closest to. It's the only kind of toy they can openly spend their allowance on.

M&G pens are not writing tools. They are crafts, props, toys that happen to write.

Based on this conception, M&G positioned itself on *creativity.* The company wanted to make the most creative and fashionable pens in the world. They wanted to be known uniquely as making creative writing implements.

M&G already made fun writing tools. Hua and Hua's core value was to inject them with the power of creative design, so that their product becomes more than a writing tool – it becomes a source of pleasure in and of itself, one that could inspire the user to be more creative.

An M&G pen is a *tool* that offers good value for the money, a *craft* that is made with high precision and reliability, a *prop* that creates value for the user, and a *toy* that is pleasurable and fun to use. This is M&G's positioning and their framework for developing products.

Based on this conceptualization, M&G no longer considered itself part of the manufacturing industry, but part of the creative industry.

Think about your own products. All products and services have overlapping attributes of a tool, a craft, a prop and a toy.

Hua and Hua's super sign approach helps you leverage your product's value as a prop and as a toy.

Every industry is a creative industry. Super signs are super creative.

The *Confucius' Blessing* series of exam pens that Hua and Hua developed for M&G leverages the power of super signs to turn their product into something more than a tool, a craft, a prop, or even a toy. It became a *talisman*.

Here's how. M&G was the first company in the industry to introduce pens specifically for exam use. It was a very successful product line. But there is no exclusivity to the exam pen product category, so other companies followed suit and soon everybody had an exam pen product line. The idea may have helped the industry, but it didn't help M&G.

So how could we leverage the power of super signs through the medium of a pen? Hua and Hua immediately thought of the super sign of learning: Confucius. We created the Confucius' Blessing Exam Pen.

In March 2008, M&G held the M&G Exam Pen Confucius' Blessing Ceremony in the Confucius Temple at Qifu, Confucius' hometown. It reached a licensing deal with the Confucius Temple to use the Confucius' Blessing branding for their exam pens.

This exam pen is more than a tool, a craft, a prop or a toy. It's a talisman that will help you get into a good school! The product caused a sensation in the lead-up to the 2008 university entrance exams. You can still see the news reports if you search for 'Confucius' blessing' (using 360, of course).

The Smile Reception Pen is another bestselling product that Hua and Hua developed for M&G. It was also an appropriation of a super sign that gave it a decisive advantage in the field of reception counter pens.

We see those pens chained to desks and counters everywhere – banks, restaurants, shopping malls, government offices. Now, the people behind the desks – regardless of whether they provide banking services, restaurant services or government services – are all expected to provide 'service with a smile'. So, a lot of people wear a smiley-face button on their chests to symbolize that. That is a super sign.

This is where Hua and Hua's creativity came in. We designed the base the pen goes into after you've used it as a smiley face. This didn't require us to change any of our manufacturing. It didn't add a single cent to our costs. All it took was to change the paint on the base to yellow, and print a smiley face on it. That created unique value.

Of course there was a name to go with it – the Smile Reception Pen.

The development of the Smile Reception Pen required just a few creative changes. There was no industrial design involved. On the other hand, the Meeting Pen that we developed for M&G was a complete process that involved both a new product concept and industrial design.

M&G was planning to introduce fineliner pens. Writing with these pens is lighter, more convenient, faster and more comfortable. You can even easily write on a napkin with one of them. They also provide a more consistent writing experience because of the fiber tip, unlike traditional metal ballpoint tips. Their construction is also much simpler than traditional ballpoint pens, so you don't have to worry about the smudges and unevenness that comes with ball-points. Unfortunately, these advantages also come with drawbacks: you can't refill them, so the pen is a one-time use product.

Hua and Hua named the new product the Meeting Pen based on its features: weight, convenience, speed, comfort. Then the industrial design was completed. Our initial idea was to call it the Journalist's Pen, because that would make its value even clearer: you could write with this pen on any surface – a notebook, a scrap of paper, a napkin – in any position – standing, lying down, sitting, crooked, upright, upside-down. But the journalist customer segment was not nearly as large as that of meeting-goers, so we settled on the Meeting Pen.

DESIGNING PRODUCTS IS DESIGNING A CHOICE FOR CONSUMERS

The purpose of designing a product is to get other people to buy it. A purchase is, in essence, a choice.

Product design is designing a multiple-choice question, or designing a logic behind the choices that the customer can quickly pick up on. That way, you can quickly become the customer's choice.

Hua and Hua developed a series of children's toothpastes for Tianqi that is a classic example of designing a choice. Our design eventually became the industry standard for children's toothpaste in China.

How does a mom choose a toothpaste for her children when she's in the supermarket? Her logic is something that the manufacturer can design. Brands have designed a wide array of choices:

Strawberry flavour.
Orange flavour.
The one with Snoopy.
The one with Snow White.
And so on ...
But Hua and Hua designed a very serious choice for moms, with only two options:
A.   Age 2-5: New Teeth
B.   Age 6-12: Changing Teeth

It was Hua and Hua's original idea to sort children's toothpaste by age: 2-5 for protecting milk teeth, and 6-12 for protecting falling teeth and new teeth. This categorization has become a standard for the children's toothpaste market in China.

A child's first teeth are very fragile, and they need to be well cared for so that the teething process is smooth. If milk teeth get cavities or fall off prematurely, this affects the normal growth of permanent teeth, and even the development of the face and the entire body. Tianqi's New Teeth Toothpaste for ages 2-5 does not contain fluoride and uses food-grade materials, so it can be safely swallowed. The abrasives are only one third the strength of those in adult toothpastes, to avoid damaging new teeth. The low-foam, non-irritating formula is adapted to sensitive young taste buds.

When children are getting their permanent teeth, they have both milk teeth and permanent teeth, with larger gaps in between and thinner enamel that makes it easier for food to get stuck and plaque to accumulate. Plus, children at that age like sweets, so it becomes even easier for them to get cavities. That's why dental health at this age is particularly important – so that they can get healthy permanent teeth. As with the formulation for ages 2-5, Tianqi's Changing Teeth Toothpaste for ages 6-12 does not contain fluoride and uses food-grade materials, so it can be safely swallowed. Similarly, the abrasives are only one third the strength of those in adult toothpastes to avoid damaging just-emerging permanent teeth, and the formula is non-irritating to the gums.

When a mom is facing the serious choice of 'new teeth' and 'changing teeth' that the toothpaste shelf gives her, all of the other options – strawberry flavour, the one with Snoopy – become irrelevant. She'll immediately buy the right toothpaste for her child's age. This is the most important choice. This is also a choice that applies for every potential customer, because all potential users of children's toothpaste fall into either the 2-5 age category or the 6-12 age category.

The most important thing is to make our customers think the way we've designed the thought process, so that range of choices, their train of thought and their conclusions are all exactly as we expected.

Think back to the real estate example we discussed a few chapters ago: 'One Beijing city, four Peacock Cities'. This is also a great example of design choices. We designed a logic behind the choice, and also set out the range of choices. This design also determined our product development: a series of projects all around Beijing.

The essence of a product is the reason to buy it. Developing a product is creating a marketing campaign.

Every industry is a creative industry. We can develop creative new products for any industry.

For old products, the marketing and creative team's task is a product re-development task. What are we re-developing? The reason to buy, and the way to efficiently communicate that reason.

CHAPTER 7

BUILDING YOUR BRAND
– A ONE-TASK APPROACH

MARKET RESEARCH IS FOR REFERENCE AND INSPIRATION, NOT PROOF

What is the purpose of market research? For reference in your decision-making, and for inspiration in your creative process. Market research is for reference and inspiration, not for proving your ideas.

A lot of people think of research as proof. The Hua and Hua method is at odds with this. Research does not constitute proof.

Why? Because research can never provide more than an incomplete picture. Research is by nature unreliable. In particular, statistics provided through research are often answers to the wrong questions.

Who would ever make their decisions based on just one research report? If a research report were all it took to ensure high-quality decision-making, then management would truly be a science rather than art. In a world where management is a science, anyone would get the same result as long as they used scientific methods and formulas. The owners of market research firms would be the richest people in the world.

But in the real world, the greatest influence on a decision-maker is often a sudden inspiration that came from knowing one person, having one conversation, reading one article, or having one thing happen. These seemingly random strokes of inspiration can drive immensely important decisions and creativity.

This chapter will give you a systematic way to find these flashes of inspiration.

RESEARCH IS ABOUT THE CUSTOMER'S STORY: WHEN, WHERE, WHAT, HOW

The least valuable part of a market research project is the report you get at the end of it. There's nothing you can get out of a report; it's just an interpretation from whoever wrote it. If you never visit the real-world environment where your customers are, if you don't get into the habit of going there whenever you can, then you'll never be a successful business person.

A research report doesn't have the *context* of the customer envirnment. All the most important secrets can only be found on-location. If you don't experience the context yourself – the store environment, the display shelves, customer behaviour, the purchase process, the user experience, what customers do with the product after they use it and how they describe it to other people – then what you get from reading the report will be 10% superficial and 90% misleading.

The owner of the budget airline Ryanair would never use market research firms or read their reports, but he would take four Ryanair flights a week so that he could interact directly with customers. The clothing retailer Zara's president would call eight of his store managers first thing every week and ask them what was happening in their stores. Toyota's executives spend several days a year at a dealership, not for chitchat with low-level employees but to observe the customers and the purchase process. The Super-Pharm drugstore chain's location in Guiyang in southwestern China once worked with the chain's Israeli headquarters to improve its performance. The Israeli Super-Pharm's senior executive came to Guiyang and spent 12 hours in a store on his first day, from opening to closing. He never left, not even for lunch; he ate a burger at the store. He wanted to see with his own eyes what happened in the store every minute of those 12 hours.

The key to research is understanding the story of a successful transaction. The elements of the story include who, when, where, what happened and how they felt about it. All of these elements must be familiar to you, because developing your products and your marketing is writing the script to this story. If you have no story, only numbers, then you will have nothing.

Not to mention, most numbers are actually wrong.

TRUE WISDOM LIES IN HISTORY: RESEARCH THE HISTORY OF YOUR FIELD

All fields of study are studies of history. The academic knowledge that we have today represents the history of their respective disciplines, whether it's math or physics. In business, as well, each industry builds its present on its past. The wisdom, experience and learning of each generation of the industry is contained in its history. That's why we need to understand the history of each industry we are involved in – definitely its history in China, and preferably its history around the world as well.

In most cases, the wisdom contained in your industry's history is all you need. Generation after generation of your forebears have devoted so much of their minds to making your industry run better. Why not use the wisdom they left behind?

For example, suppose you're creating a commercial for cold medicine. All of the cold medicine commercials from every country in the world, in every era, would provide decades of creative inspiration for you.

Steve Jobs liked to say that good artists copy and great artists steal. The great advertising genius David Ogilvy also said to search the world and steal the best creativity.

Don't think that stealing makes everything easy. There are two key skills in stealing. First, you need to know what to steal.

History is like a boundless ocean, and you need to know what is useful to you. You need to steal the things that fit your industry, not things that won awards for being 'creative'. Second, you need to steal from the people who are at your level. You might be using the same running technique as Usain Bolt, but you need to be as fast as he is for it to be 'stealing'. If you're not, then you're just a pale imitation.

The more material you have from history, the more creative you'll be.

Next, you'll want to zoom in on one piece of history: your industry's market competition history in your domestic market over the past ten years.

By market competition history, I'm referring to what the market's brands did and how they did it. Who grew and who declined. Compare what each brand did and how the market changed.

What happened in the market in 2012? In 2009? In 2006? Lay out the growth and decline of every brand on the market throughout the years. Look closely at this information.

Be particularly detailed when it comes to the key points on this timeline. Compare your advertising to your competitors' advertising. What did your commercials look like in 2008; how about your competitors' spots? How did the market react? Go into detail. It's fine if this takes you three or four months. Just dig deep so you can produce something truly comprehensive. That's the right approach to things. These are all things that Hua and Hua has done on behalf of its clients, through interviews with industry people.

This approach allows you to easily find information that is valuable to you. Of course, it's only 'easy' if you have good judgment.

My experience is that a good strategy can last 50 years.

It's guaranteed that somebody in your industry has used a 50-year strategy sometime over the past decade.

Of course, the company that used the strategy probably didn't stick by it. They probably stopped after three years or so. It's a lot easier to find the right way than to stick to it!

Plot a new course and follow the path to success your competitor gave up on.

This is important, so I'll say it again: I guarantee you that some-one else had already taken the right way. But it's a lot easier to find the right way than to stick to it.

Companies often feel the urge to change direction just because there's someone new at the top. Like wild animals, people always feel the need to rub on a new tree with their own scent.

When you're first embarking on the right strategic path, improvement feels fast and easy. It's only after half a year, or two years, that things inevitably slow down. But when the people in charge get used to rapid improvement, the slower pace will irri-tate them. They start thinking that maybe doing something else, maybe going in a new direction, could bring back the amazing improvement that they'd grown accustomed to. And so they give up the path that could have taken them to prosperity. In fact there is no better path. The right path is to slowly accumulate longer-term qualitative changes in the face of quantitative changes. You need to remain committed to win your final victory. Very few peo-ple have this insight, so pearls of wisdom are scattered across the history of every industry, unnoticed. Your goal is to find them.

Your dedication to strategy is like romantic love. When you meet the one, it could be love at first sight. You're swept off your feet and nothing in the world matters. But then the passion fades and your life returns to calmness. This calmness is what real love needs to crystallize into happiness that could last for a lifetime. But some people mistake the fading of passion for the fading of love, and they end up divorcing to seek that thrill of 'love at first sight' again.

What people often don't realize is that there is no one else. People forget that divorces are not free; they could take away half their money. Two divorces could leave them with a fourth of what they used to have.

Lost treasures are the most valuable ones of all. Researching your industry's history is going on a hunt for the treasures that have been forgotten.

RESEARCH REQUIRES TALKING TO FRONTLINE SALESPEOPLE

When you're doing research, you need to go in person. Don't just send a questionnaire. Go to the frontlines and talk to your store clerks and salespeople. No research tool is as valuable as a conversation, so you make sure you delve deep.

Don't ask salespeople 'scientific' questions. Ask them regular, plain-language questions. In fact, this applies to any question you ask anybody.

For example, don't ask questions like: What's the gender ratio of our customers? What is their age spread? What is the ratio for each age segment? What are their professional demographics? What would you say is their average monthly income? These are questions you need to answer through statistical analysis, not questions that your salespeople should be expected to answer.

Don't ask questions that require a whole thought process behind them. Ask questions like:

How many customers came in today?

How much product was sold?

What was the first customer like? The second? The third?

What did the customer ask you? What was your answer?

Ask specific questions about the store experience of every single customer.

Ask about specific, concrete occurences and processes. The judgment and analysis is your job. Don't expect your salespeople to do those surveys for you.

CREATIVITY LIES IN THE STORE: OBSERVE THE ENTIRE BUYING PROCESS

When you're visiting frontline locations to do market research, it's better to spend one day at the location closest to your office than an extended tour of every location. Customers are the same across the country, and in fact around the world. If you want to understand them, you need to look deeply, staying in one place.

Once you've talked to the salespeople at one store, try staying for two hours and just watching.

You might be watching how customers buy toothpaste in a supermarket. When you look at people approaching the toothpaste aisle, you might see something like this: One customer approaches with a cart, browsing the toothpaste brands on the shelf. They stop and focus for a moment on one box in particular. They start walking again, then stop, pick up a box, look at it, then put it back down. They pick up another box, look at it, read the copy on the back, and put it back. They walk two steps, go back to the very first box of toothpaste they looked at, read the copy on the back, and put it back. Then they go to the box of toothpaste they picked up second, put it in their cart, and their decision-making process is over.

Or is it? They might come back a few minutes later, put the toothpaste in their cart back on the shelf, and take the first box of toothpaste they looked at instead. Or they might take both so they can try more options.

Now you've seen the entire decision-making process for buying toothpaste: seven steps! Now you can approach them and offer a small gift in exchange for an interview: "May I talk to you for a few minutes about your choice of toothpaste?" And you can walk them through those seven steps they had just taken, asking them what went through their minds at every step.

If you can have this kind of interview with just three customers, you'll learn more than from a whirlwind tour across the country. Just one day of this kind of research will teach you more than three years at a bad company.

Once you've observed ten people to this level of detail, you'll know how long it takes for a customer to decide which toothpaste to buy and what factors influence their decision. Your product development and packaging design needs to focus on choreographing this entire process, like staging a play.

These specific stories and specific details are the biggest influence in your decision-making.

How do business people make decisions? What is the basis for their crucial strategic choices? Not reading reports. But just one sentence that somebody once said to them could change their entire life.

The purpose of research is to find these specific small things that could swing a decision. Nobody ever wishes they had more reports to read. What they really need is creativity. Creativity is what ultimately solves our problems.

CONSUMER BEHAVIOUR IS THE KEY TO RESEARCH

What are we really looking at in our retail store observations and interviews? The answer is consumer behaviour.

How can we comprehensively study consumer behaviour? The most effective way is through a focus group. A group of maybe eight people is brought together, with one moderator who employes techniques bordering on hypnosis to help them explore their viewpoints and actions.

This method is commonly used, but also commonly misused. If the questions are poorly designed, or the moderator is bad at their job, then the focus group will be ineffective.

Here are some of Hua and Hua's keys to conducting a successful focus group.

(1) QUESTIONS ON INFORMATION SOURCES

Most market research questionnaires ask about the customer's information sources right at the top: "How did you find out about our brand?" In my opinion, this question is not worth asking. It's not a meaningful question. And I can tell you right now that at least 50% found out through their friends.

A lot of market research companies like to ask this about information sources: "What information source do you trust the most?" Most of these reports show that the most trusted information source is family and friends, while TV commercials rank near the bottom.

What is the point of this kind of research? A young mother might confidently assert that she doesn't trust TV advertising when she's answering a market research questionnaire. But when her child gets an awful cough and she rushes to the pharmacy, she'll see the packaging for the children's lung fever coughing and wheezing syrup, remember the commercial she saw on TV, and buy it without even hesitating. Why? When you asked her if she *trusted* TV advertising, she would never have said 'yes'. That sounds too thoughtless. She's only heard the commercial talk about the product, and she's never tried it herself, so she can't say she believes the commercial. But she's willing to *try*. So why ask her if she trusts the commercial? Isn't that an impossible question?

It's very strange how everyone is obsessed with the two types of questions we discussed above. There are even research companies that issue 'reports' that purport to rank 20 information sources by trustworthiness, reports that people read and circulate as serious business. I have no idea what anyone learns from these reports. How do they help you in your work? Are you going to allocate your ad buys based on a ranking like this?

(1) Recommendation from friends (2) Online reviews (3) Editorial content (newspaper articles, etc.) (4) Official brand websites (5) Subscribed mailings (6) TV commercials (7) Sponsorships

(8) Magazine advertising (9) Outdoor advertising (10) Newspaper advertising (11) Radio advertising (12) Cinema pre-show commercials (13) TV product placement (14) Search engine advertising (15) Online video advertising (16) Social media advertising ...

This kind of research is pure pseudoscience. It's easy to imagine the research method: design a questionnaire listing all the different sources, ask respondents to rank them, and then collect and calculate the results. What's the point?

(2) QUESTIONS ON EXISTING COMMUNICATION BEHAVIOUR AMONG CUSTOMERS

We discussed previously how when researchers ask "How did you find out about our brand?" what they really want to know is the sources that customers receive brand information from – what percentage is from television, what percentage from the internet, and so on. And as we said, there isn't much point in answering this question.

But when this question inevitably yields the answer 'recommendations from friends', there is one golden opportunity to ask a follow-up question that most researchers miss: How did your friend recommend it?

The Hua and Hua way emphasizes *propagation* over communication. Spreading information is not just about the company communicating to customers, but also about getting customers to propagate the information for us. A slogan is not just something the company says to audience, but also something that the audience can repeat to other people.

By asking focus group participants how their friends recommended the product, you can gain a greater understanding of what you are in customers' eyes and find out why customers buy your product. You can also find out the unfiltered version of what customers say about your product. A lot of the time the things customers say can become a slogan itself. Use the power of propagation!

After you've asked about how their friends recommended your product, you can also ask: "Have you ever recommended our brand to a friend? What did you tell them?"

If the answer is that they haven't, you should just drop it. Don't ask: "What would you tell them if you did?" Don't try to get the participant to come up with something on the spot. Our goal is to find out what is *actually* happening in the market, not ask the customer to do our creative work.

(3) QUESTIONS ON CONSUMER KNOWLEDGE AND THINKING

Perception shapes action. The point of this section is to learn about the subjects of your research: their knowledge and experiences as consumers, and the perceptions they have formed based on such knowledge and experiences. By knowledge, I'm referring to what the customer knows about the product category; and by thinking, I'm referring to the criteria they use to evaluate the products. We often say that facts don't matter, the customer's perception does. That's because the perception is the basis for your communication with that customer.

Let's say you're doing market research for a pill for stomach problems. What does the customer know about stomach pills? What do they know about stomach illnesses? There are three categories of knowledge that your customer needs: about stomach illness, about stomach pills, and about the lifestyle of patients with stomach problems. The last category includes the lifestyle choices that can cause stomach illness and the lifestyle changes that patients need to make to alleviate those ailments. These all fall under consumer knowledge.

When you're trying to find out what your customer knows about stomach illness, you need to first understand what their problem is, what symptoms they're experiencing and listen to how they describe it. Then ask what exactly their illness is – for example, gastritis or ulcers. You'll find that a lot of people have no idea how to answer that. Why do pharmaceutical commercials talk about symptoms and not diagnoses? Because everybody knows what symptoms they're suffering, but a lot of people have no idea about what disease they actually have.

(4) DON'T ASK QUESTIONS THAT REQUIRE
THINKING OR ANALYSIS

Of course you want to know why customers buy your products. A major problem for many companies is that they don't know why customers choose to buy from them, so it's natural to want to ask: "Why do you choose our company's products?"

Is this the right question to ask? No, it is not.

Why is it the wrong question to ask? Because you're passing the buck to your customer. Why customers buy your products is something for *you* to find out, not something for your customers to analyze. And when you ask the customer this question, they start analyzing away.

This is what you should ask them: When was the first time you bought the Sunflower stomach medicine? What happened to make you buy it? Where did you buy it? Did you consider any other brand of stomach medicine? Did the store clerk say anything to you? How many bottles did you buy, and why? How did you feel after taking it? How long did you take it? How many times did you buy more afterwards? Did you keep using Sunflower only, or did you buy other brands as well? What happened to make you buy another brand?

The key is to have the customer recount their experiences, not offer a summary.

(5) QUESTIONS ABOUT HOW CUSTOMERS
USE YOUR PRODUCTS

Finding out how customers use your products is immensely valuable for both your product development and your advertising strategy. When Hua and Hua designed the packaging of Zhenshiming eye drops as an eye chart, we were making the package part of how the customer used the product.

One common problem with pharmaceutical products is that customers often take them only when they're experiencing symptoms. They stop taking the medicine when the symptoms go away, or they just forget to take the pills even though – as with antibiotics, for instance – they know they need to finish the course of treatment. Of course, this is a problem for pharmaceutical sales as well.

Some pharmaceutical companies, attentive to customer behaviour, began educating consumers to finish their course of treatment in their advertising. This strategy proved effective, but as pharmaceutical advertising regulations became stricter, the Chinese government prohibited advertisements from mentioning how long to take the drug unless the course of treatment was explicitly mentioned in the usage instructions. So this type of advertising vanished, with one exception – the antifungal ointment Dakening, which told customers to "continue using for seven days after symptoms disappear." This set Dakening apart from its peers.

FOUR MAJOR TRAPS IN RESEARCH

People often talk about the importance of market research while ignoring the problems with so many studies. Top-level design is sorely missing from many studies, whether in their approaches, methods or the actual surveys sent out. Decision-makers base their decisions on research without participating in conducting the research themselves, or putting real effort into designing the studies. Here we'll discuss four common traps that render research useless.

First, bad survey questions.

Research is about asking questions. But questions are subjective and open to misinterpretation. Research subjects respond to their own subjective and possibly misinterpreted reading of a question, and give an answer that is subjective and open to misinterpretation itself. The researcher then puts down a subjective and possibly misinterpreted reading of the answer as the result. Research is like a game of telephone; you never know what will come out at the end of the line.

In addition, questions are a major headache in and of themselves.

Now let's talk about one very common form of question, the 'why did you buy our product' question. Most people (including research firms) are obsessed with *why*. They think that if they keep asking 'why' they will eventually get the answer. Remember the 'why' questions we're all asked at school? "Why do you study?" "Why do you help your classmates?" "Why didn't you hand in your homework?" "Why were you mean to that girl?" Children might answer something like this: "I study so I can help China become stronger." "Because the five disciplines and four graces say so." "Because I had a stomach ache last night." "I didn't do it on purpose." But the real answers may very well be: "I don't actually want to study." "Because he gave me some candy last week." "Because I was out playing too late." "Because she didn't let me copy her answers last time."

Why do you get completely unbelievable answers when you ask 'why'?

First of all, in most situations people will only give answers that show themselves in a positive light or are socially acceptable, hiding the real answers that reflect badly on themselves or are socially unacceptable. People never freely talk about their true motivations. This kind of 'lying' happens all the time in research.

Second, when you try to understand a respondent's motivations by asking them 'why', you're really asking them to think back to their *memory* of what motivated them. Memories are often inaccurate and sometimes flat-out wrong.

Third, people's motivations are not always conscious. People might not even be aware of their motivations, so naturally they wouldn't be able to talk about them. How can you expect to gain a deep understanding of people's true reasons just by asking 'why'?

Research should primarily be based on observation. Observation always comes first. That's why we stress the importance of in-store observation far more than surveys.

The second trap is letting quantitative data obscure thought processes.

Customer thought processes can be discovered only through communication. A thought process is living and dynamic, but many studies turn it into a few cold, dead numbers. If you're only looking for trees, how would you ever see the forest?

Once again, we have to emphasize the importance of in-person observation. Observation allows you to see the entire process for yourself. We also emphasize qualitative research through in-depth interviews. Comparing what people say in interviews with what they do in your observations allows you to truly understand the customer's story.

The third trap is that many studies fail to consider how regular people would understand survey questions. Most surveys are poorly designed.

For an example, let's look at two studies on societal attitudes that gained widespread attention in China in 2013.

One was the *2012 Survey of Educational Equity Attitudes in China's Major Cities*. Media reports focused on the statistic that 24.3% of the public did not agree that 'education can change lives'. There was much hand-wringing over this assertion.

Let's take a step back and think about how the survey questions were designed. It was probably something like this:

Do you believe that education can change lives? (A) Yes (B) No (C) Not sure.

Which one would you choose? Changing lives is an awfully big thing to do. A lot of people would probably say they can't be sure.

Companies often ask similarly silly questions in their market research. Let's take a small variation on the above question:

Do you trust television commercials? (A) Yes (B) No (C) Not sure.

How many people would you expect to choose (A)? Why would they? But a lot of companies ask stupid questions like this.

Think back to a Hua and Hua slogan – 180 days of brewing is what gives Chubang Soy Sauce its great flavour! Suppose I'm feeling indecisive, so I decide to commission a 'consumer attitude study'. I pass out surveys in a few major cities asking:

Do you believe this? "180 days of brewing is what gives Chubang Soy Sauce its great flavour!" (A) Yes (B) No (C) Not sure.

Why would anyone believe you? They don't even know who you are. Imagine walking down the street and being stopped by a stranger, who recites an advertising slogan and asks if you believe it. There's no way you would say yes! Saying yes means that you trust this stranger who just stopped you on the street. Would you trust him? No, and certainly not anything he says. Will you still use the slogan when the report is sent to the company president showing that 80% of customers responded 'No'? But consider if we asked a different question:

180 days of brewing is what gives Chubang Soy Sauce its great flavour. Will you buy Chubang Soy Sauce? (A) Yes (B) No (C) Not sure.

Now there's nothing about believing or not believing. "180 days of brewing is what gives Chubang Soy Sauce its great flavour!" becomes a given. So why wouldn't the customer want to buy it? Most customers will choose (A).

You might ask: so what kind of research can show us whether the "180 days of brewing is what gives Chubang Soy Sauce its great flavour!" slogan is a good one?

The answer is that you don't need to do any kind of research. If you can't even make this kind of judgment, you shouldn't be running a company.

The question decides the answer. A lot of 'research' doesn't actually need any field work. Once you see the question, you know the answer.

A friend once told me that studies over nine years have shown that Chinese consumers do not believe in health supplements. When I heard that, I immediately knew how the survey was designed. The key question was almost certainly: "Do you believe that health supplements have positive effects?" You can ask the same question for the next 99 years, and people will still answer no. *Believing* is a very serious thing. But people don't need to believe you to buy your product. If they're interested in what you're promising, they'll be willing to give it a try. *Believing* comes after they try it, so why ask if they believe? If you ask women if they trust their husbands, very few of them will say with 100% certainty that they do. If people can't even fully trust their significant other, why ask them to trust you? The question of trust or belief is a false one.

Countless research reports assert that consumers believe that quality is the most important factor in their decisions – that the effectiveness of a drug is the most important factor – but that advertising is the least important factor. These studies are completely meaningless.

At the beginning of this chapter, we said not to use research results as evidence. Sure enough, some people look at how consumers respond to questions like this, see that people rank '(G) Advertising' toward the bottom, and say that advertising is useless because it is not important to consumers.

The option 'Price' is also a mistake. Price is a prerequisite, not a factor that can be ranked. Customers choose which product to purchase based on a certain budget. The price factor supersedes all other factors, but when you ask customers to rank its importance, they are certain to rank it toward the bottom.

I've encountered a very interesting survey myself.

Eight of us ate at a Hunanese restaurant one time. The food was great, the portions were satisfying and the bill was only 180 yuan a person. Great value.

The waiter gave us a customer survey to fill out. One of the questions was: Did you find the price of your meal: (A) Too high (B) Just right (C) Too low.

The person in our party who filled out the survey was not feeling charitable that night – or perhaps he didn't even have time to think about being charitable before he unconsciously checked off: Too high!

I wondered if the restaurant owner would actually lower the prices when they saw the survey results all saying that the food was too expensive.

Let me say a little more about price surveys. My advice is not to do them. These surveys will only mislead you. They are all downside and no upside.

We see a lot of survey proposals that describe a product and then ask: "How much will you be willing to pay for a product like this?"

I can say with utmost certainty that no one knows how much they are willing to pay for a product. Only with a specific price, in a specific sales context, can a customer know if they're willing to pay. In different contexts, they'll be willing to pay different amounts. They'll be willing to pay different amounts for the same product in the same store if they're shelved in different aisles. And different customers are again different in how much they're willing to pay.

This is the fourth trap of research – confusing the company's responsibility with the consumer's responsibility. That is, forgetting what a company is all about.

The responsibility of making decisions and doing creative work lies with the company, not with the consumer. But many consumer surveys are no longer about *studying* the consumer, they've become about *consulting* with the consumer. This is particularly common with surveys about creative work.

Marketers will say: What we think is not important. What the consumer thinks is important. So ask consumers what they think about this creative execution. This is pure nonsense. It is the decision-maker's responsibility to choose a good creative approach. This is not a question to ask the consumer.

Roles are a major part of research. When you ask the consumer a question, you are asking them to play a role.

Do not ask the consumer to play the role of a decision-maker. When you do that, the consumer is no longer a consumer, they are a decision-maker. Do you really want the consumer making your decisions? Of course not, but a lot of business people do this nonetheless.

Maybe they're faced with a brand image design, a packaging design, or an advertisement proof. They can't make a decision, so they decide to do a consumer survey and let consumers make the choice. They even make it a vote! Or maybe it's too much work to actually go to the consumers. And so, they distribute the survey to 200 low-level employees who are in some way thought to represent the consumers.

If this were all it took to make the right decision and avoid risk in decision-making, then any idiot could be the boss.

"Do you think this is a good advertisement?" "Which packaging do you prefer?" When you 'test' your creative output by asking this kind of idiotic question, you are demanding that consumers to play the role of the decision-maker. Now the consumer becomes your creative director and marketing director. This one's good, that one's good, I hate the other one.

Research firms have even designed more 'scientific' questions so that we can gain a more 'scientific' understanding of what consumers think about our creative work. Now consumers are asked to rate how much they agree with a series of statements on a five-point scale:

This advertisement is easy to understand.
This ad is convincing.
This ad is about a product that fits my needs.
This ad introduces new information.
This ad conveys the differences from other products.
This ad is believable about the product it advertises.
This ad makes the product more attractive to me.

And finally, the points are totaled up and the highest-rated creative work is identified. This kind of 'scientific' research is pure absurdity.

Too much of the 'science' we see out there is foolish witchcraft that the stupid wield against the wise. Science is now a religion, and research a mysterious rite. This is something we all need to look out for.

What is the problem with research on creative work? First, the survey should never ask which creative treatment the consumer prefers. It should not even use the word 'creative' because it is a cue to abandon the consumer role for the decision-maker role. A lot of people ask "Do you like this advertisement?" right off the bat. But this question has nothing to do with what you need.

So what should we ask?

The Hua and Hua way is to ask four questions:

1. What company is this?
2. What do they want you to do?
3. Will you do what they say?
4. Why or why not?

Once you've learned to ask these questions, you'll discover that the first question alone is a key test. A lot of creative work that you feel very pleased about will fail right out of the gate, because the audience doesn't even know who you are. But they might say they like it a lot – perhaps simply as an entertainment – if that's what you ask.

Learn to ask these questions and you'll come to understand why the advertising you look down on is so successful. Those advertisements make the answers to all four questions as clear as can be.

RESEARCH IS PLANNING

Research is part of planning, not an individual task. As we said when we discussed military strategy, camping and marching are all part of battle, not a break from it or preparation for it. In fact, marching is the most important part of battle. If you don't realize this, then you know nothing about camping, marching or war.

There is no such thing as objective research. All research is subjective.

You start with an assumption or a projection before you do your research. Research helps validate your assumption. It is not a task you randomly assign: "Go do some research and get a report out of it!"

Research is like scouting in war. Napoleon's scouts were different from those of every other army. Napoleon thought through every possibility on the part of both his side and the enemy's side, and made in-depth plans for the battle. And so, when he sent out scouts, they didn't disperse in random directions to find information; they went to specific places to prove or disprove his assumptions.

Napoleon's scouts weren't for discovering where the enemy was, but for discovering what the enemy intended.

RESEARCH NEVER STOPS

Clausewitz said that strategy is a task that never stops. The same applies to research.

Painters say that they are mentally sketching all the time when they take in stunning mountain landscapes. With every peak, every river, every flower, every blade of grass they look at, they are sketching in their minds for their future work.

A military strategist in ancient China knew he wanted to be a strategist from his youth. So he travelled across the country, taking note everywhere he went of good places for camps and ambush attacks. When war came, he knew the land by heart.

The calligrapher friend who created the stylized 'Hua and Hua' used by our company once visited the Shanghai Museum with me. He would stop in front of every work of calligraphy and write in the air in front of him – practicing how he would write the characters. When he talks to me, he's also writing in the air all the time – he does it whenever he is struck by inspiration.

The children's pharmaceutical strategy we proposed for Sunflower in 2007 actually originated from a brief newspaper article I read in Shenzhen in 1999, discussing the problem of dosage for children's medicine in China. Once I read the article, I wanted an opportunity to create a children's pharmaceutical brand in China. The opportunity didn't come until we began working with Sunflower.

The most valuable research is life.

CHAPTER 8

A METHODOLOGY FOR RESEARCH – ALL RESEARCH MUST BE ON-SITE

In previous chapters we discussed corporate strategy, branding, product development, advertising and market research. What we haven't discussed yet is the customer.

The Hua and Hua way starts at the end: every step is determined by what we want to happen next. Marketing is a very late step in our process, so we use the theories of communication and semiotics to devise an entire system that encompasses corporate strategy, product development and brand marketing.

Although we say that marketing is a late step, it is not the last step. The last step is the purchase. Everything is ultimately decided by the customer. Every customer votes with their wallet and this determines whether a company can survive. The customer's purchase decision determines whether a brand prospers and if products sell. That's why everything a company does is for the customer. Everything ends with the customer. Because we start with the end, everything that we do in marketing must start with the customer.

Everything in this book centres on a method that starts with the end. In Chinese, we say that we're *tracing the vine from the fruit*. The fruit is the consumer, and the vine is our marketing creativity. So let's talk about the customer.

ALL MARKETING CREATIVITY MUST START WITH THE CUSTOMER CONTEXT

'We're thinking from the customer's perspective' is something that everyone in marketing thinks about themselves, but in truth very few people think about what the 'customer's perspective' really means.

People talk about 'the customer' all the time. Everything they talk about is peppered with 'the customer' and 'thinking about the customer'. In creative meetings, people say: 'From the customer's perspective', or 'As a customer, I think ...'.

What these people are really doing is erecting a strawman and labelling it *the customer*. But the tendency is then for everyone in the room to start treating the strawman as reality. They start nodding: "That's right. What would the customer think?" But the truth is, you're not the customer. When you're trying to sell something, you can never be the customer.

When you're reading this book, you are a customer of ours, the authors. But when you're applying what you just read to your marketing activities, you are not a consumer – you are a business person.

So even when you start a sentence with, 'From the perspective of the customer' your perspective, language and context are still those of the company. Seeing things from the consumer's viewpoint is in truth a highly specialized skill. This means that, when we use the word 'customer', we need to place everything we're discussing in the context, the scenario, the situation, the information environment of the customer.

LANGUAGE GAMES AND WORD RULES

Wittgenstein said that the creation of language is making up the rules as one goes along, and using language is changing the rules as one goes along.

Sometimes it's necessary to temporarily remove a certain word from language for a little 'washing' before it becomes useful again. So now let's do that with the word 'customer'. When you're looking at things from the customer's perspective, you're placing yourself in the customer's context and taking on the customer's role.

The Hua and Hua way that we've talked about in this book is a method that uses signs and language. By leading you into the customer's context and simulating a purchase scenario, we help you design your corporate strategy, product development and marketing creativity.

Are you ready? Now let's start our role-playing exercise. The customer has four roles, corresponding to the four steps of the purchase, each with a different context: different times, places, information, reactions, purposes, methods, activities, etc.

The four contexts are:

1. Before the purchase. = AUDIENCE
2. During the purchase. = INFO GATHER/DECIDER
3. Using the product.
4. After using the product.

Before the purchase: The customer has not yet arrived at the place of purchase. They are not at the store or browsing a shopping website. The product is still on the shelf or in the warehouse. Although the customer has not yet bought the product, they have likely heard about it through advertising or word-of-mouth and made a mental note of it. Remember these three situations: they saw or heard an advertisement; they heard someone talk about it; or they saw the product itself. These three situations correspond to three things you can do.

During the purchase: The customer is at the place of purchase. They are in the store or on a shopping website. They are browsing, observing, experiencing.

Using the product: The customer has possession of the product and is actually utilizing it.

After using the product: The customer has used the product and may share their experiences or opinions with their family, friends, neighbours and work colleagues.

Now let's break down each of these four phases, as there are marketing opportunities and tools at every step of the way.

THE CUSTOMER'S
FIRST ROLE: AUDIENCE

What are customers before they buy anything? They are members of an *audience*. Before they buy, customers engage with the product though a variety of media: television, newspapers, subway billboards, fliers, internet ads, word-of-mouth from family, friends, neighbours and co-workers. When customers engage with products through media, they do so as members of an audience. So how do we study audiences? What kind of characteristics do they have?

The key is to remember two words: audiences are *inattentive* and *forgetful*.

The most essential characteristic of any audience is that they are not paying attention. You might be shouting at the top of your lungs, you might be using every sweet-talking trick in the book, but they'll still be inattentive. You need to remember that when you communicate through media, you are communicating with people who are going about their daily lives, distracted and paying zero attention. They might be on the toilet. They might be doing their homework. They might be talking to their kids. Any other thing they might be doing is more important than what you have to say. Any other piece of information is more important. A gust of wind that blows away a few leaves might be more important. It's difficult under these circumstances to talk to the customer and make them want to give you money. *Extremely difficult.*

That's why you need to make the customer snap to attention so that their focus is on you. You don't want them to care any more about what floor the elevator is on, when the next train is coming, whether the bus has arrived, what the headline in the newspaper is. You need to make the customer ignore all of that and pay attention to you. This is the first thing you need to do. If you don't succeed, you'll be ignored. All the advertising you bought will be junk. You need to get the audience to pay attention. Getting the audience's attention is the first key to communication.

How do you do this? First you need to *stimulate* the audience to get a reaction. What kind of stimulus is most effective? One that triggers instinct. The most efficient kind of communication is the kind that can trigger instinctive reactions in the audience. So you need to let the audience discover from the very first second that what you're saying is relevant to them. This is the most important and most effective point. You need to find the word that triggers an instinctual reaction and choose that word.

For instance, if the product is a stomach pill, you absolutely need to shout the words 'stomach-ache', 'heartburn', 'gas' as early as you can. People with these problems will have the instinctive reaction to listen, because these symptoms are more important to them than anything. Anybody who has had minor but recurring symptoms like these will know that a pain in the gut could become the worst thing in the world. In the long run they would look for anything to solve the problem.

Imagine a completely inattentive audience, maybe a crowd on a busy street. They are walking around, paying no attention to anything. You need to get a few people's attention. You don't know who they are, you don't know anyone's name. All you know is one thing – you're selling stomach pills. What's the first thing you'll shout into the crowd? "Do you have stomach problems? I've got just the medicine for you!" Is there any other choice?

Here's another example of triggering instinctive reactions. If you've seen the real estate advertisements in the airlines' in-flight magazines, you'll know that most of them never make it clear exactly *where* these development projects are. You need to read the tiny fine print to find that information. I've never understood the point of this kind of ad. If the audience doesn't see the name of the city, there will be no instinctive reaction. Surely seeing the name of the location might trigger a reaction: "I'm interested in buying in that location, it's possible, it's in my plans." Or maybe it's in another location, and there's another reaction: "Hmm, I'm not looking to buy there. It's a thousand miles from where I want to live." But if there's no city named, then there's no reaction, no attention.

The page is turned without leaving any impression. The audience wouldn't look at your advertising in-depth because so many more important things are going on around them. The flight attendant might be coming along. The plane might hit turbulence.

If you want the audience to react, it's important to make them feel that what you're advertising is highly relevant to them. In our chapter on super language, we talked about Wang Fuzhi's concept of *xianliang*, or 'direct perception'. In fact, Wang got this concept from the Yogacara school of Buddhist philosophy, which draws a distinction between 'direct perception', 'inference' and 'non-perception'. This is actually a perfect framework we can use to discuss what goes on with audiences.

Let's go back to our busy street. There are all kinds of people in the crowd: men and women, old and young, a variety of sizes and races. You see them all very clearly, but none of them triggers a reaction in you or leaves an impression. They all pass you by. This is direct perception: inattentiveness. When your audience flips through a magazine and sees all the ads, they see every page clearly but there is no reaction. The pages just pass in front of their eyes.

Additionally, the problem we see in a lot of advertising is that it makes assumptions about the non-perception level. These advertisers think they can use the audience's imagination without ever triggering their direct perception. When the audience has no reaction to what you're saying, when they're not finding anything unique about you, the non-perception part would never work. You will be just as insignificant as all the other million details that are part of their direct perception. This is why you need to develop brand association.

In addition to being inattentive, audiences are forgetful. You worked so hard to get their attention, but then they turn around and forget everything. They're back to inattention. How do you get them to remember you? Through repetition.

You can never have enough name recognition! Some marketing people insist that brand recognition, brand reputation and brand loyalty are the 'three cornerstones' of a brand. This is an immensely wrongheaded way of looking at things, particularly when people starting thinking of them as three *steps* – as if you could 'graduate' from one to another. This is tremendously detrimental to marketing work.

You could never have enough name recognition. Coca-Cola is one of the most recognizable brands in the world, but it's still one of the biggest advertisers. It's impossible to imagine Coke no longer spending billions on advertising. Why? Because the audience would forget about it! Coca-Cola is not nearly as important in people's lives as you would imagine.

The power of advertising lies in repetition. This is something every political propagandist knows, but many corporate marketing departments have forgotten about it. Repetition represents continuous investment in an idea. When you change your creative strategy, you're investing from scratch. Would you succeed in anything if you invested in something new every year? The Naobaijin health supplement brand invested in a single slogan for more than ten years: 'This year's holidays, give the gift of Naobaijin'. This may be the only advertising slogan in history that all 1.3 billion people in China know. If you can't be a hundred percent sure that a few hundred million people know your slogan by heart, then you better keep repeating it. Don't ever think that you have 'enough' name recognition.

Now let's talk about the so-called next step: brand reputation. In fact, brand reputation is not a step. It's not even a goal. It's a *consequence*. Your actions determine your reputation. Whether you're talking about a country, a company, a brand or a person, reputation is determined by the impression given by that entity's or individual's words or actions – not through 'reputation building' or 'image advertisements'.

"What kind of advertising should we do to improve our brand's reputation?" This is a hypocrite's way of thinking. It's not what reputation is really about.

Chuang Tzu said that if you can do good without wanting yourself to be known as a do-gooder, they will admire you. The pursuit of 'reputation' has too many companies trying to be seen as do-gooders. In the end, they're self-satisfied while everyone around them rolls their eyes. The so-called good that is done to make people think you're a do-gooder – those actions taken for the sake of reputation – are the things that you need to stop doing.

Stop thinking in terms of reputation. Corporations are like people: just be sincere and do good. Loyalty is also at the centre of a lot of wrongheaded thinking. Can people be unconditionally loyal? Why would they give their unconditional loyalty to your brand? Brand loyalty always comes with conditions. People are loyal to the *value* that your brand creates for them. If one day you can no longer create value, they will abandon you. Apple fans may seem unwavering now, but if Apple stops providing top-notch products and services, it will be abandoned in a heartbeat.

Just as brand reputation is a hypocrite's way of thinking, brand loyalty is an egotist's way of thinking. We said this earlier, but it bears repeating: Never count on your customers being loyal to you – *you* need to be loyal to your customers. Customers have no obligation to be loyal to you. Your entire responsibility is to be loyal to the customer. If you start by being loyal to the customer, you will succeed. If you start by trying to make your customer loyal to you, all of your efforts will be in vain.

The 'three cornerstones' view of recognition, reputation and loyalty is faulty because people think of recognition as a preliminary phase of building a brand. But in truth, brand recognition is a brand's ultimate advantage. The brand with the highest recognition is the brand that is the first choice for the most consumers. Most of the time, the company with the highest market share is not the 'best' company or the one with the best reputation or fiercest loyalty. It's simply the company with the highest name recognition. Every other metric is relative and subjective. Name recognition is absolute and objective: it's a reflection of the number of people who know the brand. You can even count it out.

Always invest in your brand's name recognition. It will always pay off. Your brand value is the product of your positioning and your name recognition.

THE CUSTOMER'S SECOND ROLE: SHOPPER

Now let's take a look at the customer during the purchase. Before the purchase, customers are members of an audience. During the purchase, they are shoppers. It is important to understand the distinction between these roles. When you're thinking about *shoppers*, don't refer to them as customers. When you're thinking of audience members, don't refer to them as shoppers or customers. By referring to people with the right name at the right step of the process, your thought process will become much clearer. As discussed earlier, the common characteristic of audience members is that they are inattentive and forgetful.

What is another characteristic shared by all shoppers? They are *information gatherers* in the purchasing environment. The purchasing environment could be a shopping mall, a supermarket, a restaurant or a computer or phone screen. These environments are all the same in essence. Either shoppers are standing in front of a shelf, or they are clicking around with a mouse, or they're tapping around with their finger. But their ways of thinking are the same, and our best practices are the same.

Once we think of customers as information gatherers, we can treat our displays and packaging as media. We can then design packages, shelves and entire shops so that they function as media.

THE HUA AND HUA WAY: WE-MEDIA AND FULL MEDIATISATION

As noted earlier, some people call social networks like Twitter and Facebook 'we-media'. But we take an even wider view of we-media here at Hua and Hua. We believe that *everything about a company* can be a form of media. Everyone is their own biggest media source; every word and action is communication. For a company, every product is a form of media; product packaging is the most important media source to propagate a brand. Exposure rates are much better for products themselves than for media advertising. *Full mediatisation* means that every part of how a company engages with customers and sellers must be designed as a media source.

Marketers talk about *winning the customer end*. How do you win at the customer end? Do you send out your own salespeople to every supermarket? That takes a huge amount of manpower and money. You want to win at the other end, but where will you get that win?

Your product's packaging is your most important media source.

Use signs to stimulate shoppers' instinctive reactions.

Treat display shelves like billboards.

Turn your packaging copy into a purchasing guide.

Let your products talk for themselves; let the packaging act as your salespeople.

Design your packaging to create a display advantage.

Design your product structure to occupy more shelf space and create more sales opportunities.

Note that nothing about the above adds to the cost of your market displays. Once again, let's go back to that busy street where you considered conducting a survey. Every supermarket aisle is like that street. The products on the shelf are the people that pass by, of all ages, genders and sizes. A shopper could never find something unique about all of the thousands of products they can find in a supermarket. All of them are part of their 'direct perception' as they pass them. How can you make shoppers engage with your product on the 'non-perception' level?

Packaging is your brand's most important media source. This is a crucial part of the Hua and Hua method. Giving up on using your packaging is an even greater loss than giving up ad time on television.

The idea that one's self is one's most important media channel applies to everything. The most important media channel for your office building is the building itself. It's a media channel that can be around for a whole century.

In our view, the information environment of a supermarket is a media environment. Every product is a channel, putting out content to attract viewers. And the eyes of every shopper are remote controls.

Your first weapon in this environment is colour. Colour is the most important factor in visual communication. One of our clients is a *baijiu* liquor brand called Huangjin. We chose to make its packaging blue. Why blue? Don't Chinese people like red for items like this, which are often purchased as gifts? Of course, we know that, but when we noticed that most *baijiu* are packaged in red – that *baijiu* shelves are a sea of red – we realized that blue could create an enormous display advantage for us. Every shopper's remote control will be turned to us.

Use signs to stimulate instinctive reactions. Chubang Soy Sauce uses the green checkerboard pattern sign in its packaging, creating positive feelings of familiarity in shoppers. It could even stimulate the appetite and salivation. The Pavlovian response! Consider display shelves like you would a billboard and your packaging like a media channel. Every Chubang Soy Sauce bottle is printed with the slogan: 'Seeing is believing. This is Chubang's subtropical riverside drying field for soy beans. Our beans are dried for 180 days right here.' Every year several hundred million of these advertisements end up in customer hands, right there on their bottles of soy sauce. This is much more effective than any television ad campaign.

Turn your packaging copy into a purchasing guide. If you've seen how shoppers choose toothpaste or laundry detergent, you'll know how powerful good packaging copy can be. Making your shopper read your copy, and keep reading it until the end, and then put your product in their cart once they've finished reading it ... these simple few steps are a huge accomplishment for a marketer that could take a lifetime's work.

The bulk of your communication should always be done through your packaging. Shoppers are serious and rational in reading packaging. Every bit of copy on your packaging needs to point to the value of your product. You need to be absolutely sure that your copy will make your customer willing to pay money for the product.

Effective use of colours and signs is just the first step. Next you need to begin a quick but serious communication with the shopper. Note the words 'serious' and 'quick'. Serious, because it's a serious decision to buy something. Quick, because you have very little time to influence their decision. Plus, you have to be quicker than everybody else! Quick communication with the shopper is how you can beat your competitors.

If your communication is slow and takes a lot of time, complications could crop up. The shopper might put the product back on the shelf. If they pick up your product and they don't know where to start reading, they'll put it back. If they start reading and realize they have no idea what this product is, they'll put it back. They wouldn't be curious or patient. They're not in the mood for joking. When they pick up the product, they want it to tell them what exactly this is and why pay money for it. You must tell them quickly and seriously.

In the Hua and Hua way, we call this letting the product speak for itself. You start with a bang – an instinctive reaction created by colour and signs. Then you draw them in. You draw them to the purchase and you draw them to purchase more, all with your packaging copy. Thinking from the shopper's perspective isn't just about packaging design, it's also about product development. You should develop different products for different sales channels and locations, creating a comprehensive product structure within your category. This can help you win the biggest display space possible.

Cooperation policies with retailers will also shape your development of products at different specifications and prices, so that you can work with them on the best possible terms. In the market, we actually have two kinds of customer: the shopper (the people who buy your products) and the retailer (the people who sell your products for you). So marketing is really about two things: getting customers to buy your products, and getting retailers to sell them for you. If you can create more value for a retailer's business, then the retailer will devote more effort and resources to selling your product.

Most people will think that they can achieve this in two ways: the carrot, giving retailers bigger margins for selling their product; and the stick, making their brand so influential that the retailer has to sell it even if the margin is low.

But have you considered that you could also become a consultant to your retailers, so that they can not only sell more of your product but also improve their business in your product category overall? Or even improve the performance of their store as a whole? In fact, a lot of companies are already doing this. What is missing is only a systemic awareness and methodology.

THE CUSTOMER'S THIRD ROLE: EXPERIENCER

What do customers buy a product for? To use it. The process for the customer does not end with the purchase, because the customer still has to use the product. Using a product is, in essence, an experience. The customer experience will determine a brand's ultimate fate.

The marketing plan must be based on a deep understanding of the behaviours and the experience of the customers as 'experiencers'. Product development must start from the experiencer context. Different products have different usage experiences. For services like restaurants and entertainment, the experience comes with the purchase. The service sector has therefore developed a comprehensive methodology for the experience economy. The experience economy methodology divides the process into the following three phases:

1. The 'before' phase, where you create expectations.
   Expectations are what draw customers to you.
2. The 'during' phase, where you create surprises.
   Satisfaction is what happens when expectations are exceeded, so you need to carefully design your expectations and your surprises. In addition to individual surprises,

you also need to design an emotional climax for the entire process. Think of amusement parks: When you've finished the ride and you're still on the emotional high, the next stop is always the stall where you can pick up a photograph or souvenir. This is where you're most willing to take out your wallet.

3. The 'after' phase, where you create a willingness to think back to the experience and talk about it. It's also crucial to create a souvenir to bring back. What is a souvenir? It's a talisman, a sign, a media channel.

The last part is key. When you buy a little model of the Eiffel Tower after visiting the real thing, and put it on your shelf, then your shelf becomes a free advertisement for marketing Paris and the Eiffel Tower. You'll also be glad to talk about the experience: "Oh, we visited Paris this spring. Let me tell you about the Eiffel Tower." And that's an advertisement – perhaps the most effective kind.

But suppose you're in the consumer products business, the real estate business, the agriculture business, the B2B materials business. Can you do user-experience marketing like this? Of course you can, but you need to be aware of it.

You can create experiences through your products. Colgate toothpastes have their 'mini breath strips' that are clearly visible but dissolve into the toothpaste. When you see the mini breath strip, you feel an extra rush of freshness.

Laundry detergent manufacturers add blue bits to white detergent, saying that they are enzymes that help make your laundry cleaner. But the enzyme isn't actually blue, and the blue bits probably have nothing to do with the enzyme. It's just to create an experience, so that you can see the 'enzyme' with your own eyes. The manufacturer didn't lie to you – they did add the enzyme, but it's not in the blue bits. This is just one way of making it tangible and real for the consumer.

Packaging is also a way to create an experience. Sanjing used blue bottles to symbolize something pure, rich and good-tasting.

Let's say that you're drinking juice. The packaging that has better pictures of fruit will taste fresher and more flavourful than the ones that have less appealing pictures. Different products need to create different experiences. Some people complain about the 'over-packaging' of products, particularly health products that are often given as gifts. They always come in enormous boxes that seem to be mostly full of bubble wrap. What a rip-off, what a waste!

But when customers think about how they can get this grand-looking gift for their friends, they realize this is the most appropriate packaging possible. The product's developer and designer have a deep understanding of user needs, usage scenarios, the psychology of the user and the price point the customer would be willing to pay. A lot of thought has gone into developing this product. How can you just say it's 'over-packaging'? This kind of gift box has been a bestseller for 20 years.

What is packaging? It's a ritual to wrap up my heart before giving it to you. Would a wedding with lots of flowers be considered 'over-packaged' and 'wasteful'?

The packaging of a pack of cigarettes or a food gift is a different user experience. A pack of cigarettes is very much part of its user's life. It stays in the user's pocket for days, and is taken out every now and then and put back. Or it could be placed on a desk. So the design of a cigarette pack is like a work of art.

A toothpaste box must be an advertisement, a poster. The communication during the purchase is very important, but once it's taken home the box is thrown away.

The user experience can be designed. We designed an experience in advertising Tianqi Toothpaste: yelling 'Tian-qi' instead of 'cheese' when taking a picture. In another advertisement we designed a different experience: brushing your teeth, then saying 'Tian-qi' to the mirror to check if they're clean.

THE CUSTOMER'S FOURTH ROLE: COMMUNICATOR

This is the final step of the process: the customer *after* using the product. As marketers, many of us put most of our attention on the customer as an audience member, and then as an 'experiencer'. A lot of marketers never think about their customers as communicators. Being a communicator is the customer's final role, and in fact it's the most important one. If you have a good handle on communicators, your job becomes much easier.

The Hua and Hua way focuses on *propagation* over *communication*. We say that the key to spreading your message is in propagation, not communication. Communication is about maximizing the number of people who hear the message, so we talk about 'cost per thousand' and 'audience exposure'. But propagation is about putting something out there that people will be willing to spread. In this way customers do propagate for us and we focus on letting the customer communicate for us. It's about successful transmission at no cost.

Tianqi Toothpaste provides a classic example of propagation. Our commercial started broadcasting in March. By May, it was propagated around the world. Every tourist site in China had people saying 'Tian-qi' as they took a photo. Why do we say it was propagated around the world? Because Chinese people travelled everywhere for the May Day holiday. By the Eiffel Tower you could see people yelling 'Tian-qi'. It was the same alongside Victoria Harbour and at Mt. Fuji.

You must think about how customers who have already used your product can become communicators for you. How do you make them spread your brand message? In the previous section on the customer as experiencer, we said that you need to make the customer willing to think back on the experience and talk about it. *Talking about it* is extremely important – in fact, it's one of the most important parts of marketing. We can even say that it's where all advertising creativity must start from. People need to be willing to talk about you to communicate your message and transmit your brand. We say that a good product can create word-of-mouth. That's true, but what does the word-of-mouth *say*?

Your goal in creating your advertising is designing this word-of-mouth propagation. That's why the Hua and Hua way says that advertising is not about telling your customers something, it's about designing a sentence that they can repeat to their friends.

You need to plan and drive word-of-mouth. When writing copy for a product, you can't just think about how to talk to shoppers about it. You also need to think about how to help customers who have already used the product communicate it to others, and how to make sure they use the same language that you do. Consequently, it's important to leave no room for doubt in your description, no room for misunderstanding. And the language needs to be memorable. For example, "180 days of brewing is what gives Chubang Soy Sauce its great flavour!" This would never go wrong in the repetition.

Advertising slogans are not about telling the customer something, they're about designing a sentence for customers to repeat to others. The same thing applies to visual design: it's not about designing an image for the customer to see, but designing an image that they can describe to others. Our design needs to extend not only to what the customer says, but also the scenario and process in which they say it. The design can be based on this scenario and process, because we have studied the roles of the customer *after* using the product – the repeater, the communicator.

Chubang Soy Sauce is an image that can easily be repeated. We laid out this scenario earlier, but it bears repeating. You're going out and your wife tells you to bring a bottle of soy sauce back. She says she wants the Chubang. You close the door and you forget – which brand did she want? But suppose your wife said that it's the one with the green checkerboard pattern. That's something you'll remember. Even if you forgot, you would remember as soon as you saw the real thing in the supermarket.

Let's look back on this process. You were the audience – you received the information that your wife wants you to buy soy sauce. You were inattentive; you were just going to buy a newspaper and never wanted to run this errand for her. You could have just gone to the newsstand but now you had to go to the supermarket, so you weren't really paying attention. The word *Chubang* went in one ear and didn't even have a chance to go out the other – it bounced right back out.

Your wife was the communicator. She told you that she wanted the one with the green checkerboard pattern. If she knew you weren't paying attention, she might have emphasized why she needed the Chubang. The beans were dried in the sun for 180 days. Maybe that would help you remember it for three more minutes.

Fifteen minutes later you arrive at the supermarket and now you become a shopper. You head for the soy sauce shelf. Undoubtedly, you'll see the enormous collage of the Chubang green checkerboard from far away. Now it's all coming back to you. You go there and pick up a bottle. The drying field is there on the bottle. Seeing is believing. You think back to that advertisement about 180 days of drying. And now you understand your wife's choice.

Back home, you become the experiencer of dishes cooked with Chubang Soy Sauce. The bottle with the green checkerboard pattern is the most memorable part of countertop. Then more and more Chubang products appear in your kitchen. Does this really happen? Of course it does. Because Chubang's marketing creative work is entirely based on this scenario.

The customer's role as the communicator is a major focus of the Hua and Hua way. All of our design and advertising is based on the idea of how to make customers spread our message themselves. If something can easily be communicated by customers, then we can easily communicate it to the customer.

Now take on a role and begin a silent play. 'Silent play' is a technique in traditional Beijing opera. Hours before an actor takes the stage, they 'play' the part in their heads, usually without making a sound.

The customer is your role, the products are your props, the process is your play. What we do every day is a 'silent play', in the roles of audience, shopper, experiencer and communicator. If you cannot or do not do this silent play, you will never write a good play, and never become a star in the theatre of the customer.

CHAPTER 9

REAPPRAISING THE CUSTOMER – FOUR CUSTOMER ROLES

Did we propose any 'new theories' in this book?

No?

People often want to discuss 'theory' with me. They talk about trendy, buzz-generating new theories, or whether something is inconsistent with another theory. You see bestsellers proclaiming that certain theories are 'outdated' and saying that their novel new theory is the way of the future.

What is a theory? What makes it outdated? The essence of a theory is its explanatory power. If it can explain everything, then it is a theory. A theory can be formulated based on practice, or devised based on a hypothesis. Either way, something is a theory if it can explain what it describes. If the theory fails to explain something that happens, then it becomes bankrupt and a new theory is needed.

Remember that a theory is essentially an explanation. If it fails to explain something, then it fails as a theory.

For instance, people say that the Chinese entrepreneur Shi Yuzhu uses 'crude' methods that don't fit 'Western marketing theories'. But this is absurd! If his success cannot be understood under that theory, then the problem lies with the theory. Nothing that Shi Yuzhu does goes beyond what modern marketing and communications theory can explain.

Geniuses do not need theory, but theories rely on geniuses. Theorists have long agreed on the definition of genius and the relationship between genius and theory. Clausewitz said: "Pity the warrior who is contented to crawl about in this beggardom of rules, which are too bad for genius, over which it can set itself superior, over which it can perchance make merry! What genius does must be just the best of all rules, and theory cannot do better than to show how and why it is so."

We criticize people for knowing something without knowing why, but geniuses can, in the words of Chuang Tzu, "simply be without knowing why." Everything comes naturally to them.

How about the idea of theories becoming 'outdated'? Liddell Hart, a renowned military strategist of World War II, expressed admiration for Clausewitz's ideas, but he reserved his highest praise for Sun Tzu. He had this to say: "Sun Tzu's essays on 'The Art of War' form the earliest of known treatises on the subject, but have never been surpassed in comprehensiveness and depth of understanding ... Among all the military thinkers of the past, only Clausewitz is comparable, and even he is more 'dated' than Sun Tzu."

Clausewitz was born more than two thousand years after Sun Tzu, yet Liddell Hart found Clausewitz to be outdated and Sun Tzu to be at the forefront of military thought.

Few marketing-related theories have been described as 'outdated' more often than the *4 Ps* of marketing. The 4 Ps include: Product, Place, Promotion and Price. This is one of the field's most important and authoritative theories, so anyone who wants to propose a 'new theory' begins by trying to overturn the 4 Ps. This is the cause of a lot of muddled thinking that we must work through here. Perhaps the biggest attack on the 4 Ps has been the so-called *4 Cs* theory.

In his book *Integrated Marketing Communications*, the academic Don Schultz tells us that the world of marketing should now focus on the 4 Cs: Customer value, Cost, Convenience and Communication. Schultz says that companies need to stop thinking about products and start thinking about customer needs and desires – about selling the products that someone is certain to want to buy. Stop thinking about pricing, he argues, and start learning about the costs to the consumer of fulfilling their needs and desires. Stop thinking about sales channels and start thinking about convenience. And, stop thinking about promotion and call it 'communication' instead.

Schultz said that the 4 Ps were entirely from the company's perspective instead of the customer's perspective. In pivoting from the 4 Ps to the 4 Cs he suggested thinking about:

Customer Value instead of Product.

Customer Cost instead of Price.

Customer Convenience instead of Place.

Customer Communication instead of Promotion.

How did a theory like the 4 Ps become so influential? I would say the biggest reason is that, like all true knowledge, the 4 Ps suggest a path of hard work and true effort. There are no false steps or skipped steps. You must be diligent and smart, and it may well be exhausting.

Many people could never truly understand it or use it. Other 'alternative' paths, which make themselves seem easy, take advantage of people's desire for new and quick shortcuts. Whereas the 4 Ps represent major strategic decisions that encompass all of marketing, the 4 Cs provide nothing more than a skewed perspective. The 4 Cs theory may help one gain some new insights, but not nearly enough to justify its fundamental errors.

Let's walk through the 4 Ps and the 4 Cs one by one.

First, let's compare Product vs. Customer Value.

Is the 4 Ps theory ignorant of the fact that products represent customer value? No. The textbooks are clear – customers buy holes, not drills. Ever since the first product was produced thousands of years ago, products have been made to bring value to customers. Should we spend our time trying to find out what customers want, or creating new products?

Steve Jobs said it best: "Some people say, 'Give the customers what they want.' But that's not my approach. Our job is to figure out what they're going to want before they do." Nearly a hundred years earlier, automotive pioneer Henry Ford said that if he'd asked customers what they wanted they would have said faster horses.

Customers don't know what they want. You need to know what customers need and create the product that fills that need. The idea that you should 'sell products that someone is certain to buy' is absurd. No one can ever be certain of what product they want to buy. The responsibility to find out lies with companies. Modern companies are now increasingly cognizant of product-oriented thinking, and product managers have been elevated to a higher status. Thinking of customer value instead of products brings no new insight and creates only confused thinking. Products are more than this. Products are your company's development strategy.

Product is the first of the four Ps. In marketing thinking, what's important is not how to position a product – this is a relatively low-level question – but rather how to create your products, how to plan and design your product structure, and how to design your business portfolio. This is a matter of strategy.

Our work for Sunflower's children's pharmaceuticals strategy began with planning out a business portfolio and product structure for children's pharmaceuticals and health services. As we've said, the mission of Sunflower's children's pharmaceuticals business is to provide safe medications for Chinese children. Its products and services represent the solution it is offering.

With this in mind we can say that the question of 'product' is ultimately the question of the company's strategic roadmap.

Now let's take a look at the next considerations in our 4 Ps vs. 4 Cs comparison: Customer Cost instead of Price.

This change is simply ignorant of reality. Price is a key determining factor in purchase decisions. The customer cost factor is half as important, if that.

Your pricing decides if you live or die. Price point design is a top-level decision in marketing. It's a strategic issue. Why? Because your price point decides your allocation of profit and marketing resources. Your price point decides how much profit and resources there are to allocate, and how much goes where. This is a hugely important marketing decision. Your price determines your marketing model: how much you invest into marketing, and how your profits are distributed.

Your price point should not primarily be decided by what customers would accept – different customers have different reasons for buying and thus different price tolerances. Your price point primarily defines your choice of marketing model, your product value and your revenue-sharing model with sellers. Marketing is not just about benefits to the customer and the company, but about benefits for the middlemen as well. Only when all three get what they want can sales occur.

Here's a simple example: Amway, Huangjin Dadang and Theragran all sell multivitamins, but with completely different pricing strategies.

That's because they have completely different sales channels: direct marketing, supermarkets and pharmacies.

Pricing is one of the core elements of marketing. Several factors influence pricing: how much you want to sell your product for; your choice of sales channel and how your revenue is shared with them; how you persuade customers that your product is worth the price. We often see different brands sell products of similar quality at wildly different prices. The price point is a result of work that you put in, not something you get from 'understanding the customer'.

There are two classic examples of pricing strategy in China; Wang Lo Kat herbal tea and Yunnan Baiyao toothpaste.

Wang Lo Kat's pricing is one of the key factors in its success. If its tea hadn't been priced so high, at over three yuan a can, Wang Lo Kat would never have been able to sustain its enormous advertising spend, and its business model would never have succeeded. If it had been priced at two yuan a can, Wang Lo Kat would never have become a legendary brand.

The same goes for Yunnan Baiyao toothpaste. Without its jaw-dropping price point of over 20 yuan per tube, there would be no way that the company would have been able to pay those extortionate rates for television commercial airtime – not to mention the crucible that is Carrefour and Walmart shelves – with just a single product.

Pricing is a subtle and complex art. For companies, pricing is a question of marketing models, profit allocation and sales strategy. For customers, pricing is not simply a question of cost. The price of the product is not simply a cost the customer pays to obtain the value of the product. Oftentimes the price of the product *is* its value! Why is it that some things sell better the more expensive they are? Well, a product wouldn't feel exclusive without an exclusive price. When you truly understand marketing, you'll realize that the hardest part is pricing.

The third terms in our assessment of 4 Ps vs. 4 Cs are Customer Convenience vs. Place.

The question of place is first and foremost a question of your marketing model, an issue of strategy. Essentially, this is the question of your company's 'political system'.

Your sales channels are an important part of your marketing team, and yet they are not part of your corporate structure. How can you incorporate these people outside of the company into your management's orbit, so that you can make them an extension of your company's brand? The answer is that your company needs to become a friend, teacher and guide to the owners of these sales channels.

The 4 Cs theory is shockingly irresponsible in its understanding of sales channels. It wants us to forget about sales channel strategies and think about 'the convenience of purchase'. If convenience is all there is to sales channels, then there's no point to studying marketing.

The 4 Ps theory defines sales channels as the sum of all the steps and driving forces in the process of getting products from the manufacturer to the customer. What are these 'steps and forces'? Not the customers, but the sellers: a group of people with a strong profit-seeking motive.

'Place' is about your ability to mobilize and control these segments of the chain. To put it in simple terms, marketing is about two things:

1. Persuading customers to buy our products.
2. Persuading sellers to sell our products.

Your sales channel strategy involves coming up with a solution so that sellers will be willing to sell your product, and to do so proactively. What's needed is a solution that allows you to integrate and leverage your sales channels' resources to the greatest extent. If customers are willing to buy from you, but no sellers are willing to work with you, where would all those customers go to acquire your product? Where would 'customer convenience' come from?

Some years ago, a businessman in Guangzhou made waves in the media when he launched a 'one-yuan cold medicine'.

But he forgot one problem: who would sell his medicine? When none of the stores would carry his product and he had to find a way to deliver it to millions of homes, only 100-yuan cold medicine would cover his costs.

The sales channel issue is a political issue. It involves trusting and following a vision, designing and implementing a profit-sharing system, rewarding and punishing behaviour with rigour, and mobilizing and controlling marketing organizations. A successful company needs to be able to meet its sales channels' demand for profit and development. It needs to become a guide. This is the essence of place strategy.

The issue of place also involves the control of your price system. Why do many traditional companies struggle with e-commerce? Because online sales channels have disrupted their old-school pricing system, which was geared toward traditional channels. The disruption of the system has disrupted their marketing as well.

Place is also closely tied to market. You need to develop different products for different channels. This allows you to meet the individual needs of each channel, as well as your own need to set up your pricing system. Finally, place is about your funding chain, your supply chain and business model innovation. These are all fundamental questions in marketing. So how can we say that the 4 Ps are outdated? How can we even try to replace them with the 4 Cs?

Finally, the fourth piece in our comparison of the 4 Ps with the 4 Cs is Customer Communication vs. Promotion.

The traditional theory identifies five components of the 'promotion mix': advertising, sales promotion, personal selling, public relations and direct marketing. These five elements encompass basically everything there is to know about brand communication, and we won't go into further detail here.

But the 'customer communication' view is enormously problematic. It simply misses the forest for the trees. It's a half-baked theory from 'the customer's perspective' that stems from a lack of comprehensive understanding of business management. If a young person learns about the 4 Ps before they start out in marketing or advertising, they will have a solid framework of knowledge that will benefit them for their entire career. But if they start down a dead end that is the 4 Cs, they will never understand what marketing is all about, even with a lifetime of work. Sadly, we see this kind of misguided person all too often!

The 4 Cs may be somewhat illuminating as a perspective for considering business problems. But claiming that they can replace the 4 Ps is simply irresponsible. All told, this chapter touched on common sense, theory, methods, insights, consulting products, models, panaceas and proverbs. Having done so, we've demonstrated that the 4 Ps approach is vastly superior to the flawed 4 Cs model, no matter how *au courant* the new 'theory' may seem.

There are a lot of theories out there in our society, prompting more misconception than insight. People are making up new terms all the time; the battle to eliminate jargon rages on. But let's go back to the issue we brought up at the beginning of this chapter: Do Shi Yuzhu's 'crude' methods fit 'Western marketing theory'? They absolutely do, because the 4 Ps can explain everything that he does.

Product: He defines his product's value as a gift for parents, superiors and teachers. The gift of a Naobaijin herbal health drink is a way to show filial piety.

Price: He set the price at a bit over 100 yuan, but not too much. It started at 118. For customers, this is a gift in the '100-plus' range. If the price were 99, people wouldn't buy it because they don't want to give a gift that's 'less than 100'. But people wouldn't buy it at 199 either, because that's too much for a '100-plus' price range. So the pricing strategy for Naobaijin allowed the product to be positioned more precisely as a '100-plus gift'. When most people go gift shopping, they decide on a price range before they start looking at their choices.

Place and promotion are obvious. Big advertising campaigns, big supermarkets, big sales. Why have they kept the same slogan

– 'This year's holidays, give the gift of Naobaijin' – for fourteen years? We've discussed this well-known tenet of communications theory at some length: propagation requires repetition, stimulating instinctive reactions and actions.

There is nothing in marketing that the 4 Ps don't cover. But are the 4 Ps becoming obsolete in the internet age? No. All marketing work in e-commerce still revolves around the Ps:

1. What products do you want to make, and how do you define them and communicate them?
2. What is the price point you'll set?
3. What about place? The internet is far more important as a sales channel than as a media source.
4. How will you promote the product?

Certainly, the internet has brought immense changes to every one of the 4 Ps, but product is still product, price is still price, place is still place, and promotion is more crucial than ever. That's why I say that the 4 Ps form a valid marketing theory and the 4 Cs do not. What are the 4 Cs? They are a kind of method. Theories explain; methods solve problems. The 4 Cs provide a way to solve a small number of problems in marketing. They merely won over some unsuspecting folks by packaging themselves as a theory, but they don't form a comprehensive system of marketing theory.

Many bestselling books on business are packaged more like a 'consulting product'. I say this because they employ two commonly seen claims on product packaging. The first is declaring itself to be 'all-new'. It's fine that writers have their own ideas, but why do they always need to assert that their ideas make the 4 Ps obsolete? Because they need to step on the 4 Ps to sell themselves. When they proclaim that the past is gone and a new era has begun, audiences gladly follow along like little lost lambs, thinking that they have found salvation!

The second claim is that they can immediately solve your problems, that it's a miracle cure. Like those seven-day skin whitening solutions: Just do what I do. *It's that simple!* Consulting products, particularly most successful ones, sell by promising miracles. They are selling a fantasy of allowing you to make all the money you want as long as you do what they say. "See, so-and-so company did it and succeeded."

Everyone is lost and looking for a panacea. Everybody wants a miracle. That's why 'new theories' will always have a place in the market.

But the truth is, nothing in the world is that easy. If you take a shortcut, or overlook one element of your work, you will not succeed.

It's more than those 'new theories' and consulting products that influence the way we think. In our work we often encounter 'models'. Too many people use models blindly without realizing that each model works only in a specific context. If you are not in that context, it's not for you – you shouldn't use it blindly.

Take the Boston Consulting Group's (BCG) matrix. This grid is one of the most commonly used models out there for people working in business portfolio strategy. Marketing directors often use it to analyse their business and products. But this is inappropriate for their role. Let me explain why.

The BCG matrix is also called the growth-share matrix. It divides products into cash cows, dogs, stars and question marks based on their market share and growth.

High-share, low-growth products are called the 'cash cows'. They generate huge amounts of cash that can be used for investing. Low-share, low-growth products are called the 'dogs'. They generate no cash, but at the same time they need very little; they offer low return on investment and could turn out to be a cash trap. High-share, high-growth products are called the 'stars'. They may be self-sustaining in terms of cash, or they may not. Low-share, high-growth products, called the 'question marks', require large amounts of investment.

The problem with the BCG matrix is that it's not really a strategy tool. It is a policy tool for people with capital, not a tool for people running a business. What policies am I referring to?

They include the policy of a company's headquarters toward its branches, the policy of a venture capitalist toward businesses. The BCG matrix is for people who do not understand or control the businesses in question, not for those who *do* understand and control the business.

Executives based in the headquarters of a multinational company – one that sprawls across multiple business units and products – usually don't know much about the semi-autonomous departments and businesses the company owns around the world. And so, they need to formulate policy based on financial performance and market data: invest or withdraw, expand or pull back.

Beyond the BCG matrix, McKinsey and General Electric (GE) worked together to introduce the so-called nine-box matrix, adding a third possible outcome. Besides the options of increasing or decreasing investment, this matrix looked at potentially selling the business to another company. This was considered the greatest contribution of the nine-box matrix to management strategy models. It recognized that the ability of a company to capture value from a given business unit must be measured in the context of the ability of *other* potential owners to capture value from it. This introduced the concept of opportunity cost to business strategy. If a certain business is efficient and profitable for us, but may prove even more efficient and profitable in company B's portfolio, then perhaps it will be more valuable to sell it to company B.

If you know GE, you'll know why its legendary leader Jack Welch needed a tool like this. The BCG matrix and the nine-box matrix are oriented toward a capitalist's way of thinking, not a business person's. A major flaw in business thinking today is the misconception of the *context*, which is something we've talked about all through this book. Many people are just starting a business – or struggling to make their small enterprise survive, grow and succeed – and yet they're discussing business problems in the context of the world's richest people.

Another commonly used model is SWOT analysis, which assesses strengths, weaknesses, opportunities and threats. This tool is widely used, perhaps because there's such a low barrier to entry. Anyone faced with any problem can fill in the four boxes in the SWOT analysis and enjoy an 'analytical illusion' – the illusion that they're thinking about the problem analytically and getting results. Yes, I say it is an illusion because this tool is only a framework to *start* thinking. It offers no way to solve problems. It is simply a matter of course. Strengths, weaknesses, opportunities and threats are neither a sufficient nor a necessary condition to solving a problem. But the biggest feature of SWOT is that anyone can fill in the four boxes. That's the only reason it's so popular.

Consulting products sell themselves as panaceas through the promise of a miracle; models sell themselves with the analytical illusion. We often see BCG matrices and SWOT analyses in PowerPoints because the presenter just randomly included them to create the illusion that they've 'analysed' the problem. And we see listeners keep nodding along. But if the boss cares about the true essence of things, then they'll have to point out the truth.

We have too many bestsellers, too many false theories, too much new jargon. All of these bring more confusion than true value. We are facing an explosion in the amount of knowledge at our fingertips ... and an explosion of pseudo-knowledge as well. I can only stress that common sense must be your guide. Use common sense to look at your problems and solve them.

Find the essence of things, and use common sense to find the force that can push you forward. That is the true way of strategic marketing creativity. Rely on common sense, not pseudo-knowledge. There is no such thing as a panacea. You need to put in the work.

Finally, I'd like to share four stories that represent four levels of our work.

1. THE BLIND MEN AND THE ELEPHANT

The blind men and the elephant, which we referred to earlier, is a story you can find in first-grade textbooks in China. Four blind men have no idea what an elephant looks like, so they each touch one. One of them touched the tusk, so he said that an elephant is like a long, thick, smooth stick. Another one touched the ear, so he said the elephant is like a huge fan. One of them touched a leg, so he said the elephant is like a pillar. And the last one touched the tail, so he said the elephant is like a rope. 'The blind men touching the elephant' has become a Chinese saying that means not truly seeing the full scope of something.

My son laughed and laughed when he read this story. "They're so stupid!" he said. I could only sigh: "Well, your father is touching an elephant every day."

Don't ever think this is someone else's story. You are a blind man touching an elephant every day in the office. Leaders around the world are blind men touching an elephant when they're trying to solve the latest financial crisis.

How about China's real estate and stock market problems? Go look through the papers from the last few years, and you'll see that the elite in the country – the people with immense amounts of power and resources – are just blind men touching an elephant. They touch the leg, and they think they can do something. It's important to realize that you can't avoid this trap. You're in this trap every day. Everyone in the world is at some point a blind man touching an elephant.

Being blind is not the problem. Not knowing it, that's the problem.

Not knowing it is not a problem in and of itself. Not knowing that you *don't know* is the problem.

Then again, not knowing that you don't know is not a problem. Not knowing that you don't know, and thinking that you know everything, is a major problem.

People are decisive and forceful. They dive into things headfirst. They have a solution for everything. And yes, I'm talking about all of us. That's why it's essential to know that there are things you don't know. It's also important to be decisive and forceful.

When you're making any decision, remind yourself: *I am a blind man touching an elephant. I don't know everything.* When you're aware of this, you'll make fewer mistakes.

It's said that this is the era of big data, an era of knowing everything about something, past and present. But I suspect that in the end we'll still be blind men touching elephants. Because there's more than one elephant. Because the elephants are always changing. And because our competitors are touching the elephant too.

2. THE PONY CROSSING THE RIVER

My son's textbook has another story called The Pony Crossing the River.

A pony wants to cross a river, but he doesn't know how deep it is. He asks the buffalo, who tells him that it's perfectly safe – the water is hardly up to the knees. The pony is happy to hear that and prepares to cross the river. But the squirrel stops him: "It's very deep! One of my friends drowned last year!" So the pony doesn't dare cross. He goes back and asks his mother, who tells him that it's impossible to know without trying for himself. So he does, carefully, and it turns out the water is just the right depth for him to cross safely.

This is another wonderfully true-to-life depiction of our work: We want to do something ambitious, but can we really cross this river? There are plenty of companies that did, so clearly there's a chance. But there are also plenty of companies that failed; we just don't remember them. Consequently, it's useless to look at what other people do. You have to forge your own way.

When you run a company, you must cross river after river. Like Deng Xiaoping said, we must 'cross the river by feeling the stones'. There might be a bridge, but it's not necessarily a bridge for *you*. You need to build your own bridge. You might not be able to build the same bridge as someone else, and yet you might succeed at building a bridge that someone else fails at. Other people might have crossed already, but that doesn't mean you can cross. Other people might have failed, but that doesn't mean you will.

3. THE OIL SELLER

The oil seller story is one I remember reading in my Chinese middle-school textbook. Its main character is a young man called Chen Yaozi, who is a great archer. Once he was practicing archery in his yard, when an old man selling oil sets down his barrel of oil and watches him for a long time, long enough to see Chen Yaozi hit his target eight or nine times out of ten. But the old man seems unimpressed, giving only a slight nod.

Chen Yaozi says: "Do you shoot? Am I not an excellent archer?"

The old man replies: "There's no secret to what you do, you're just familiar with the skill."

This angers Chen Yaozi: "How dare you talk about my mastery of archery like this!"

The old man says: "I know this because of my experience with pouring oil." He takes a gourd-shaped barrel with a narrow opening and sets it on the ground. He places a coin on top of the opening, and slowly starts pouring oil through the hole on the coin. No oil splatters onto the coin. The old man says: "There is no secret to my art either. I am merely familiar with the skill." And Chen Yaozi could only send the old man away with a smile.

I have always aspired to be 'merely familiar with the skill'. The goal of Hua and Hua's creative work is to be *reproducible*, to become *routine*. We follow templates in our design, and we follow routines in our planning. By doing this, we ensure that eight or nine out of every ten arrows we shoot hit the target. Nothing is as reliable as familiarity.

Some people think very little of routine. "It's all you know!" they say.

Yes, one routine is all we know. Not even two routines will do, because with two routines you have half the familiarity. You might think other people's routines are simple, but they would never work for you. You might pour oil like the old man, but you won't be able to flawlessly pour the oil into the barrel. You might try to shoot arrows like Chen Yaozi, but you'll never be as accurate. So you need to be the best at your routine. You need to be deeply familiar with it. And to reach that level of deep familiarity, you'll need to stick to one routine.

What if you encounter a problem that your routine can't solve? I say, then leave this problem to someone else. You can't do everything. Only the people who aren't good at anything worry about the things they can't do. Once they can do one thing very well, they don't care about all the other things anymore.

4. THE BUTCHER AND THE COW

The butcher and the cow is a story told by Chuang Tzu. He tells of a cook who butchers cows for King Hui of the state of Liang. When he is taking apart the cow, the sound of flesh being ripped from bone emanates everywhere – where his hand moves, where his shoulder leans, where his feet rest, where his knee touches. The sound grows louder as his knife is plunged into the cow. The sounds form a harmonious tune with the rhythm of the most elegant and noble dance.

The king says: "Excellent! How did you become so skilled?"

The butcher puts down his knife and replies: "I have spent my time exploring the patterns of nature, far beyond my pursuit of butchering skills. When I first began to butcher cows, I knew nothing about the structure of a cow's body. I saw only a whole cow.

"Three years later, I saw the interior musculature and tendons of the cow. I couldn't see the whole cow anymore. Now when I butcher a cow, I make contact with the cow's body only through my will. I do not need to see it with my eyes. All of my senses have stopped functioning, and I move only by my will. I go with the grain of the cow's body, and I move my knife through the crannies between the tendons and the bones, the spaces in the joints. Everything I do is based on the structure of the cow's body. My knife never touches anything that joins tendon to bone, or muscle to muscle. Certainly it never touches the large bones either.

"A skilled cook needs a new knife every year, because they use the knife to cut down meet. A mediocre cook needs a new knife every month, because they use the knife to cut through bone. But I've now used my knife for 19 years, and I've butchered thousands of cows with it. Yet the knife is as sharp as if it had just been sharpened on the whetstone. Spaces exist in the joints of the cow's body. The blade is thin, and by moving the knife through the spaces, there is plenty of room for manoeuvring the blade. That's why my knife is still sharp as the day it was sharpened on the whetstone, 19 years later. Even so, when I encounter a knot between tendon and bone, where it is difficult to cut through, I am still cautious and careful. I focus my sight and slow down my movement. The knife moves only slightly, and the bone and the meat separate with a great sound, the meat scattering on the ground like a pile of dirt. I stand with the knife, looking around in pride for my success. I am satisfied and relaxed. Then I wipe down the blade and store it."

This is the story of the butcher and the cow. He knows all there is to know about things. Perhaps this is what is meant when one says that 'every possibility is accounted for'.

However, I have yet to encounter a single figure in history who has reached such a level. Even the greatest of heroes are at the level of the blind men, the pony, the oil seller. The cook may be good at butchering a cow, but there is no way his understanding can transfer to our problems. So let's treat this as a fairy tale. If anyone says that they've 'accounted for every possibility', I'll be sure to avoid them.

The Hua and Hua way is about mere familiarity with skill.

A BRIEF STORY OF

H&H

1. PROLOGUE
– MY FAMILY HISTORY

We founded Hua and Hua in Guangzhou in 2002. The company was named after the two of us – Sam Hua and Nan Hua.

We were born into a family of teachers in Daozhen County in Guizhou. I was born in 1971, and my brother Nan Hua was born in 1974. That's why my brother often says that Hua and Hua has been around "since 1974."

We were born during China's Cultural Revolution. That was an age when people were honoured for their poverty, and Zhang Tiesheng became a hero for turning in a blank test paper on his university entrance exam. In other words, the nation idolized those without money or knowledge – and the more you disdained money and scorned knowledge, the more you were renowned.

第八课　一份发人深省的答卷

《人民日报》编者按，七月十九日，《辽宁日报》以《一份发人深省的答卷》为题，刊登了一位下乡知识青年的信，并为此加了编者按。这封信提出了教育战线上的两条路线、两种思想斗争中的一个重要问题，确实发人深省。

毛主席关于"要从有实践经验的工人农民中间选拔学生，到学校学几年以后，又回到生产实践中去"的指示，发表已经五年了。教育战线的干、社、尺，正在继续深入。我们要认真学习和坚决执行毛主席的指示，调查研究，总结经验，搞好无产阶级教育革命。

《辽宁日报》编者按：这里刊载的是张铁生同志在今年大学招生考试卷背面写的一封信。

张铁生同志是一九六八年的下乡知识青年，共青团员，现任兴城县白塔公社枣山大队第四生产队队长。他对物理化学这门课的考试，似乎交了"白卷"，然而对整个大学招生的路线问题，却交了一份颇有见解、发人深省的答卷。

80

But in 1977, when I turned six, China began holding university entrance exams again. And in 1978, China began its period of 'reform and opening'. The country began to focus on building its economy. A 'spring-time for science' began, and scientists became heroes. 'Knowledge is power' became a much-repeated quote. And my parents became excited.

My father received a degree in mathematics from Guizhou University, and at the time he was teaching maths at the high school in Shangbei People's Commune in Daozhen County. My mother first taught in the elementary school, then at the high school as well. She started school a year later than my father did, and her entrance into higher education coincided with the downfall of Liu Shaoqi. After that it was impossible for a landowner's child without connections to go to university, so she could only attend a 'labour university', and her degree later counted only as a vocational diploma. My mother saw that the university entrance exams were being reinstated, and that English would become a mandatory subject. There were barely any English teachers in our whole county, so who could help her two sons learn? That was when she decided that she needed to learn English herself.

My father was excellent with money. Even with a limited income, he was able to provide us a good life, help out relatives in trouble, and save up a little. Of course, we were not exactly poor. In the 1970s, my parents' wages combined was over 70 yuan a month – a comfortable income. After I was born, my father was able set aside 15 yuan a month to hire a nanny for me. Ours was the only family in the county, aside from the county magistrate's, to have a nanny. My nanny was a Ms Zhao, whom my parents called Auntie Zhao. She was part of our family. Once my mother decided she needed to learn English, my father spent over 60 yen on a radio. This was a fortune in those days, but it was no difficulty for him. And so, my mother began learning English through the programming on China National Radio.

Then the county started a night school where English was taught. The teacher's name was Peng Qianzhong. He had a degree in English from Guizhou University. I suspect he was the only person in the entire county qualified to teach English. Mr Peng was a good friend of my father's, and he visited me at my house in Shanghai a few years ago. Perhaps because he studied English, he was also the most admired man in the county. I remember he was the first person in the county to own a motorcycle. I always idolized Mr Peng.

My mother was in Mr Peng's class. The Shangbei People's Commune was 15 miles of mountain road from the county capital, which she took by bicycle. When her class let out, she had to ride back and get up early the next day for her own students' morning assembly. But the punishing schedule never bothered her, and she was never afraid of taking the mountain roads alone at night.

She was determined to be the best. When she finished the night school course, she got herself into a two-year course at Guizhou University's department of English, and eventually became an English teacher – not just any English teacher, but the 'third-year guardian' teacher. She always taught the third-years at her high school, preparing them for the university entrance exams. She was demanding and rigorous, like a drill sergeant. My brother and I both took the entrance exam under my mother's 'guardianship', and we both did very well in English, just as she planned.

But don't misunderstand me – neither of us can use English very well. We were good at taking English exams.

Because both my parents were teachers, my house became an informal boarding school for children on both sides of my family. Before I even started school, many of my older cousins came to stay with us as they prepared for entrance exams. One of my mother's favourite stories is about my cousin, Zhang Yaqun. He was a good-looking man, 180 centimeters tall. When he took the exam for technical school when he finished junior high, his managed to score only in the 180s for his six-subject total. He worked in a factory for five years after graduating, but one day he suddenly came and told my mother: "Auntie, I want to go to college!"

My mother made fun of him for that. She said: "How could you get into college? You didn't even go to high school."

Yaqun pointed to the two-person couch in our living room and said: "This is where I'll sleep." I took a look at the couch and imagined his feet hanging off the armrests. But he came and stayed, and in one year he went from not knowing the alphabet to getting over 80 on his English entrance exam. He got into the Beijing College of Language to study English, and now he lives in Canada.

We are in the age of Zhang Yaqun, not the age of Zhang Tiesheng.

Back to 1977 – no, back to 1976 now. My parents began my education when I was five. I had two lessons every day: In the morning, my mother would take me on a run. The school where we lived was by a valley that a creek flowed through. Upstream was a small waterfall called Baioshuiyan. And under the waterfall was a bridge, which was the road to Zunyi, the nearest city. My mother and I would run across that bridge and run halfway up the mountains surrounding the valley, where we would stop and she would tell me a story. They were all well-known traditional Chinese stories, like Wu Song fighting the tiger, Li Ji killing the snake, and Cao Chong weighing the elephant. When we came back home, I had to write down the story in my own words, using pinyin for the characters I didn't know. These were my first lessons in writing. My second subject was penmanship. I practiced my Chinese characters using pencil on grid paper, as many as I liked. My father would look over my work, and he would circle the ones he was satisfied with. My goal every day was to get 50 circled characters. These tasks gave me a strong foundation of language skills. From elementary school to high school, my teachers showed my writing assignments to other students as models. When I took the university entrance exams in 1988, I was the top-scoring student in the school for Chinese. My brother says he was the top-scoring student in the *city*. (When he took the exam, our family had moved to the city of Liupanshui, where my parents taught at the high school for their mining agency.) I am sure that the top score in our school would also have been the top score in the city. So, maybe I was the best in the city as well – but we didn't look it up back then, and he'll always have that over me.

Before I started school, my mother taught me Chinese and my father taught me maths. Our heroes were two types of people: scientists, as I said, and prodigies. And the most brilliant prodigies were the members of the Special Class for the Gifted Young at the University of Science and Technology of China – a group of 13-year-olds who were going to university. China had just emerged from an age when the more you knew, the more reactionary you were; there was an urgent need for talent in science and technology. My father's wish was that I would become part of the Special Class. Everything in China is politics, and all politics come with propaganda, and all propaganda centres on 'models'. The models for the Special Class for the Gifted Young were Ning Bo and Xie Yanbo.

My father told me their stories. Ning Bo worked so hard on his studies that he didn't even realize when his pants caught on fire from the fireplace he was studying near. This story had a great effect on me. I started studying by the fireplace to see if my own pants would catch fire. I started scooting my knee closer and closer to the fire, but it got too hot before anything could catch.

Another thing my father talked to me about was the Nobel Prize. The best scientists were the ones who won Nobels! So it became my childhood dream to become a scientist and win a Nobel Prize. A photographer came to our county capital one day when I was in elementary school. He brought a billboard of a blue sky and a airplane, with two holes cut out where the windows were. Children would sit behind the billboard and stick their heads out from the holes. Every child in the county must have taken a picture with the billboard, because our writing assignment that week was to write about our pictures with the plane. Everyone else in my class wrote that they were pilots flying the plane, but I was the only one who wrote that I was going on an observation trip abroad. My father was thrilled that his son had different aspirations from everyone else. He never stopped telling the story, which is the only reason I still remember it.

In a family of teachers, learning is the most important thing in life. My brother and I were free from our studies only one day out of the entire year, Chinese New Year's Eve. Even on New Year's Day, our learning continued. That's how learning became a lifelong habit for me. To this day, every day I don't learn brings a feeling of guilt.

This brief history of Hua and Hua begins with my family and my childhood, because this is a company founded by two brothers. Everything we have accomplished can be traced back to how our parents taught us. My parents could never have imagined how much China would change in the years to come. The best life they could have dreamed for us was to go to university and teach, or to study abroad and come back to serve the country. They didn't know anything else.

Here I also need to offer an account of my family roots, because my family is the perfect specimen of the traditional Chinese family. Our story has been a typical story for millennia, and it is also part of what made me what I am today. Our family records can be traced back with some clarity for 1,600 years, and we know the names of every family member starting from 800 years ago. Starting from 300 years ago, we have detailed records of every generation.

Three hundred years ago, my ancestor Hua Youduan left the family village in Liancheng in Fujian Province and moved to Ziyang in Sichuan Province to live with his older brother, Hua Youjun. Youduan started off as a traveling salesman, selling little things like knitted items and toys. He eventually saved enough to buy a small plot of land, become a farmer, and start a family of his own. His house was one of a cluster of three, the other two belonging to his brother Youjun and his in-laws, the Liaos. Youjun's house still survives as one of my family's ancestoral shrines.

Hua Youduan's good life didn't last long. A flood of the Tuo River took away his wife and two daughters, as well as his house. Youduan went bankrupt and had to start over, working hard and saving up. This is a common refrain in our family records – working hard and saving up, building a foundation for success. The goal of the ancestor is to work hard, save up, and build a foundation for the success of future generations. As the Chinese proverb goes, 'the ancestors plant the tree, and the descendants enjoy the shade'. This is the tradition in China.

Hua Youduan married his second wife when he was 42. His new wife changed the fate of our family, by the introduction of knowledge, culture, and civilization. Her family name was Wei, and she was 24 years old when she married into the Hua family – an old maid by the standards of the time. Her father was Wei Xianbang, a local Confucian scholar who held private classes for the children. Miss Wei studied with her father from a young age, and she knew the Four Books – four great classics and teaching texts of Confucianism consisting of the *Great Learning*, the *Analects*, the *Mencius*, and the *Doctrine of the Mean* – by heart. She became an important figure in the family after she married, because she was cultured and told wonderful stories from *Legends of the Past and Present*, a collection of stories from the Ming dynasty that even today I am familiar with.

Miss Wei changed the Hua family. The Hua became a prosperous family of scholar-farmers by the time of her son, Hua Zhouhui. Our family records are full of poems and writings from the family guests back then. My father's great-grandfather Hua Guangyao was a prodigy in his time, one of the three brilliant students of the county collectively known as the 'three lights of Ziyang' because all three of them had the character *guang*, or light, in their names. My family recorded the county magistrate's comments on Hua Guangyao's writing when he took the imperial examination: that it had the grandeur of the rainbow, and the strength of a thousand troops. Unfortunately, none of his actual writings remain.

I am the ninth generation descended from Hua Youduan, but I still feel the influence of Miss Wei. I suppose this is what they say when they talk about a family's way, destiny, style, or learning. In addition to running my company and writing books on brand marketing, I also write about history and philosophy. *Sam Hua on Sun Tzu's Art of War* sold over 400,000 copies in China, and has been published in South Korea and Thailand. I hope that it will one day be published worldwide. *Sam Hua on the Analects* has sold 50,000 copies, and *Sam Hua on Mencius* was recently published. My next projects are *Sam Hua on the Grand Learning and the Doctrine of the Mean, Sam Hua on Wang Yangming's Teachings*, and *Sam Hua on the Zizhi Tongjian*. My hope is to bring Chinese traditional values and wisdom to the entire world.

2. MY MISSED SHOT
AT RICHES

High school is three years in China's education system, and all students must choose between the humanities track and the sciences track in the second year. I did well in my humanities classes and didn't like the science subjects, so I wanted to choose the humanities track. But my father said: "Learn maths and science well, and you can do well anywhere. If you go into the humanities, what happens in politics could destroy you!" I was not happy about it, but I always did what my parents said. The thought that I could disobey never even occurred to me, so I found myself in the sciences track.

When I took the university entrance exam in 1988, my father said: "Our car industry is going to take off. Choose the best school in China for learning about cars and go there!" So that's how I ended up studying motors at the Jilin University of Technology.

When it was my brother's turn to take the exam, my father said: "In the future there will be five-star hotels everywhere in China. Go study hotel management!" So, Nan Hua majored in hotel management at Sun Yat-sen University.

My father had an excellent sense of what was going to happen in China, but his judgment of our abilities was less sound. I was not good at mechanical engineering. In my lab course, I took apart simple 195 diesel engines but I was never able to put them back together. There were always a few parts left over.

Other than getting past my exams, I spent my four years at university doing three things: I dated, I played soccer, and I read. A major topic of my reading was the philosophy of ancient China, particularly from the age when the various schools blossomed more than 2,000 years ago: Laozi, Confucius, Mencius, Chuang Tzu, Hanfeizi, Shang Yang, and the like. Another major topic was military tactics and strategy: Sun Tzu's *Art of War*, of course, but also Wuzi, Wei Liaozi, the *Six Secret Teachings*, the *Three Strategies*, and Guiguzi as well. I liked strategy, not intrigue. I loved the *Art of War*, but I despised Guiguzi. I was also very familiar with the *Strategies of the Warring States*, but there was too much emphasis on intrigue and conspiracy for my liking. And I also read a lot of history. The two most important works of history in China are the *Records of the Grand Historian* and the *Zizhi Tongjian*. The *Zizhi Tongjian* is over three million Chinese characters, all in classical Chinese. Everyone in China knows of it, but very few people have read it in full. I have done so four times, and I am doing a fifth reading of *Sam Hua on the Zizhi Tongjian*. I expect this project will take seven years and ultimately be five million characters long.

I spent much of my university days reading about Chinese history. I'd given up my dream of becoming a Nobel-winning scientist, because I knew I wasn't cut out for that. Now I wanted to be a philosopher, a thinker – at least a columnist. I thought having a column would be pretty cool. What I wanted was to have ideas, and write things that would change how other people think too, so that they could form their own ideas. Influencing and shaping public opinion is what a marketer does, but that hadn't occurred to me yet. In truth, though, that was what planted the seed of my career in advertising.

3. A HEAVY FOG OVER SILVER LAKE

I graduated from university in 1992. University graduates in China were still given jobs by the state at that time, but it was already 14 years since the reform and special economic zones like Shenzhen and Zhuhai were already the places to be. Graduates were free to refuse their state-assigned positions and 'dive in'. That was what I decided to do – I wanted to find my own job. But the atmosphere in my Northeast university was still conservative. My classmates asked me three questions:

1. You didn't study business or management, so how can you work in business?
2. What would you do with a *hukou*, a legal registration in those cities?
3. How will you get a house in the future?

To the first question, I said that the president didn't go to university for doing presidential things either, and it didn't seem to be a problem.

To the second question, I was very familiar with *The Book of Lord Shang* because of my reading. I knew that keeping the people poor and limiting their ability to migrate were the two cornerstones of China's legal school of ruling. At the time, the government made it official policy to let some people get rich first. With the first cornerstone gone, I thought the second would never survive on its own. So, I said that I was certain the *hukou* system would be abolished. My classmates thought I was insane. I never would have imagined that today, 26 years later, the *hukou* system would live on – but it's a completely different system now. There are no longer limits on where you're allowed to move, and my lack of *hukou* has never been a problem for me.

The last question was about a house. I didn't know. At that time no one thought that we would be able to *buy* a house. I just said:

"My grandfather had a house, my father has a house. There's no reason I wouldn't get one. I don't know where it's going to come from, but I'll get one." This is how I always think. You could never predict the future, so I don't see any point in thinking about what is going to happen. I simply decide what I'm going to do today, and I leave the future to fate and luck.

My father was very supportive of my decision. He said: "You should go! We can help you out with money if the first few years don't go well. I would definitely go if I were still your age. Your mother and I wanted to go when they started looking for people in Shenzhen in the 80s, but we didn't because we were worried about the education there. We didn't go because we didn't want to hurt your future. But now it's clear that we shouldn't have worried." This was the first time I ever heard about my father wanting to go to Shenzhen. He was already thinking about it when the rest of us didn't even know the place existed! Our family had a shot at riches, but my father didn't take it. Now he was willing to help me out while I established myself there. As it turned out, it took me three and a half years to stop needing his help.

I went straight to Zhuhai after I graduated in 1992. But in my first few years there, I had no idea what I was going to do. I had no direction. I took two jobs that brought me to Xinjiang and into the coal business. One of them was at an international trading company in Zhuhai, where I was in charge of selling Guizhou coal to Guangdong. I was there the better part of a year, but I only sold about 300 tons of coal. It wasn't much, and certainly not enough to keep myself afloat. It was time to look for something else.

Between 1992 and 1995, I never made enough money to support myself. As he promised, my father helped me out with his money. I relied on dad's money for three and a half years, so I can empathize with people who do that now. But the important thing is it can't become a habit. You can't end up afraid of the real world and relying on your parents forever.

At that point I was really at a loss at what I should do. I felt like I had a lot to offer, but no one was taking it. Still, I was ambitious.

I had no money, but I wanted the world. I carefully read all the papers every day, so I could keep up with the country's reform and opening as well as its economic developments. I drank Haizhu beer at roadside stalls with my friends, talking about how we were going to become rich.

In 1995 I wrote an essay, "On China's Economic Development and Direction of Investment." I wrote it purely for myself and my friends, and I focused on the industrialization of agriculture, corporate mergers, and home appliance chains. My friend Deng read it and said, "This is good! It reads like Wang Zhigang!"

I said: "Do you know Wang Zhigang?"

"I met him once," he replied. "I have his card."

I said: "Well, let me have it!"

Wang Zhigang was a famous reporter at the Xinhua news agency's Guangdong branch. We were all loyal readers of his articles. I got his card from Deng and sent a copy of my essay to him with a letter signed "Sam Hua, a presumptuous reader." In the letter I asked him for his thoughts on the essay.

From what Wang Zhigang told me later, he got so much mail every day that he'd thrown my letter away after skimming it. But his father, a lifelong educator and a retired high school principal, fished it out of the wastepaper basket and said: "I think this presumptuous kid has potential. You should meet him!" And so, my pager rang. On 6 January 1996, I went to Guangzhou and met Mr Wang. That was the day my career truly began.

I was very excited to meet Mr Wang for the first time. Two things he said left a particularly strong impression on me. The first was: "I want to create a business planning industry in China, and establish a database of business thinking here." The second was how he started so many sentences with: "In China I can say that I ..." This brought me back to when I was considered a prodigy in my little county. Back then I could probably start sentences with, "In Daozhen County I can say that I ..." After a few moments I wondered, when would I be able to say that for China?

So, I said: "Mr Wang, I want to work for you."

He said: "Well, you have to pass my test first."

I said: "I'm ready!"

The test was to write a suggested plan for a cultural centre project in Guangdong. I spent three days in the Sun Yat-sen Library in Guangzhou writing it. Mr Wang read it and said he would give me an 85 for it, so I was hired. I became part of the Wang Zhigang studio, making 1,000 yuan a month with company housing provided.

My first assignment was to write a script for a television feature on an expensive private school. Mr Wang had a group of moonlighters from the arts-and-culture world, and one of them, Luo Yong, became a great friend of mine. Lu Yong worked on the script with me. We got together and talked about some of our ideas, and soon we were getting excited. He said: "Come on, I'm a fast typist. Just start talking and I'll type it." And so, I started pacing around the room and talking, while he sat at the computer and typed. We were done in no time. I was good at this!

Soon it was Chinese New Year, and my first project was over. The commissions were paid; everyone else but me was part-time, and they were paid only on commission for the projects that were completed. I was paid a salary, so I wasn't expecting anything, but Mr Wang gave me a share anyway. It was 3,000 yuan! This meant that I made 4,000 just for my first month! I booked a plane ticket home – no more trains; the age of aviation had arrived for me.

Mr Wang was very much in demand for his business planning services. I'm don't know if he created the industry in China, but certainly he was a pioneer who inspired many, including me. He also ended my money troubles. My starting salary of 1,000 a month lasted less than three months, and my salary and bonuses skyrocketed. The second year I was there, I married my girlfriend and bought a home in Zhuhai – where there was almost a view of the sea, if you stood on your tiptoes.

For so many years now, Mr Wang jokes whenever he sees me: "Your shirt didn't even have a collar when I first met you. But when you started working for me you had a cell phone in your hand in no time." Mr Wang knew how to pay his people.

In 1997, a troublemaker came to the Wang Zhigang studio. His name was Chen Zhufu, and he previously worked at an ad agency. Now he runs one in Shanghai, called Tiana.

Why do I say Chen Zhufu was a troublemaker? He said to me, "Sam Hua, you can't keep working for Mr Wang."

"Why?" I said. I had gone from rags to riches working for Mr Wang. I was feeling very good about my job, and I hadn't thought about anything else.

He said: "Mr Wang is the traditional brain trust type. He's not a professional at anything in modern business. If you keep working for him, you won't be a professional either, and you'll never become him. You should go work in advertising. I think you'll be good at it."

"Advertising? Isn't that just selling calendars?" Back then companies printed calendars at the end of every year for the next year, and ad agency salespeople would go around selling them. They had a base salary of 200 yuan. "That's a low-end job, isn't it?"

"Advertising is anything but low-end! Do you know who David Ogilvy is?"

"No."

"There have been six ad men who made it to the cover of *Time*, and Ogilvy is one of them. He has two Rolls-Royces."

"That's the car the queen of England gets driven around in, isn't it?"

"The queen only has one. Ogilvy has two!"

So, I learned that, if you're in advertising, you could be on the cover of *Time*. You could also have one Rolls-Royce you drive and one that you just keep in the garage.

"Are there any books by ad men?" I asked. So Zhufu gave me a list. That Chinese New Year, I read Ogilvy's *Confessions of an Advertising Man*, Claude Hopkins's *Scientific Advertising*, James Webb Young's *The Diary of an Ad Man*, and a book by an ad man called Liu in Taiwan. I realized that advertising was perfect for me. I knew how I could do it, and I knew how I could do it differently from everyone else. I knew how to do it better. So, I wrote

251

a long essay titled "Our Strategy and Tactics." It was my business concept for the advertising industry. My thesis was that if your plan didn't cover everything, it wouldn't help you do any one thing. Everything the same thing. This was the root of everything Hua and Hua does: strategy consulting, product development, and advertising. And of course, doing everything means that our project contracts are bigger and more lucrative.

When we returned to work after the Chinese New Year in 1998, I told Mr Wang that I was quitting. Mr Wang was very disappointed. He disdained any kind of 'profession' – he aspired to be the traditional gentleman and scholar, who was broadly knowledgeable and insightful. He didn't like the idea of me becoming a professional. But he saw that I was determined, and so he supported and encouraged me. I was sad to be leaving too. By then our office had moved from Guangzhou to Shenzhen, in the Yinhu district – the name meant 'silver lake'. I left on a foggy day. I left behind a poem, or perhaps a lyric – but it didn't match any of the classical Chinese lyric patterns. Later I found out that this was a new literary form, the 'return poem' – just hit Return every time you finish a thought, and you have something that looks like a poem. Here's the return poem:

A Heavy Fog over Silver Lake.
The gentle wind is bathed in fog,
And the fog conceals the rustle of the trees.
The sharp peak reveals boundless sights,
And the trails are the home of fairy folk.
I want to scale the heights and compose a song,
But where do I start my journey?
I dither and linger, and I'm lost,
In the heavy fog over Silver Lake!

4. MY ADVERTISING CAREER

In February 1998, I started working at Lichuang Brand Image Design in Shenzhen. Lichuang was one of China's first corporate image design firms. Their flagship projects included Jialing motorbikes, Yangzi home appliances, and Lucky film. Lichuang started an ad agency subsidary for me, so my first job in advertising was actually heading an agency.

Nobody ever taught me how to do advertising, so I developed my own methodology by working over 20 years in the business.

My first task as the head of the Lichuang ad agency actually had nothing to do with advertising at all. The head of our design company was swamped with work, so I had to lead his team on a business trip to Guiyang to present a corporate logo proposal to South Huiton, one of our clients. It was my first exposure to the world of graphic design. In my time at Lichuang, I got to know almost all of China's top graphic designers of that generation. This also helped me develop my own sense of aesthetics for graphics and typography, the latter in particular. Later I read in Steve Jobs's biography that he was greatly inspired by a calligraphy class he took in college, which resonated with my own experience. This sense of aesthetics also helped me realize that I did not have the talent for professional design. That's why, for Hua and Hua's design work, I would always ask a master of the field to give a look-over after we complete the designs in-house. In the beginning I often asked Chen Shaohua for his advice; the logos and fonts for Chengguang stationery, Heimei toothpaste, and Ergun city all benefited from his work. Since we did the bulk of the design work and only asked him to do some final edits, he was never very enthusiastic about it. Oftentimes I had to go to Shenzhen himself and visit him at home for an evening, looking over his shoulder as he did the edits. But great craftsmanship comes with its rewards! What takes Chen Shaohua two hours

I could never do in two years. This was the truth that I had great respect for.

Eventually it was too hard to get Mr Chen for our final design edits, so I began working with another master of graphic design: Liu Yongqing of Huathink in Shenzhen. He enjoyed learning from me, and he was enthusiastic about working with me as well. He still does the final edits for all Hua and Hua designs.

Back to my career in advertising: My first account was Hiyeah Ginseng, based in Shenzhen. We designed their packaging and advertising around a central brand image of a Native American. The designs were very successful, and the project helped open the door for me in the business. It was very important for me that I started out on the right foot.

In 1997 my brother Nan Hua graduated from Sun Yat-sen University. He taught for a year at a tourism college, then went into advertising himself. He immediately became famous in the business for his talent at copywriting. His very first project was a housing development in the Haizhu District in Guangzhou. Haizhu literally means 'pearl of the sea' in Chinese, so one of the slogans was: 'Where is the pearl in Haizhu?' I thought this was a great line, so when I handled another real estate project in Zhuhai called Phoenix Gardens, I used something similar: 'Pearl of Zhuhai, Crown of the Phoenix.' It's a pity that we hadn't developed the Hua and Hua method then. Now if we were in charge of the project, I would buy the rights to the song 'Pearl of the Orient' and have it play everywhere in Zhuhai: 'The pearl of Zhuhai and the crown of the phoenix is right across from the Xiangzhou Wharf on Qinglu Road!'

Nan Hua had a few short-lived jobs at the Hizone and Inyoung ad agencies, then he struck out on his own. I told him he should hone his skills at an international agency like Ogilvy, but he wanted to make money for himself. He and two of his friends started an agency called Pingfang. That was when Guangzhou was the centre of TV advertising in China. They would find out what companies were looking to produce a commercial, then put together proposals. They made their money through production fees when clients greenlighted their proposals. Anta Sports's first commercial with the table tennis player Kong Ling-hui was Nan Hua's work.

Four years later, in May 2002, Nan Hua came to me and suggested that we go into business together. In July 2002, we officially registered the Hua and Hua name in Guangzhou.

5. EVEN A CONSULTANCY NEEDS A CONSULTANCY

Hua and Hua was officially founded in Guangzhou on 8 July 2002. The company started with five people. We rented an office designed for 16 in the Jianhe Centre in Guangzhou's Tianhe District. But we never filled all 16 seats in our entire time in Guanzhou.

Our first client was Zhulin Zhongsheng's Chinese goldthread oral formulation. The contract was for one million yuan a year. On 1 November that year – I remember it very clearly, because it was the opening day of the 16th National Congress – I signed KBD. Our slogan "KBD cures your cold with Chinese and Western medicine" would be familiar to readers who were around back then. And in January 2003, we signed Dalian Merro. This gave us three clients and over three million yuan in revenue a year. In my eyes, this meant the company was on track.

In May 2003 we signed Tianqi toothpaste. That contract was three million. At that point we had nine people and contracts worth over six million a year in total.

"Only the first two extractions – Zhulin Zhongsheng Chinese goldthread formulation."

"KBD cures your cold with Chinese and Western medicine."

"Stomach ache? You must be working hard. Take some Merro stomach tablets."

"Take a picture. Say 'Tian – qi –'. Tianqi toothpaste."

All across China, our advertisements were on everybody's lips. We got several more clients, and soon we were making over ten million in revenue a year. At the end of 2003, we still only had 11 people.

The year 2003 was also the year when we decided to move to Shanghai. It didn't take long to put the plan into action. On 24 December that year, Hua and Hua officially moved to the Zhongxin building on Nanjing West Road in Shanghai. The building was also the site of GE's Asia-Pacific headquarters, and next door from our office was Sina on one side and Yamaha on the other. This has always been my style. We're a creative consultancy, and we needed an office among the top echelon of business.

Our first new client after we moved to Shanghai was M&G stationery in 2004. Then we got Sanjing pharmaceuticals, GNT GoldBrew, Huangjin Dadang health supplements, and Sunflower pharmaceuticals. The company was growing fast. That was also the golden age for television advertising in China. We were making a new commercial nearly every month. Around 2008, I was reading a magazine and came across a list of China's top ten companies in terms of advertising spending. Four out of the ten were Hua and Hua clients: Tianqi toothpaste, Sanjing pharmaceuticals, GNT GoldBrew, and Huangjin Dadang. When I turned on the TV, our commercials played on every channel.

Hua and Hua's explosive early growth had a lot to do with one man: Yu Xiaosheng, who ran the Xiaosheng ad agency in Harbin. He was a distributor for TV advertising space across China, and most of his clients were in the pharmaceutical industry. I met him early in my career, when we were both working at Yibai pharmaceuticals. Once I signed Zhulin Zhongsheng and KBD, I introduced them to Yu Xiaosheng so they could buy airtime. After that he started referring his clients to me – *all* of his clients: Sanjing, Sunflower, Furen, Topfond, the list goes on. I told him later that without him, Hua and Hua would have had three more years in the wilderness before we found real success. It was thanks to him that everything happened so quickly for us. He said: "I tell you, Sam Hua! Companies grow up quick! Once it's on track, it gets going! Not even you can stop yourself!"

There are three features of Hua and Hua's work:

First, of course, is the super sign. Nan Hua was the one to coin this term, so we say that Hua and Hua invented the concept of the super sign. Every brand that we created centres on a super sign, whether a visual or aural one. To use Sun Tzu's terms, super signs are the 'signs and signals' that allow a general to command a large army. Visual signs are signs; aural signs are signals. All of our work

257

on a brand is guided by the super sign. Super signs are signs that everyone knows and follows.

Second is the super slogan, the encapsulation of why a customer should buy the product. The super sign creates customer awareness, but the customer still needs a reason to buy. When we make TV commercials, we always emphasize that the goal is to convince the viewer to buy a product they discovered for the first time – in 15 seconds. We need to give the viewer a reason to buy. We also emphasize the assumption that this is the *first* time a viewer has heard of us. The communication needs to start from scratch. Never assume that the customer has already heard of the product you're advertising, or that they care about an 'upgrade'. In 15 minutes, we need to convey a message that is clear, familiar, and viral to the first-time viewer – and make them want the product. This is the basis of the super sign. Later, Nan Hua identified four major components of the concept: shelf-based thinking, the reason to buy, the cultural basis, and the super sign.

The third feature is that everything we do is the same thing. Hua and Hua does strategy consultancy, product development, and advertising. From the beginning we've said that everything is the same thing. At first what we meant was that packaging and advertising needed to be designed as one. We did both graphic design and TV commercial production, and we considered packaging to be a brand's most important media source and strategic tool. The packaging and the advertising must all be designed around a super sign, so we said that the two are the same and requires a common approach. That is the best way to leverage brand assets. Then we developed the idea that packaging design is the *redevelopment* of a product, because when we develop new products we're designing new reasons for customers to purchase. To take this further, this means we should first design a reason to purchase – communicated through packaging design – before formulating our product development plans. This is the methodology we used to develop successful products like the 'New Teeth' and 'Changing Teeth' toothpastes for Tianqi, the Confucius's Blessing pen for M&G,

and the 30-minute Relief Cough Drop for Yibai. These are examples of how product development itself has become Hua and Hua's killer product. Corporate strategy involves the structure of the company's industry and its business portfolio. We developed our corporate strategy consulting business on the basis of our product development services. Our most successful examples include our strategy for Sunflower's pharmaceuticals for children and 360's strategy for its internet security business. Throughout this entire process, every step we take is determined by what we want to happen next. We start at the end. This is how Hua and Hua developed our own unique business: strategy, marketing, brand, and creative consulting.

We published *Super Signs Are Super Creativity* in 2013, discussing the Hua and Hua way and related case studies. The book became a business bestseller, and a second edition was published in 2016.

Sometime around 2007, I read a comic book by a Korean author on Toyota's business practices. This was the first time that I had read about the Toyota Production System (TPS). I read the book in one sitting, marvelling at how the book described exactly what I was doing. This is universal wisdom, conclusions we arrived at independently. This was the fundamental truth of how we should do things! I bought several copies of the book for my clients, including Chen Huxiong of M&G. He still hadn't read the book two years later, when he took a trip to Europe with his executive team and his best distributors. He finally read the book on the plane, and became obsessed with TPS. He even changed his itinerary and held group study sessions in hotel conference rooms on the way. When he came back, I went to M&G for a meeting and saw that there was a copy of the book on every desk, and that they had an expert from Taiwan come and talk to them about TPS.

I said: "Well, well! It took you two years, but you finally read the book."

"What do you think the essence of TPS is?" Huxiong asked me.

I talked through the highlights: lower staffing, multi-skilled workers, the U-shaped production line, guidance by next steps, total attack and defense, just-in-time manufacturing, *kanban* management, one-page plans, and so on.

He said: "Hah! You still haven't talked about the core of TPS."

I knew that true learning was achieved by doing. Chen Huxiong had a better handle of TPS than I did, because he had a bigger company and he had the opportunity to do things that I didn't. So, I immediately asked him what he thought.

He said: "The way I see it, the core of the Toyota Production System is *kaizen* – continuous improvement! If every employee in a company is conscious of this, then it would be a great company indeed!"

Hmm. I didn't quite get it, but I remembered what he said.

A few years later, in 2014, I went to Chubang's ribbon-cutting for their new plant in Yangxi. I met Masaki Hashimoto and Hu Guangshu of Showa Consulting, who were the TPS consultants for Chubang. I took the opportunity to ask the two of them to be consultants for Hua and Hua as well. They thought I was kidding. Wasn't Hua and Hua a consultancy itself? I said: "Even a consultancy needs a consultancy!"

In 2015, Hua and Hua began implementing the 5S methodology part of TPS. We started with *seiso*, the sweeping and cleaning. One hour every Monday morning was devoted to cleaning. Every month we had two days devoted to 5S activities, and every year we had a team visit Japan to learn more about TPS, consisting of everyone from the general manager down to entry-level employees. Unfortunately, there's not enough space to go into the details of this activity here – this could be another book.

In 2018 we began seeing the preliminary results of our 5S implementation. An awareness of continuous improvement has been established among team members, and the awareness can be seen in their work. The services we provide keep getting better. We just helped the Juewei food company with a *kaizen* project. The client said that the project was worth 100 million yuan, and it was based on what we learned from Uokuni Food Services in Japan. It's been said over and over that it's been too easy to make money in China over the past two decades. Money practically fell from the sky, and nobody wanted to bother with the money that you need to bend over to pick up. Now money doesn't quite fall from the sky anymore, but people still aren't willing to bend over – all they do is complain. The quality of work in China is still too patchy; all it would take for someone to gain an overwhelming advantage is to slow down and refine their work. Look at Japan and their obsession with refinement, the work they put in for the smallest of improvements. Are we still going to chase high volume and low quality in China? I talked about our two killer products at Hua and Hua: super signs and super slogans. Now let me add continuous improvement!

Now I know continuous improvement! I've never forgotten my conversation with Chen Huxiong on TPS. I didn't wait to introduce Hu Guangshu to him, and now Chubang is also one of Showa Consulting's clients. Just like how Yu Xiaosheng referred his clients to me, I recommend Mr Hu to all of Hua and Hua's clients as well. This is my way of sharing with him what I built over more than a decade. Showa Consulting is also quickly expanding its presence, thanks to Hua and Hua. This is what gratitude is – not a quid pro quo, but paying forward the spirit and values that helped me.

6. SICKNESS IS GOD'S GIFT

Everything was going well at the company in 2009. I worked like a madman, from early in the morning deep into the night. But I never stopped thinking. My brain was always whirring along without a moment's rest. I sometimes wondered if it was going to overheat. It wasn't just when I was awake – even in my dreams – I was coming up with new ideas! Sometimes I would wake up in the middle of the night with something I absolutely had to write down, so I had a pen and notebook on my nightstand.

Even today my brain still works when I'm asleep. I often dream about meetings with clients, and sometimes I dream of entire projects. I talked about killing a man in my dreams, and I can definitely see how that could happen.

I was spending much of my days in the air. I might be on a plane to Harbin in the morning, meet with the client in the afternoon, have dinner at the airport, and take a late flight back to Shanghai. The next afternoon I might be flying to Guiyang. I racked up over 200 flights a year, sometimes visiting two cities a day. I felt sick even looking at an airplane, and felt the urge to escape whenever I was in one.

Then my body gave out. The doctors couldn't name a specific illness, but I just couldn't sleep. Once I went three days and three nights without sleeping. It was terrifying. I told my mother that I hadn't slept for three days, and she said: "That's impossible! I heard you snore!" I suppose I had very short naps without even realizing.

Then I lost the ability to drive. One time I was on the Yan'an expressway and my body froze. I couldn't move my limbs. I was terrified, thinking I was going to cause a pileup. I never drove after that.

I wasn't sleeping, I felt anxious all the time and I was exhausted. Sometimes I felt too tired to even breathe. We never think of breathing as something that takes effort, but I could barely muster the energy to do it. Then there was the anxiety. How bad was it?

I would sit next to someone and suddenly feel like I was sitting on pins and needles – an overwhelming urge to leave. One day at the office I genuinely felt like I was about to die. I called Nan Hua to me. He asked if I had any last words. I said: "Everything I own goes to my wife. Mom and Dad go to you!"

I saw doctors. None of the Western doctors found anything, so I went to traditional Chinese ones. I tried acupuncture and all kinds of herbal remedies for more than a year, but nothing worked. That was when one of my friends recommended Anding Hospital in Beijing, saying that they knew someone who suffered the same symptoms as I did, and was cured by a doctor there.

I only had the vague impression that Anding Hospital was a psychiatric hospital, but I had nowhere else to go, so I made an appointment with the doctor he talked about. When I went to the appointment, the nurse looked up and said: "Where's the patient?" I said, "That's me." The nurse stared. She probably didn't think I looked like a psychiatric patient. But it would take a psychiatric patient to come to a psychiatric hospital without a psychiatric illness, wouldn't it?

I met the doctor and described my symptoms. I was taken to a room that was like a classroom, where I sat down at a desk, with the other patients around me, filling out forms as if we were taking an exam. I was sure I aced it. There was a brain wave measurement. As I was hooked up to the machine, my mind started wandering: surely geniuses would have abnormal brain waves? If your brain waves were completely normal, you were probably mediocre. But then, I didn't think of myself as a genius, I just worked hard. My thoughts were interrupted by the doctor, who said: "You have a mild anxiety disorder. That's what's causing the insomnia and the physical symptoms. I'm prescribing a treatment course. I can't say it will make everything go away, but you should see results in a month and a half."

I was very happy to hear that, and I asked what my brain waves looked like. The doctor said: "It's borderline." I asked him what that meant. He replied: "You're at the edge of normal, not quite atypical."

Exactly as I thought: I might be smarter than normal, but I wasn't exactly a genius.

The doctor prescribed one anti-anxiety drug and two sleeping pills. When I did my own research, I learned that psychiatrists usually start off with large doses, to get the patient to sleep and start treating the symptoms; then they start tapering off the doses. But stopping the pills is a difficult process, which is why there are so many jokes about it. I only realized that it's no laughing matter when it happened to me.

I used to believe in the old Chinese proverb that all medicines are part poison. I resisted the idea of taking medicine, and sleeping pills because I associated them with suicide. I only learned how wrong I was when I started going to the doctor more often. Not taking the drugs they prescribe does much more damage than any side effect!

A month and a half into the treatment regiment, I was feeling much better. I was sleeping, and the anxiety attacks stopped. Everything was back to normal! About two years into the treatment, I started tapering off the doses. But then work started becoming stressful again, and the symptoms came back. I went back on the drugs, and things went back to normal. Then I stopped the pills, and the symptoms came back again. I'm still taking them now. I follow everything that the doctors say, and know that I need to err on the side of taking the drugs longer.

I was actually prescribed sleeping pills when I first started having trouble sleeping, but I refused to take them. I was afraid of becoming dependent on them. The doctor said: "So what if you're dependent on them?" I didn't understand that back then, but now I do. So what if I'm dependent on the pills? People with high blood pressure are also dependent on pills to control it. Why was I so worried about this relatively minor problem far off into the future that I wouldn't solve this major problem affecting me right now?

People want there to be nothing wrong with them, so they just try to grit through symptoms without taking action. Not only don't they do anything about it, they're also good at poking holes in other people's suggestions. Doesn't this sound like a lot of people in business meetings?

I've written such a detailed account of my illness and treatment because I think a lot of people need to read about it. Too many people aren't taking the medicine they need. I started talking to my friends who clearly suffered from anxiety or depression about the importance of medication. Many of them refuse to take any, and their friends and family also prefer that they don't. Some of these friends and family members even think of psychiatric medicine as an insult or a conspiracy against their loved one.

After I realized that I had psychiatric issues, I started talking to a therapist, and said: "Everything's going great for me! My work and my life are both as good as it gets. I have nothing to be anxious about! Why would this happen to me?"

My therapist said: "You're still not accepting this. No matter what happens to you, you need to accept it and make peace with it. What reason do you have not to accept this? Why do you think that your job, your life, and your body all have to be perfect?"

"You mean I need to live with the illness, and not try to fight it?"

"Yes," said my therapist. "You have to accept it, make peace with it, face it. Then you do something about it."

A Peter Drucker quote came to mind: "Don't try to solve all of your problems. Live with them and learn to move forward with them." And I immediately understood what my therapist had meant. One thing I'm good at is finding connections between everything that happens to me, everything I read, everything I hear. I use them all, and what I do is always informed by what I know. There was nothing extraordinary about this talk with my therapist, but it was extremely influential for me.

Then in one session I asked: "Everything is going well, but sometimes I still feel stressed, I feel the anxiety coming back. What can I do?"

My therapist said: "What, you want a hundred on the test? Maybe you should thank God for this flaw of yours. Otherwise you wouldn't know yourself."

This really helped me let go. I've met a lot of people who really want a hundred on the test. You put them on a task, and they wouldn't do anything unless they think they have the perfect plan. I get very frustrated with these people, but it turns out that I have something in common with them.

My illness was a gift from God. It was a cleansing, a restructuring, of my outlook and values, and it made me much wiser. Here's what I learned from it:

First, I learned to accept failure. I learned to do my best with what I could do, but to leave the result in the hands of fate and luck, and accept it when I fail. This doesn't mean the results don't matter. When you say the results don't matter, you're still focused on the good result. What this means is a true acceptance of failure. If you can accept failure, then it's okay to have some flaws, and it's nothing to compromise a little. Applied to life, accepting failure means that you don't fear anything, not even death. This means you can be guided by your principles and your will.

Second, I learned to wait and not rush to solve problems. We need to learn how to live with our problems and move forward with them. If you learn to wait, then you won't be anxious. You won't do anything rash. You won't make mistakes.

Third, I learned to accept the side effects. I learned to focus on solving the problems, not on poking holes in solutions.

Fourth, I learned not to demand the best result. There's no such thing as the best result, only the least worst result. The least worst result is something you need to build up.

These four lessons were all learned through my illness. These lessons, together with all the other wisdom I learned, formed my new values. When I wrote *Sam Hua on Sun Tzu's Art of War*, my conclusion was that the *Art of War* is not a book on warfare, but a book on avoiding warfare; it is not a book on gaining victory, but a book on never suffering defeat. I truly learned these lessons not from reading the *Art of War* but from my own life experiences. Without these experiences, I wouldn't ever have understood Sun Tzu.

In addition to changing my values, my illness also changed my lifestyle. After I got sick, I started strictly following my own schedule and cutting back on social events and nonessential things. I learned that when you have a task ahead of you, you don't start by working as hard as you can, you start by asking if you really have to do it. Don't do any task that you don't have to do. Focus on your own work, learning, exercise, and rest.

My illness over the past few years was a watershed moment in my life. It changed me and changed Hua and Hua. It brought Hua and Hua's business to a new stage and a new world.

This new stage started in 2014.

7. BECOMING A BUSINESSMAN

Nan Hua founded Dookbook in 2006.

The publishing business is a natural fit for us. From the perspective of the Hua and Hua way, publishing is developing product concepts and designing good packaging. We were successful at both, and by 2010 we had bestsellers like *The Tibet Code*, *Notes from the World of Government*, and *Twenty Years in Underground Society*. Dookbook took up more and more of Nan Hua's time, and it became hard for him to take part in Hua and Hua's work.

Unfortunately, that was also when my illness was at its worst. I was not sure if I could even keep working. So, I talked to Xiao Zheng about taking over as company president. Xiao Zheng has worked with me since 2000, and he followed me to Hua and Hua. He was a vice president at the company then.

Before this, Hua and Hua was always a small company of 20 or 30 people under the two of us. Nan Hua was in charge of the production and creatives, and I handled the sales work, prospecting for clients and doing proposals. Sometimes I would meet people from other consultancies or ad agencies at client meetings, sometimes young women who were eloquent and comfortable giving presentations. I would think: *Why don't I have anyone at Hua and Hua who can come out and do proposals on their own like this?* I hadn't realized back then that I was the problem. I needed 100%; I refused to accept even 99%, so I insisted on making every presentation myself. There were no opportunities for anyone else.

But now I was no longer able to do everything myself, so I had to let other people take over. I didn't choose to do this willingly, but it actually opened up a new world for the company. Xiao Zheng did a fantastic job, and in 2012 we promoted Yan Yan to vice president. Yan came to Hua and Hua in 2004, one of the first people to join us after our move to Shanghai.

In 2012 I was feeling better, and the company had a whole new face. My illness didn't affect our business at all, and we gained two talented executives. That year I went to do an EMBA program at the China Europe International Business School. The two years I spent in the program were extremely helpful for me. I never learned how to do business; I just figured it out as I went along. And I realized that what I had wasn't really a *business*; it was more like a craft shop, with a master and apprentices who took commissions for creative work from brands. The two years I spent at CEIBS helped me get over my blind spots and complete the missing pieces of the puzzle. Now I had a clear panoramic view of what a business is, and I became much better at what I did.

I went to CEIBS on the advice of a businessman friend of mine. I was skeptical at first, because I thought business was something you learned by doing, not at school. But he said: "A business is this (he drew an enormous circle in the air). What you do is this (he drew a much smaller circle). You might be the best at what you do, but if you don't have an understanding of what goes on in the entire business, you don't even know what it's like, then you wouldn't understand what we're talking about. You can't join in on the discussion, or even have a feel of what we're saying. You don't know enough about the entire business, and your professional knowledge has its limits."

He also said: "You need to have partners. This can't go on forever. You have a craft shop with your apprentices, not a business."

What he said – becoming an entrepreneur and establishing a partnership system – was shocking to me, and it completely changed the course of Hua and Hua. I realized that I was running a business, so I needed to be a businessman and not just a creative. That's why I wanted to go the CEIBS. I later did another finance EMBA program at Tsinghua PBCSF, which helped me build a comprehensive understanding of business operations as a whole.

I met Zhang Haimeng, a global partner at McKinsey, when I was working with China Fortune Land Development. I invited him to our company for a chat, and took the opportunity to ask him to give a talk. He said: "Consultancies usually go through four phases:

The first phase is establishing a methodology and proving that it works through solving problems for clients. It looks like you've already done this. The second is teaching this methodology to people other than the founder, and proving that the methodology is transferable. I don't know if you've been doing this. The third is internationalizing. The fourth is the founder leaving and the company continuing without him."

I started thinking about Hua and Hua in terms of these four phases. We had our own methodology: the Hua and Hua way. We had made progress in teaching the methodology to other people, but we needed better efficiency in doing so. Internationalization wasn't a focus for me at that time, and I was just going to see what happened on that front. The founder's departure was something I definitely had to think about, since sooner or later everybody has to leave.

The second phase was really the most important. How do I transfer everything I know? When we brought on Showa Consulting to help us improve our management, Hu Guangshu said: "You have to turn the skills of individuals into the capabilities of the company."

Mr Hu's words helped me see our problems with the old apprentice system. This was the system Hua and Hua was run on. Our core team all apprenticed with me. But the apprentice system has a cultural problem. One old Chinese saying goes, "The master brings the apprentice in, but how much he learns is up to him." The master teaches by example and by word, and what the apprentice learns is up to his 'insight'. In other words, the responsibility for learning falls on the apprentice and not the master. This is not an efficient way of teaching, and it means that all we have is the master's skills and the apprentice's skills; none of this becomes the capabilities of the company. This means the master needs to take more responsibility when it comes to teaching. We need to have teaching materials. Then I read the Wanda Group's *Operation Management for Commercial Real Estate* – it was a detailed handbook of their procedures. I decided that this kind of handbook was what Hua and Hua needed. Every step needs to be detailed in specificity, and the whole book could be published. This is what we're doing now.

Back to the partnership system. I had a decent understanding of how the partnership system at McKinsey was set up, but I was still not sure how a rational system could be implemented at my company. Finally I decided to just try it. I instituted a two-tier system: managing partners were given a percentage of the company's income, and regular partners were given a percentage of the income generated from their own responsibilities. I decided to start with this and gradually iterate on the system, with the ultimate goal of a profit-pool distribution like McKinsey's. But my reasoning was that in the early stages, the company was going to invest heavily in advertising and training. A profit-based distribution system was going to be less attractive, so I decided that the partners shouldn't have to worry about investments – they were being paid based on revenue, not profits.

The partnership system was implemented in 2014. We also brought on a consultant for this, from a company called Open Quest Facilitation Technology in Taiwan. They specialized in *facilitating*. They held a vision-building meeting for the entire company, under the title 'Nuclear Fission'. This was a new experience for me, because I was used to being the only one in charge. I talked, I acted, and everybody followed. But now everybody needed to talk, write things down, even draw pictures. We produced posters of our own ideas about the company's vision and action plan, posted them on the wall, and searched for consensus.

The meaning of the title 'Nuclear Fission' was that the partnership system was going to create the energy for more talented team members and a bigger company. The three-year target that we decided on in the company was 150 million yuan in consultancy income in 2017. At that time, the number was only 40 million, so this was quite ambitious. Our actual income for 2017 was 135 million.

In a group discussion, I heard Chen Jun say: "If creativity is so important to the company, why not offer a million yuan for great creativity?" I thought this was a great idea! I immediately talked to Nan Hua and Xiao Zheng, and on the same day I announced an annual prize of one million yuan for the best project in the company. The first winner in 2014 was the Xibei Youmian Village project, with the next few winners being 360, Jilin Yuntianhua, and Hanting Hotel. Everyone was excited about the million-yuan prize, and later I announced an even bigger prize that would be awarded every five years: one million US dollars, awarded every five years to the project team that was best able to create long-term values for the client. Maybe it's because I know I'll never win a Nobel for myself, but I do love giving out this prize.

After 2014, we also increased our investment in training. Our partners and core directors all attended EMBA programs on company funding. The entire company went to Japan in groups to learn about TPS. The core strategy and design teams could go on one company-funded overseas learning trip a year. This September I'm bringing a team of 30 to the US East Coast, with stops at West Point and Harvard.

It is now 2018, 16 years since the company's founding. My first group of apprentices are now experienced executives. The partnership system provided the incentive for everyone to work hard, driving explosive growth in the company. We now have 150 employees. And I think I've officially become a businessman, not just a project planner. It's been 22 years since I started doing consultant work in 1996, and I've worked with China's best entrepreneurs and businesspeople. It's taught me a lot about the theory and practice of business. Jia Guolong has said that Xibei's most important product is its people, and I understand this on a deep level. This is why we've been spending more and more time on training. The responsibility of a leader is to make other people better, to nurture new leaders. In our operations, I now have a sense of our scale. My sense of scale is still on the 0.5 to 1 billion yuan range. Could we reach McKinsey's level of 7 billion US dollars globally? I have no sense of that yet; I'm focusing on 1 billion yuan first! But how will I achieve that? The answer is the Hua and Hua value system.

8. THE HUA AND HUA VALUE SYSTEM

The Hua and Hua value system is essentially a Confucian value system. Its basic driving force is simply the passage of time. This is what we have hanging on Hua and Hua's walls:

Our Mission: Putting Companies on the Right Path.

Our Core Values: No Deception, No Greed, No Exaggeration.

Our Corporate Spirit: Real People, Real Hearts, Real Skill.

Our Central Concept: Please Those Near and Attract Those from Afar.

All four of these slogans are based on Confucian thoughts. On first glance, one might think our mission and core values are too conservative: We just want to put companies on the right path, not help them aggressively expand and conquer the world. The first item in our core values is 'no deception', not expansion, not being the best, not innovation, not winning. This in itself is part of our values: When we talk about core values, it is a low bar we can never fall under, not a high standard we need to strive for. But if you're serious about the low bar, you realize that it's never as easy as it looks.

It was with a purpose that we set our mission to put companies on the right path. It's always been a human weakness to look for easier and faster ways, the shortcut, the 'back roads'. In the *Analects*, Confucius said: "Who can exit a house without going through the door? But why do people never follow the right way?" People say that the open wide road is the easiest road, but their actions never show it. They don't take the simple path, they want to take detours that they think could get them there faster. And so they encounter dead ends and hard conditions – not the right path.

The best efficiency means never starting over; the quickest way to improvement is never backsliding. Do solid work with no expectations or assumptions about what it might bring. Focus on the process, not the results. Do not give up, and do not take shortcuts you think will lead to better results. You might think shortcuts give you an advantage, but all they lead to is traps. We see this all too often in today's China.

Clients who come to us are often looking for shortcuts to success. They think: you've helped such-and-such company achieve so much, so now help us do the same! Either that, or they expect quick solutions to their problems. A consulting firm could easily take advantage of their expectations and desire, persuading the company to make big bets – on the consultancy itself, and on the market. And of course, this also represents a bet for the consultancy, using the client's money. If the bet pays off, the glory goes to the consultancy. If it doesn't, the company suffers the losses. No loser would ever come out against their consultancy – it's too embarrassing.

This is the innate power imbalance between the consultant and the client. That's why many consultancies lie, get greedy, and exaggerate. They attribute their clients' success to themselves, and construct elaborate stories with them as the hero. And then they dangle a carrot in front of the client – if the client falls for it, then another human weakness takes over: the sunk cost fallacy. It could take years before they finally face up to mounting losses and cut the consultant loose.

What we believe is what I wrote in *Sam Hua on Sun Tzu's Art of War*: "*Art of War* is not a book on warfare, but a book on avoiding warfare; it is not a book on gaining victory, but a book on never suffering defeat." We don't aim for total victory, but rather to gain a position where we cannot lose. That is because the ultimate goal of a company should be sustainability, to be in business forever. We've been through so many ups and downs that we know success is nothing. What matters is thriving forever. Businesspeople need to suppress their passion for conquest, and develop their passion for their mission, because that's what counts in the long run. For companies who came to us because of our success, I tell them that the success belongs to the clients. The fact that other companies succeeded does not mean that Hua and Hua could help them succeed as well. A consultancy needs to keep its distance with their clients' successes. Whether clients win or lose is their business. We can only do our best at what we do. Sometimes a client would ask: "What are we paying for, when we work with you?"

This is a dangerous question, because it focuses on expectations for results. They want guaranteed things. But this isn't a good mindset. This is a mindset that unscrupulous companies take advantage of. At Hua and Hua, my standard answer is: "Work with us only if you accept that the money might not get you anything!"

If I'm this blunt, I can confidently say that I've fulfilled our core values: No Deception, No Greed, No Exaggeration.

To let your words surpass your deeds is a shame; to let your deeds surpass your words is good. Our core values are also a way to keep us on the right track ourselves. Mencius said that morality is about the accumulation of the small, like water piercing a stone, and not about single towering achievements.

This little passage is also from *Mencius*: "A stream that springs from a source flows day and night, eventually filling up creeks, joining rivers and oceans, and eventually find the sea. What springs from a source is to be commended. But water without a source – the water that falls from the sky in the summer – may fill up creeks and streams much more quickly, yet they dry up just as quickly. This is just as when a man's reputation exceeds what he actually is, and a true gentleman should consider this a shame."

People are good when their achievements surpass their reputation; it is shameful when their reputation surpasses their achievements. People with unearned reputations might be able to fool the world for a short time, but eventually the truth will come out. And when this happens, reputation turns to shame.

A true gentleman knows where he comes from. When he fails at something, he looks inward and strives to improve himself – to build up a more solid foundation. When this leads to success, reputation follows. This reputation is like a spring with a source, and it will flow always and never run dry. Regardless of how great his reputation is, it is always backed up by true ability!

Here is a passage from the *Doctrine of the Mean*: "The Book of Odes says to wear fine dyed silks, but to wear plain cloth on top. This is so the silk cloth is less prominent. The way of the gentleman is the same way: it is initially hidden by the plain cloth, but the fine silks beneath eventually becomes apparent. The way of a poor character is to seem deceptively attractive, so they present a wonderful façade; but their true nature could never support this, and with time the façade is bound to come down."

Real People, Real Hearts, Real Skill is our fine silk. No Deception, No Greed, No Exaggeration is our plain cloth. We wear the plain cloth on top of the fine silk, and eventually our true nature comes through. This is how we keep ourselves on the right path.

When I talk about Hua and Hua's corporate spirit, I often quote from Zhu Xi: "Keep the nature of the world, and eradicate human desires." Some people really don't like this – they think this mean celibacy. But what did Zhu Xi mean? In his terms, eating food would be part of the nature of the world, but gourmet eating is only a human desire. Perhaps this is still too much of a challenge, so let's say this: Gourmet eating is part of the nature of the world, but excessive eating that endangers your health is human desire. So now everyone can live up to this quote with every meal! How does this apply to what we do? For us, the nature of the world is to create value for the client; human desire is to keep the relationship going and renew the contract every time. So, when we keep the nature of the world and eradicate human desires, we're not guessing at what our client wants and appealing to that. We are simply doing what we think is best to create value for the client. We give the client what they need, not what they want. This is what is meant by "real people, real hearts, real skills." If a client isn't smart enough to recognize this, then we take the Confucian approach: Value me, and I will do all I can and help the entire world. Don't value me, and I'll retreat and keep my abilities within me, but it's no loss to me.

Hua and Hua's value system is to never obsess over results and never change what we're doing based on gains and losses. We do everything in good conscience, based on what we believe is right. When we do this, we would never deceive, be greedy, or exaggerate.

There is actually a follow-up to "Real People, Real Hearts, Real Skills," and that is "The Heart of a Teacher, Friend, and Parent." A consultancy is always a client's teacher and friend, and an important one.

But a consultancy is not just a teacher and friend, because they also have the heart of a parent. We must think of ourselves as a parent to the client. This is not from a feeling of superiority. My driver once got himself into terrible road rage, and I said that he should have the heart of a parent – if he were driving his child around, he would never be so angry. He never had road rage after that. If a doctor has the heart of a parent, they would be careful with every treatment and every prescription. If a powdered milk manufacturer has the heart of a parent, they would never put out low-quality product. That's why the heart of a parent is a treasure. Some people think it must be difficult for us to find clients, but it's really much more difficult for a client to find us! If you really live up to "Real People, Real Hearts, Real Skills" and "The Heart of a Teacher, Friend, and Parent," then people take notice.

Of course, this is very difficult. But what in life isn't difficult? Do solid work, and you'll achieve the last part of our value system: Happy Clients Near and Far. This is another concept I took from the *Analects*. A lord asked Confucius about good rule, and Confucius replied that a good ruler "pleases those near, and attracts those from afar." This is our goal. Think of how much work, energy, and investment it takes to go out and find clients. But it costs nothing to attract them so they come to you.

When we please those near and attract those from afar, this means our traffic is zero-cost.

Zero-cost traffic is what Mencius talks about when he talks about "the way of the king."

To take the way of the king, we need our values, and we need time. We don't focus on expectations. We don't look for shortcuts or results-oriented methods. We focus on the process and not the results. We simply do solid work day after day, and wait for the work to accumulate and the water to pierce the stone. Confucianism tells us that the benevolent are free from worry, the wise are free from bafflement, and the brave are free from fear. When we have focus, determination, and hard work, we will achieve a level far beyond anybody else can imagine!

9. PASSING ON A LEGACY OF LEARNING

Companies are organizations that deal in knowledge, consulting firms particularly so. We use knowledge in our business, so we should also leave behind a legacy of knowledge for the world. I've always loved to learn, to synthesize, and to write. Writing has become my second job when I'm not working at my first one. And for me, writing is also part of running my business.

Professor Gao Zhongyu of Tsinghua University actually wanted me to write a book ten years ago. Back then, I said I didn't have the material. I had some experience, yes, but not enough to organize into a book. He said: "Ah! When responsible people all say they don't have enough material, it's the irresponsible people that become major authors." That stayed with me, and in 2013 I finally worked up the courage to co-write and publish a book with Sam Hua: *Super Signs Are Super Creativity*. This was when I was in the program at CEIBS, and I asked Professor Jiang Jiongwen of the marketing department to write an introduction. Professor Jiang wrote an enthusiastic introduction full of praise for the book, but he also told me: "This is very different from a usual bestseller. If you're writing a book about super signs, usually I'd expect that the entire book would be on that one topic. You might talk about the three major features of super signs: clear representation, a large amount of information conveyed, and a strong power to influence action. Then you might say that super signs are familiar to everyone, so they could influence everyone and turn a new brand into an old friend for millions of consumers, driving brand preference and sales. This is enough theory for one book. You could have followed it up with some case studies all proving your theory. That could be your book, and would be very helpful for the reader. But the book you wrote had much more information and many more topics than this!"

Professor Jiang was right. *Super Signs are Super Creativity* was about far more than super signs. I published a revised version in 2016, with even more content that wasn't directly about super signs. In fact, this book is a distillation of the Hua and Hua way. I plan to publish a book next year with this title: *The Hua and Hua Way*. This will be a reorganized systemic description of what we do. Based on what Professor Jiang said, this book covers enough ground for ten books. And this is what I plan to do, what I think of as my mission. But as I said to Professor Gao – I don't have enough material. Maybe in ten more years, I'll have read enough, experienced enough, worked on enough cases. I want every example that I write about to be a real case that I've worked on, because there's always something missing when you're analyzing things other people did. Sometimes I see other people's analyses of my own work, and they can miss the mark very badly. That's why I only want to write about my own work, so I can be sure that the theory and practice go together. Writing these books will be like building a skyscraper: the structure, the supports, the roofs, the windows, the division into different units. And when I'm done, I'll be able to tell you exactly where every room is, with the confidence that every room stands on its own, and there's no space left over. Everything will be 100% clear! But this is no easy task, and it will be the work of a lifetime.

As I collected the material for my book, I also wanted to do other things. If there's any topic I've been familiar with since childhood, that's almost instilled in me, and I've put into practice in all my life, it's certainly Chinese military strategy and Confucian values. I live and breathe these things, so I decided I wanted to write commentaries on the Four Books of Confucianism. But as a business consultant, I doubted that anybody would want to read my thoughts on the *Analects*. So, I decided to start by writing *Sam Hua on Sun Tzu's Art of War*. It's less jarring to see a consultant write about military tactics, certainly! If people read my commentary on Sun Tzu, it meant they accepted me as someone who knows Chinese thought. Then they'd accept my commentary on Confucius.

I dug up my copy of *The Art of War with Annotations from Eleven Masters* at home, and started working on it every day. I woke up at five every morning to write *Sam Hua on Sun Tzu's Art of War*, and finished the book in 183 days. For me, this was no difficult task. It was just putting everything in my head on paper, because what I was writing about was really myself. The book was published in 2015 to great success. It's sold over 400,000 copies in China, and the rights have been sold for South Korea and Thailand. The Korean version is already published, and I understand the Thai version will be published this October. A traditional Chinese version has also been published in Taiwan. My hope is that the book will eventually be translated into ten languages and published around the world. In 2018, Luo Zhenyu invited me to produce a series of 30 podcasts on the *Art of War* for his Dedao app. The series was also a huge success. A lot of readers said that my book completely changed the way they thought about Sun Tzu, but I said that I was just correcting popular misconceptions. None of this is original research, it all comes from the annotations of the eleven masters. It's just that people aren't familiar with classical Chinese anymore, and commentators have become so preoccupied with inventing new perspectives that the original meanings have been lost. All I did was wipe the dust off the original and give it some polish. But this is how we carry on the legacy of the old masters.

After the book on Sun Tzu, I published *Sam Hua on the Analects*. It's sold 50,000 copies so far, which isn't a bad start. And then came *Sam Hua on Mencius*, which hasn't sold through its first run of 25,000 yet. I've completed the manuscripts for *Sam Hua on the Grand Learning and the Doctrine of the Mean* and *Sam Hua on Wang Yangming's Teachings,* which will both be published the next six months. This will complete my series of commentaries on Confucian thought.

Ultimately, I hope to write a book on Confucian corporate culture. I've been learning a lot from Japanese companies. Peter Drucker, widely known as the first master of modern corporate management, said that Japan was where his ideas were best put into practice. He also said that Japan is the country that has best combined Western ideas of management with local culture. What is this 'local culture' that Drucker talked about? In my view, it's simply Confucianism! The Japanese people I learn from all like talking to me, because when they talk about an element of TPS, I can always think of a passage from the Four Books or Wang Yangming that it came from. They found it illuminating as well. And of course, they admired Sun Tzu.

Chinese companies have focused too much in recent years on learning from the US, and not enough on learning from Japan. I want to bring together Sun Tzu, Confucianism, and the experiences of American and Japanese experts, and see if I can build a system of Confucian corporate culture and management theory that belongs to China. I don't know if I'm good enough to do this, and it will take a very long time. But what I can do is write my commentaries on Confucian classics. For me, these writings are in my blood. I know it and I live it. And putting them down on a paper is like studying them once again.

Dripping water can pierce a stone. When you practice what you know and stick with it, you'll find that no stone could withstand the water. Drip ... drip ... drip ... pierce one stone, then move on to the next. I spent four years on Sun Tzu, the four books, and Wang Yangming's teachings. I was going to go back to writing the next book in my series on the Hua and Hua way, but I realized I didn't have enough material yet. Still, I've grown used to spending my early mornings writing, and I couldn't stand the thought of stopping. So, I found a bigger stone: the *Zizhi Tongjian*. This stone could last seven or eight years, enough time for me to work up the courage to write about my profession.

There is also a strategic element to my choice of the *Zizhi Tongjian*. It's such an enormous book that hardly anyone would try to write commentary on it. Modern Chinese translations of the *Zizhi Tongjian* fall into two types. The first type is the work of dozens of people, each working on one part of the book. This type of translation is usually very poor quality, because it's just a product for the publisher. The translators lack passion and hardly put any work into their work, making for extremely boring reading. Even the passages that are readily understandable to a modern reader become dull as dishwater, lacking the power of the original. The other type is the version by Bo Yang. Bo put a lot of effort into his work, and it is a great contribution to the field. But he is so critical of Chinese history he practically rejects it. Not to mention, he produced his translation when he was in prison, and projected his hate for Chiang Kai-shek onto historical rulers.

His entire book is tainted by this hate, and he adds too much that wasn't there. This is why I want to write my own version. First, I want to produce a translation that strikes a balance between readability and accessibility. Second, I want to interpret this history through the lens of Sun Tzu and the Four Books. I want to add my own commentaries to the ones by Sima Guang, the original author. Sun Tzu will be useful for understanding the war-related events, and the Four Books for the politics. It was said in the past that truly understanding half the *Analects* is enough to rule the world. With the entire *Analects*, plus the *Mencius*, the *Great Learning*, and the *Doctrine of the Mean*, we can read through the *Zizhi Tongjian*, turning the history into a casebook for these great philosophical works. I believe this is valuable work.

Peter Drucker said that, in a society of knowledge workers, a person's professional knowledge is often out of date when they turn 45 and they become less competent in their work. This is when people should look for a second profession or a second hobby to avoid a midlife crisis. But I'm lucky in that my learning and knowledge has progressed along with my work.

I plan to complete my writing on Chinese history and culture by the time I'm 55. After that, my writing will entirely focus on my profession: business. I will focus on corporate strategy, brand marketing, and corporate management and culture. This is an ambitious goal. But I think this is about devoting myself to formulating and passing on knowledge for good. Generation after generation, good has always battled evil. The paths of good and evil have always hung in the balance. People want the fast and easy way to success, so often they succumb to the side of evil. This is true for every field. So, I want to draw on the theory and practice of Hua and Hua to establish and pass on a system of knowledge for the good path, and I want to find my fellow travellers. When I read Wang Yangming and his lamentations on how he could save the people of the world, I want to be like him – I want to build a school of the mind like his, but for corporate thought!

In 2013, shortly before my father passed away, he kept repeating this to himself: "Work hard! Work hard!" This is his final legacy to us – work hard!

AUTHORS' BIOGRAPHIES

SAM HUA

Board chairman and founding partner of
Shanghai H&H Marketing Consulting Co., Ltd.

Well-known expert in creative strategic marketing

Chief brand adviser of National Real Estate Manager Alliance

Sam Hua has been dedicated to marketing strategies
and creative marketing services for nearly 20 years.
He established the first systematic marketing methodology
– "H&H Methodology" – in the domestic marketing circle.

NAN HUA

Founding partner of Shanghai H&H Marketing
Consulting Co., Ltd.

Board Chairman of Dook Media Group Ltd.

Co-producer of several movies such as
So Young and *Old Boys: the Way of the Dragon*